Does the Crew Sleep on Board?

*From Cruise Ships to
International Game Shows
A Memoir By*

Bruce J. Starin

Does the Crew Sleep on Board?
© 2021 by Bruce J. Starin

All rights reserved. No part of this book may be reproduced or transmitted in any form or by any means, electronic or mechanical, including photocopying, recording, or by any information storage and retrieval system, without permission in writing from the author and appropriate credit to the author and publisher.

Unless noted otherwise, photographs in this book are from the collection of the Author. The Author has attempted to locate the owner of other photos. Any photographs in question will be removed from future editions upon presentation of proof of ownership by their copyright proprietor.

Although the situations in this book actually occurred, certain names have been changed to ensure the privacy of the individuals and/or other entities who were involved.

Starin, Bruce J. 1951 -

 Published in the USA by:
BearManor Media
1317 Edgewater Dr #110
Orlando, FL 32804
www.bearmanormedia.com

Paperback ISBN 978-1-62933-762-3
Hardback ISBN 978-1-62933-763-0

Edited by: Nat Segaloff
Design by: Robbie Adkins, www.adkinsconsult.com

Dedicated to
Nat Segaloff
Who was first to say,
"Hey, you can write."
And to
Geraldine and Peregrine
who lovingly scream,
"You wrote about what?"

WARNING: *Many readers may find memories of the famous people encountered, as well as the adventures and situations recounted on the following pages, to be ribald, nasty and offensive. If this is true, the author thanks you in advance for your discerning opinion and suggests you quickly turn the page.*

Table of Contents

Part I: At Sea 1
Arrival 3
Woody Trail—One Tiny Side Street in the Hollywood Hills 5
Welcome Aboard, or Call Me Fishmeal, Babe 19
The Capitano 27
The Chief Purser, Would You Like To ... Dance? 33
Cruise Director Marty, or Joey, or Johnny, or Lonny 37
The Assistant Cruise Director, and His Solid Gold Penis 51
The Ship's Doctor, A Kiss Is Just A Kiss 57
The Entertainers, or, One, Two, Three, Kick 61
Mr. Myron Cohen 67
Rowena—Just a Singer From a Smokey Cafe 71
Kenny Kingston—Psychic to the Stars 73
Izzy the Comic 77
Babette and Robaire—Los Danse Stylists Parisian 81
Lindy Shore & Vivian Avalon, We're a Closing Act, Period! ... 85
The Tours, the Drunks, and Even More Complaints, or, You ... 89
    Don't Have to Be Drunk to Enjoy a Tour, But It Helps
The Revolution in Grenada, or, I'll Give You Three Key Chains .. 109
    for the Hostages...You Can Keep Their Cameras
The Croupier, or, Wherever There's Cash, Someone Will 119
    Figure Out How to Steal It
Of Bella Fica's, Busy Asses, and Women Who Had Cars 125
    of Their Own

Of Cherry Boys, Religious Girls, and Women Who Wear Their 133
    Boots to Bed...or, Twenty Dollars Gets You Twenty Minutes
Cast Thy Bread Upon the Water 165
The Funeral at Sea 175
The Party Night, or: Ho, Ho, Ho, Ha, Ha, Ha, Arbeit Macht Frei!...181
The Arrival of Bobo Natale, or, Isn't It Amazing Around 185
    Christmas Time Everyone Looks Like an Angel
Concerning the Removal of Luggage 195
The End, or, It's Great When Your Ship Comes In; It's Even ... 199
    Better When you Are On It

Photo Gallery 200

Part II: Still at Sea... But Attempting to Plant My Feet 221
    in Hollywood
Oh Brave New World, That Hath Such Creatures In 223
The Return of the Prodigal 233
Chuck Barris 241
Al and Flo Joyner 249
Mike Tyson 257
Dick Clark, or, Let's Rock Around the Clock 263
Andrew Dice Clay and the American Music Awards 269
Monty Hall and Clint Eastwood 271
Will Geer, America's Grandpa 279
Uncle Moishe 283
George Abbott—Producer, Director, Playwright, ... 287
    Screenwriter, Legend
Aunt Sara, Uncle Irving, Abbie Hoffman 291
Esther Williams, The Million Dollar Mermaid 297
Wheel of Fortune Live! 303

Edmonton, Alberta, Canada.................................. 315
Branson, Missouri 319
Las Vegas Residency, or, What Happens in Vegas, ... 321
    May Not Stay in Vegas
Tom Jones, A Close Personal Friend ... Really?.............. 327
The Emerald City Lounge.................................... 331
Harvey Weinstein, Need a Light, Sugar Lips? 335
Joe Garagiola and the Wrangled Audience................... 337
Jonathan Winters and Two Honeybaked Hams 341
Larry King, Wide Suspenders, Thick Glasses and Hot Pastrami...343
Merv Griffin.. 345
Roger Ailes, Rush Limbaugh, and Miss Eartha Kitt............349
Gerald Ford and Tales of a Fly-Away Producer 355
Jay Leno and A PA System Hitler Used at Nuremberg........ 371
Sir John Gielgud, Sir Ralph Richardson, Muhammad Ali 373
    and Elaine Stritch
Steve Landesburg - Comedian, Actor, Daddy................ 377
Charlton Heston - Lilla Heston's Big Brother ... Chucky...... 381
Lion Tamer Clyde Beatty, Otto the Dwarf, and a Grandma .. 385
    on a Skateboard
Hotel Ritz Paris 389
Pierce Brosnan & Mohammad Al-Fayed.................... 393
Ithaca 397

Part I: At Sea

ARRIVAL

In Hollywood, everyone's arrival story is different. I rolled into town in 1976 with some prior experience in assorted television series, movies, and commercials in Miami and New York. I was armed with a Bachelor of Arts degree in acting and a Master's degree in playwrighting.

Arriving in Los Angeles, I found a cheap apartment in Hollywood, dodging hookers on my way home from a nighttime job at Wallach's Music City on the corner of Sunset and Vine, thus making myself available for auditions during the day. I even called the William Morris Agency and asked to speak with Mr. Morris. The operator said, "He's been dead for fifty years, honey!" and promptly hung up on me. Could never figure out why. Had photos made, sent them out to every agent in town, excluding the Morris office, with my paltry resume stapled to the back. I received a bite from one agent and landed a few small jobs on popular television series of the time—*Barnaby Jones, Rockford Files, Incredible Hulk* and even a short time regular on the soap opera, *Days of Our Lives*—and that was it. After a year of living amidst the mean streets of Hollywood, shopping at the Hollywood Ranch Market, and being awakened during the early morning hours with lesbians beating each other up in the street, I decided it was time for a change.

WOODY TRAIL – ONE TINY SIDE STREET IN THE HOLLYWOOD HILLS

After surviving for a year in the Hollywood tenderloin, I reached out to a fellow actor I had met years before at the Mount Holyoke College Summer Theatre. We were "coeds" at the Ivy League Girls School, one of the "Seven Sisters," hired to play the male roles in various plays, particularly during their summer stock season. My friend came out to Los Angeles a few years before me and found an apartment in the surrounding hills on a street called Woody Trail. He claimed it was named after Woody Guthrie, a onetime resident, and, more importantly, there was another apartment available. That was all I needed to know.

"I'll be up there in an hour!" I said, and so began my earliest sojourn in the Hollywood Hills.

In order to find Woody Trail, one needed to first deal with Pacific View Drive, a narrow, two-lane road, mainly serving as a winding mountain shortcut that will take you from a congested Cahuenga Pass in the San Fernando Valley to Outpost Drive in the Hollywood Hills. The shortcut drops you off in Hollywood just west of the Magic Castle and a street heading up to Yamashiro's, a restaurant and bar with expansive views of the nighttime twinkling lights of the entire Los Angeles basin. While driving the curving Gran Prix-like road to Outpost on balmy summer nights, you could pull off the road at a particular spot and see the crowded Hollywood Bowl below. If the breezes off the Pacific were blowing in the right direction, you could even hear, for example, the artists of the Playboy Jazz Festival as well as the various summer pop or classical concerts. The laser light show on John Williams (*Star Wars*) Night or the elaborate fireworks display for Tchaikovsky's 1812 Overture Night and, of course, the July Fourth Fireworks Spectacular, done in sync with marches by John Phillips Sousa, were stunning and exciting to experience. Best of all, we appreciated it all free, though with one false step you could end up tumbling down the hill into someone's backyard pool.

On a promontory on the highest point on Pacific View with a commanding view of both the San Fernando Valley and the Los Angeles basin were the stone ruins of a house that was rumored to have once belonged to Bela Lugosi. Supposedly, it burned down in the thirties and couldn't be re-zoned for a house inasmuch as the entire hill was geologically "DG," or decomposing granite. Recent earthquakes didn't make it any more stable, so we would scramble up the crumbling sides and used it for a great spot to hang out and smoke a joint or two. Pre-Bela Lugosi, late twenties early thirties, the stone edifice was supposedly a hunting lodge. Various Hollywood stars, among them Errol Flynn, David Niven, and Alan Hale would frequent the place to hunt deer and assorted little critters that roamed the wooded hillsides. Older residents of the hill claimed it was actually a speakeasy and brothel, and the Hollywood stars who stopped by were not on the hunt for deer.

Woody Trail is a small road that drops off precipitously from Pacific View with a few homes clinging on either side of a dangerously steep hill. It leads to a small flat area below supporting a few more homes, and therein lies a tale.

I was fortunate enough to be offered a tiny studio apartment situated below one of the larger homes that at one time belonged to beat poet and hipster Lord Buckley. Buckley was an early purveyor of the "Spoken Word" and would re-write classics in "Hipster" as well as create his own spoken word works. His most famous piece was a rewrite of Shakespeare's "Friends Romans, Countrymen" monologue from *Julius Caesar* into "Hipsters, Flusters, and Finger Poppin' Daddies, Lend me your lobes." He also created a Christmas story called "The Naz" (nee the Nazarene) and an homage to Gandhi called "The Gahn."

Lord Buckley, sporting a Salvador Dali-esque pointed moustache, affected a stuffy English accent. He appeared in hip nightclubs all over the country as well as appearances on *The Ed Sullivan Show* and *The Steve Allen Show*. He always dressed in his signature starched formal evening wear with tails, wearing a pith helmet.

His son Fred currently occupied the house. He billed himself as "Lord Buckley, Jr." when I rented the apartment. On move-in day, Fred told me the apartment had great ghosts since James Dean and even Woody Guthrie once lived there, hence the name of the street "Woody Trail." No way to verify the lore, but the one-room apartment was rather inexpensive and it did have a small deck jutting out over an arroyo that dropped down to the Hollywood Freeway, roaring through the Cahuenga Pass. There was even a tiny ribbon of a stream that gurgled down the narrow convergence of the arroyo sides during the rainy season. When a siren from a fire engine or police car screamed through the pass below, a pack of coyotes who lived in the arroyo would start howling like a chorus of Valkyries until Fred sauntered out on his deck above my apartment and, with a booming baritone voice, shouted, "Shut the hell up!" and the baying stopped immediately.

A small herd of deer with a few antlered bucks clomped around the wooded hillsides as well. They were mainly visible on rainy days for some reason, along with smaller pals such as opossums, rattlesnakes, huge hooting owls, soaring red-tailed hawks, and chubby raccoons. The bolder, more aggressive raccoons would actually come up on the decks in the evening and forage around, occasionally rearing up and scratching on my sliding glass door.

This area in the Hollywood Hills separating the San Fernando Valley from the Los Angeles basin, in addition to the assorted wildlife, was also home to the most amazing assortment of writers, artists, celebrities, and wonderful eccentrics that a wide-eyed new arrival could ever hope to meet. Fred and his father notwithstanding, the unofficial mayor of the "Trail" was a spritely older fellow named Lancelot Hay. Lancelot came to town to be the original Robin in Columbia's *Batman and Robin* serials produced in the late 1940s. He'd made his living since then as an interior designer and carpenter who would rebuild interiors of homes with built-in curving furniture, always with indirect lighting underneath controlled by dimming rheostats. He felt the ability to adjust the lighting enabled his clients to match their moods as necessary. Lancelot did not believe in lamps or overhead lighting. In addition to being hired by various architects and designers to rebuild the interiors of the Frank Lloyd Wright and Lloyd Wright homes checkering the Hollywood Hills, he was also employed by many celebrities to redesign their living spaces

One afternoon, Lancelot told me there was a client in Malibu who owed him a few bucks and asked if I would give him a lift to the guy's "pad." I agreed, never having been inside any of the houses in Malibu clinging to Pacific Coast Highway, so I was instantly curious. When we arrived, Lancelot led me right in to the dimly lit house without knocking. We came across his client lounging inside, listening and gently grooving under what looked like a pair of state-of-the-art headphones. The client was wearing large, dark sunglasses and a long, glossy caftan bedecked in embroidered musical notes. He turned and rose, removing the headphones and the dark sunglasses, to say hello. I could not help but notice his eyes seemed dangerously large and bloodshot, but he motioned us in and directed us to sit on his huge sofa that snaked thought the living room. Just beyond the floor-to-ceiling windows, the Pacific crashed and rolled with a monotonous regularity.

"Hey man," he said in an extremely hoarse voice, "can I get you a soda or something, some chips, maybe a Nutter Butter?"

I declined politely. He nodded and said, "Cool" and, in the same gravelly voice, added, "Hey Lancelot, come with me." The two of them casually sauntered into the kitchen for a chat.

Lancelot failed to mention on the drive over that designing for this particular client who owed him a few bucks was one of his biggest claims to fame. Lancelot designed and built this forty-eight foot "S" curved couch covered in zebra hide, with indirect lighting, of course, that I was sitting on. We were, coincidently, in the Malibu mansion of jazz legend Miles Davis. Miles Davis who just offered me a soda and a peanut butter cookie! My head almost exploded.

Lancelot owned what was probably the largest house on Woody Trail. You entered the main floor with floor to ceiling windows on one end and the indirectly lit, curving furniture lining the walls. His studio and design center was on the lower level, and the bedrooms and baths on the highest level. The "lab" at the time was filled with photos and cardboard cut outs of Shamu, the Killer Whale, as Marineland had recently hired him to design a souvenir mobile of the leaping whale to sell in their gift shop.

There was a bathroom on the main floor. In a fit of creativity, he had made the bathtub into a huge desert terrarium with a collection of cacti and various plants to match. The terrarium was home to a tortoise Lancelot claims crawled into his sleeping bag during an acid trip in Joshua Tree National Park. He took that as an omen and named the tortoise Timothy. I once asked him if that was in honor of Timothy Leary and he smiled coyly and said, "Maybe yes, maybe no, wanna smoke a joint?"

Even though it was still completely illegal in those days, Lancelot was never without an ample supply of fantastic marijuana, no telling from who or where he purchased it. One afternoon, my parents were visiting from Miami. My mother was off shopping in Beverly Hills and my dad and I were just hanging out on my deck overlooking the arroyo. Lancelot saw us from his living room and, with a yell and a frenetic welcoming wave, invited us over. It seems Lancelot was a one-time circus performer and, as I had told him my dad once traveled as a "talker" or "barker" with the Ringling show during the thirties, he was dying to meet him.

As we entered Lancelot's place, my father looked around and whistled quietly to himself, as he was wont to do when surprised or introduced into any situation he considered "artistic." Lancelot showed us to his curvilinear sofa, pulled over a harlequin colored Arabian leather hassock, and sat down. He was wearing one of his signature caftans, which he wore every day. As a neighbor, I grew accustomed to his somewhat eccentric outfits, which included a caftan as well as a walking stick with a sword hidden inside.

Quite a different story for my father who, I might add, was a cross between Tevye and Archie Bunker. He didn't say anything—just stared at me suspiciously and quietly whistled.

Lancelot began chatting with my dad about the circus, and while doing so, he pulls out an elaborately decorated wooden box, opens it matter-of-factly, and begins rolling a joint by hand. He was very good at it.

My life flashed before me. I quickly glanced over to my dad, who was staring at me yet again, and let us just say, if looks could kill, I would be a dead man.

Ever the consummate host, Lancelot finished rolling the joint, lights it with a silver Victorian styled lighter, takes a quick puff, and hands it off to my father saying, "Abe take a hit, this is really good shit."

My father demurred with uncharacteristic politeness and then Lancelot, with neighborly nonchalance, offers the nicely burning joint to me.

If the windows were open, I would have jumped out; my father's stare was boring holes into the side of my head.

"Thanks man" I replied, "but we have to drive down the hill to pick up my mother in a few. I'm taking them to Nate and Al's deli. Want me to bring you back a sandwich?" desperately trying to pivot the moment to something less illegal.

Still offering me the joint, with a wisp of smoke snaking through his fingers, Lancelot says, "Hey man, hot pastrami is great after a few tokes. Take a hit."

"Lancelot, it's okay, later," and I shot a side eye to my Dad. Lancelot finally got it and offered a Pall Mall cigarette to my dad from a packet he had in his caftan pocket—coincidently, my dad's favorite brand, so he accepted and they chatted about the circus for another hour or two.

We left a short time later. My father never mentioned the incident or Lancelot again.

Sunday afternoons were reserved for unofficial "come-as-you-are" soirees at Lancelot's place. All the neighbors were invited and you never knew whom you might meet.

The author of One Flew Over the Cuckoo's Nest, Ken Kesey, dropped by one Sunday afternoon, invited by an ex-Merry Prankster named Mike Hagen, who was another homeowner on Woody Trail. Years before, Kesey organized a few fellow travelers to board a dilapidated yellow school bus they named "Further" to travel to LSD testing sites. The plan was to volunteer to be the subjects for all the experiments. The riders became known as the "Merry Pranksters." Hagan was the camera operator for the adventure and was given the nickname, "Mal Function." He had moved to Hollywood to pursue a career as a film technician. Both he and Kesey kept us all enthralled and laughing uncontrollably as they retold stories of the trial and tribulations while on the road seeking out testing sites and the copious free samples of LSD.

Timothy Leary showed up with Kesey and Hagan one afternoon. A few weeks prior I had given him a Pong® game as a gift while working nights as a clerk at Wallach's Music City on Sunset and Vine. He had walked over to the cashier's stand preparing to pay. Not looking up at him, I had to ask him his name for the receipt, and he said, "Leary."

"Oh, is that as in Timothy?" I asked, trying to be funny.

"Yes," came a modest reply.

I looked up in surprise. Standing in front of the cash register was a smiling person with a serene expression and a twinkle in his eye, the world famous guru of the "Tune In, Turn On, and Drop Out" counter culture, Professor Timothy Leary! I quickly bagged the Pong game and shoved it into his hands saying, "Here Professor, take it. My treat!"

He seemed a bit embarrassed and tried to pay, but I refused and said it was my way of thanking him for just being him. He smiled, winked, and walked out with his Pong game tucked under his arm. I added the cost into the cash drawer from my own pocket and thought how cool it was that Timothy Leary had just purchased one of the earliest versions of a video game from me. Actually, I purchased it for him, but that did not matter.

You can imagine my surprise when I noticed him standing on Lancelot's deck enjoying the sunset one Sunday afternoon. I walked over and asked, "Hi Professor Leary. Enjoying your Pong game?"

He looked at me quizzically for a moment, and then his face lit up in recognition,

"Hey, you're the kid who gave me the Pong game! How ya' doin' man?" he asked, vigorously shaking my hand, "I'll tell you what, man. That damn Pong game is really fucking me up. I mean, it's like out there! Hey, Ken, Mike, come here! This is the kid who gave me the Pong game the other night!"

Kesey and Hagan came over and started cross-examining me as to if I really gave him a Pong game. I told them it was a Friday night, the place was empty, and so I gave it to him as a gift. I didn't say anything about paying for it myself after he left. They were both amazed.

"Damn, I could have sworn you were bullshitting." Kesey said to Leary.

"No way!" answered Timothy. "He just told you what happened."

By this time a joint was being passed around and the subject of conversation quickly changed. We all continued talking about the sunset and the indirect lighting under Lancelot's sofa.

Just before they left, Professor Leary separated from the duo, came up to me and placed a small tin foil cube in my hand, and said with an impish smile, "Enjoy it."

It was a sugar cube. I never used it. It still sits in a small Mason jar in my office.

Another denizen of the group was artist Nino Russo. Nino was very proud of the fact his daughter was the model and actor Rene Russo, though she never stopped by at any of the Sunday soirees. Nino lived off Laurel Canyon Boulevard, high atop Lookout Mountain Avenue. On a clear day, you could see Catalina Island from his kitchen window. It seems this location was the highest spot and farthest inland from the coast with a clear view over the entire Los Angeles basin to the Pacific. During World War II it was designated to be the last bastion of defense if the Japanese ever decided to invade Los Angeles. Carved into the mountain directly below Nino's house was a huge artificial cavern of sorts that ran parallel with the street above for few thousand yards. It was an abandoned ruin by the time I was able to check it out, but you could still see the remnants of a military installation with posts for telescopes and such and even a few rusting government issue olive green bed frames, desks, and cabinets scattered about. Below that slit in the hill, Nino claimed that, during the fifties, the military built a Top Secret facility just below and used it to develop the stills and movies taken of the atomic detonations in Las Vegas. Known as Hollywood's Top Secret Nuclear Film Studio, the structure has since been rebuilt into an eight-bedroom, twelve-bathroom private home recently purchased by actor Jared Leto.

Nino met me at Lancelot's one afternoon. We hit it off and he asked if I would be willing to assist him when he needed some help. He created bronze statues and assorted artwork using the Lost Wax method of casting. He would carve a wax version of his work, cover it with a special clay, and then it was my job to run it down to a foundry where they would pour in the molten bronze. The wax would disappear, hence "lost wax," and, after cooling, the clay was chipped away, revealing the bronze statue in partial glory. I would then have to deliver the rough sculpture back to Nino's living room studio where he would add an assortment of chemicals to create a patina he thought appropriate. Occasionally that was hand-rubbing with hard Minwax, heating with a blowtorch, or simply letting the pieces stand outside and weather naturally. One afternoon, I asked where his bathroom was, and he asked off-handedly if I had to pee. A bit surprised, I said yes and he then directed me to pee on a bronze of a trumpet player out in the yard he had just received from the foundry. It seems he wanted an acid patina on the piece and urine had the perfect components.

Nino never seemed to have much cash on hand, even though he charged huge amounts of money for his works. Occasionally he took trade instead of cash, and once paid me with a brick of tightly wound Thai stick direct from Bangkok. On another occasion, I arrived to do an errand and noticed a huge mound of cocaine sitting on his kitchen table. I didn't say anything as I had a very cautious "don't ask, don't tell" relationship with Nino and some of his dealings. The windows were open in the kitchen on this clear spring day, and just about three in the afternoon, a huge breeze directly off the Pacific blew in through the open window, exploding the mountain of cocaine into a huge white cloud instantly spreading throughout the studio and onto everything and everyone in it. Undaunted, though himself coated with a fine white powder, Nino calmly placed his chisels down, wiped his glasses with his apron, and announced to everyone in the room, including his current girlfriend, his agent, the fellow from the foundry, and me, "Okay everyone! Lick it up!"

Which we did, like children rolling around in a room dusted with powdered sugar.

After being refreshingly alert and wide awake for about forty-eight hours, I finally went to bed and slept for three days.

One weekday, I was working on a script and was startled by someone yelling and screaming on Woody Trail. I listened for a moment and heard a voice calling Lancelot every nasty name in the book: "You can't even get it up anymore, you asshole! You couldn't even get it up if Marilyn Monroe was sitting on your face, you turd!"

I figured it was time to investigate. Walking outside, I noticed a few of the neighbors had already surrounded the screaming guy, who began waving a gun as they were trying to calm him down.

It was Nino. It seems he heard that Lancelot told someone that Nino's Norwegian girlfriend was nothing more than an over-the-hill airline stewardess. This was more than Nino could bear. We hustled him out of the neighborhood before the police arrived and, over a cup of coffee in a café at the bottom of the hill, we tried to defuse the situation. We were particularly concerned with the chrome .38-caliber pistol he had been waving around.

"Oh, come on guys, for Christ's sake, I wasn't going to kill him, I just want to scare the little fucker. The gun isn't even loaded." he scoffed, tossing the huge pistol on the café table. We all jumped back in our seats, and Yabo Yablonsky, another resident of the

Trail, grabbed the gun and immediately checked the revolver. It was indeed unloaded.

"Nino, I'll keep this for the time being, until you get it together, okay?" said Yabo.

"Fine, I don't care," said Nino, "But I'm telling you guys if he ever says anything about my old lady again, I'll come down there and beat him to death with a stick."

"Until then," said Yabo in finality, and we all got up and left.,

Yabo Yablonsky, by the way, was another homeowner in the neighborhood. He wrote *Victory*, directed by John Huston, starring Sylvester Stallone and Michael Caine. He adored Bulgarian buffalo grass vodka and, once loosened up a bit, loved singing Russian folk songs at the top of his lungs from Lancelot's deck He would serenade the entire arroyo whether residents were interested in torch songs of the revolution or not.

Drew Barrymore walked in one Sunday afternoon. She had just purchased a small Spanish house on a neighboring arroyo, and took one look at her father, John Barrymore, Jr., who was there chatting up Ultra Violet, one of Andy Warhol's favorite stars, and promptly walked out in a huff, shaking her head in disgust.

I did get to know Drew later during one of my early evening walks on the winding hillside streets. It seems everyone in the neighborhood knew Merlin, my huge black cat with a crooked Art Deco tail, as I'm told he visited many of the neighbors during the day while I was working down the hill in Hollywood by then with a production company. Drew rushed out of her house one evening and showed me a Polaroid® she had snapped of my cat Merlin terrorizing a baby rattlesnake on her patio. She had taken the snake that Merlin eventually killed and shoved it into a bottle of rubbing alcohol and asked me if I wanted it. I gladly accepted the bizarre trophy and we remained friends for quite a long time after that. I even invited her to my daughter's third birthday party, where she gladly assisted in handing out ice cream and cake. She became friends with our babysitter, a college student who lived with her parents in the hilly neighborhood. Occasionally the two of them would "sit" for us while my wife and I ran down the hill for a screening. When we returned I would pay our babysitter but when I attempted to hand Drew a few bucks she would giggle, slap my hand playfully, and say, "Oh come on, don't be silly, I should be paying you!" The two of them, laughing and giggling like teenagers, would saunter out into the jasmine scented evening on their way to a movie or who knows where.

During one of Lancelot's soirees, I met a couple who were part of an improvisational comedy group who performed in the Belly Room, a back room at the Comedy Store on Sunset. They told me they were preparing to set sail as "The Drama Duo" on a cruise ship that docked in San Pedro for a one-week stint. The ship would hire a couple to perform scenes from a number of Neil Simon plays as weeknight entertainment in one of the larger lounges. It did not pay much, but you did get first class passage for a week, had to wear tuxedos twice a week, and you were allowed to enjoy gourmet meals nightly including an indulgent dollop of Beluga caviar on French Night. The cherry on top seemed to be the ability to bring back from other countries as many illicit pills and bricks of marijuana as was prudent.

They gladly imparted this information to me after I introduced them to the iconic Viola Spolin who, with her husband, were two additional denizens of the Trail. Viola also happened to be the author of *Improvisation for the Theatre*, the bible for improv artists. During the introduction, taking place amidst the hanging spider plants and ferns in Lancelot's kitchen, she patiently instructed all three of us on the proper way to "hot knife" hashish.

On the following Monday morning, bright with promise, I telephoned the woman in charge of the agency. I told her of my desire to work on a ship and listed my meager credentials. While attending college in New England, I had held numerous positions with resorts on the Eastern Seaboard as far south as the Casablanca Hotel on Miami Beach, or Mount Airy Lodge, way up to the Poconos. I was primarily employed as a "Tummler," or social director on the pool decks, in the nightclubs, and anywhere else my services were required. This included everything from calling Bingo to hosting the "Grandmas Bragging Party." My favorite stunt was approaching a good-looking female guest who was wearing the skimpiest bikini I could find. I made a big show of whispering something in her ear. I told her to scream, slap me in the face and push me in the pool fully dressed, creating the biggest splash possible. Always good for laughs on the pool deck during steamy hot afternoons.

The booking agent listened intently, paused for a moment after I had finished, and finally said, "Well kid," (all booking agents like to call aspirants "kid"), "what are you doing on Wednesday?"

"I have nothing penciled in my appointment book and even less in ink. Why?"

"How would you like to be a Social Director" (obviously a high class version of "Tummler") on one of our cruise ships for a few months?"

"I suppose I could work it into my schedule." I replied, wanting to sound eager, yet detached.

"Fine." she snapped, "Report for a uniform fitting first thing tomorrow morning at this address."

She gave me the address of Academy Award Clothes, a huge uniform wholesaler in the Los Angeles Garment District that specialized in suits and uniforms for real estate people, airline ticket agents, and inexpensive tuxedos for Maitre'ds and waiters. Cruise ship personnel were also included and, when it comes to polyester, it was just a matter of color. Even more convenient was the fact that alterations could be had instantly with a hand-held steam iron.

"Report to the dock in Port Everglades at 8 A.M. on Wednesday. I will FedEx your plane tickets after lunch. Oh, and by the way," she interjected before hanging up, "stop by the office and say hello next time the ship docks in Manhattan. Okay, babe?"

Booking agents also like to call you "babe" once you have agreed to their offer. They think it a lot more personal than "kid."

"Okay." I answered, and a few days later I was sailing out of Port Everglades, Florida, on what turned out to be one of the grandest adventures of my life.

WELCOME ABOARD, OR, CALL ME FISHMEAL, BABE

After receiving my uniforms and white shoes from the huge wholesale emporium in the Garment District, I was told to board a taxi for the Los Angeles International Airport. It seems the ship I was ordered to was be being overhauled in Fort Lauderdale's Port Everglades and I was to meet the vessel there.

Somewhere between the Garment District and LAX I was scheduled to meet up with the ship's secretary, a woman named Lotus. Asking for a description, I was told not to worry as she was impossible to miss. This was less than reassuring; the Garment District, a charming section of the inner city, was populated by homeless folks babbling the blues, exploited seamstresses, flouncy women from Beverly Hills wearing pastel colored running suits searching for bargains, and paunchy middle-aged men wearing tape measures draped over their shoulders as though they were exclusive rag trade prayer shawls.

Having waited what I thought to be a considerable amount of time, I had run out of change for the panhandlers and decided to hail a cab and set off for the airport, figuring the mysterious Lotus would show up there.

A rendezvous with someone you have never met is always interesting, especially when the appointed location is one of the busiest air terminals in the country. Lacking even a vague description to go by, I imagined a ship's secretary to be either very business-like, favoring tweeds and sturdy shoes, or a bombshell built like Dolly Parton, not knowing how to type and having absolutely no desire to learn. I prepared to greet either.

After a few women appeared to be walking my way only to run off in B-movie horror when I smiled and asked, "Hi there. Are you going to be working on a cruise ship?" I decided to forget about finding a Lotus in an airport and headed for the gate.

Moments before boarding, every head in the terminal turned in unison toward a flurry of excitement moving though the building. Bounding through the entrance to the ticket window, then toward the gate as fast as her clicking high heels could carry her, came a woman with mounds of bouncing orange hair, a figure that could stop traffic, and was. She was pushing a carriage of matching Louis Vuitton luggage. I believe she honestly thought she was going to get it all on board as carry-on. She clutched a shrieking Shi-Tzu in one arm and what appeared to be a two and half foot long zucchini with the other.

Out of all the other people in the crowded terminal staring at her equally, she walked right up to me and placed the long green thing in my arms. I was right. It was a zucchini and weighed at least five pounds. She kissed and snuggled the wriggling Shi-Tzu who, with bloodshot eyes rolling back in his head, looked as though he was having convulsions. Unconcerned, she shunted him off to one of her accompanying entourage, said and kissed her good-byes, then turned to me and said, "Hi. So you're going to be working on the ship, right?"

"Is it that obvious?" I whispered.

"Welcome aboard. I'm Lotus." Grabbing the zucchini out of my arms, she extended her hand, giving me a hearty how-do-you-do handshake. At a loss for words, I sensed most everyone in the airport was now ogling both us rather than just her. Noticing my discomfort, she snorted cheerfully, saying, "Get used to the stares, kiddo. I mean, if it bothers you, honey, are you ever in the wrong business." Slapping me on the chest, she minced her way ahead and sashayed through the gate toward the plane. I followed her, which I did not mind doing at all.

Once we were seated, I inquired about the zucchini. She told me it was a gift for the Chief Purser, winking suggestively, licking her raspberry glossed lips with her tongue. Popping a Xanax, she settled in for a trans-continental nap, cradling the squash throughout the entire flight like a teddy bear.

Five hours later, after wading through a wall of humid air perfumed with the essence of mildew, I found myself deep in the terminal building of the Fort Lauderdale International airport. Once outside, conditions grew worse as an "autumnal" ninety-six degrees enveloped us. Lotus, not the least bit groggy from her Xanax, told me to go on ahead to the cab stand, as she wanted to make sure all her luggage had arrived intact. Furthermore, the Chief Purser, that bastard, was supposed to have sent a car for her anyway. Poor child, I thought, to travel all that way with an elephantine squash just to be stood up at the airport. Ah well, such is life in the fast lane. I hailed a cab and we were off to the shipyard.

I was warned beforehand that the ship was large. I never expected to see the superstructure looming above the neighboring buildings while the cab was still many blocks away. As we approached, more of the ship became visible, but only in segments. We turned a corner and, at the end of the lane, I saw a white wall dotted with portholes. Up another street, the tip of the bow protruded with the ship's name being touched up with gold paint by a crew of six painters standing on a scaffold suspended from what looked to be the heavens. Talk about large; they were all working on one letter. Finally, we turned down a street ending with another wall of portholes but, unlike the other, there was a small doorway in its center with a gangway zigzagging from it to the deck below. Each zig and zag consisted of some ten steps and there were five of them. This led only halfway up the side of the ship. I was in awe. If it remained floating, I was in business.

The ship, the T.S.S. Luna Sea (not the actual name, but changed to protect the guilty) according to the get-acquainted brochure, was just shy of nine hundred and fifty feet long, ninety feet wide, and over fourteen stories high, five of those levels beneath the water line. Small, "boutique size" by today's standards. For the sports-minded, we are talking the length of two and a half football fields and the distance from the goalpost to the thirty-yard line in width. When fully loaded with two thousand passengers and their luggage, six hundred crew members, their shoulder-sized stereos, and everything else necessary to keep this floating pleasure palace comfortably opulent, it displaced fifty five thousand tons, give or take a few pounds. She was able to scoot through the water at a brisk twenty-five knots like a huge iron swan in a kiddie park's wading pool.

Should God ever decide to build another Ark I thought, foregoing cubits, these would be the dimensions to consider, provided He could establish some extremely creative financing.

I began climbing the stairs. After a few flights, I paused for a moment to catch my breath and look about. Stretching before me was the town of Fort Lauderdale blending into Miami toward the south and the flat Everglades beyond that. I wondered what the view was like from the smokestack, realizing Lotus was telling the truth when she mentioned the flashing red light on the funnel was an airplane beacon. I was in awe!

Finally reaching the top of the gangway, I stepped from the bright sunlight into a reception area. Expecting to find a loggia rivaling the Pitti Palace in Florence or, at worst, a hotel lobby in Vegas, I was taken aback to see every inch of furniture, wainscoting and carpet covered with drop cloths, plastic shrouds, and carpet runners. The area resembled my Aunt Estelle's house in Queens, New York, the time my family arrived for our annual visit a few days ahead of schedule. At least at Aunt Estelle's you could smell the brisket and potato pie simmering in her kitchen. Paint, brass polish, and turpentine were the mellifluent scents greeting me a few short hours before two thousand passengers were scheduled to board.

Briefly, I thought it might be sporting to remove some of the drop cloths, but as dozens of men clad in blue trimmed T-shirts and baggy jeans were being ordered about by snarling gentlemen in starched white uniforms, I figured drop cloth removal was a union job and decided to mind my own business.

So there I was, uniforms and tuxedos slung over my shoulder, kit bag in hand, feeling completely out of place. Wherever I stood, I was hustled to another spot by a sailor struggling with a sofa, hauling a bolt of carpeting, or dragging a cart loaded with dripping paint cans. Each move initiated with a few choice words in Italian or Portuguese, and as I spoke little of either, it all sounded nasty.

Seeing what looked like an elevator, I began inching my way over to it, gingerly avoiding any collisions with wagonloads of linen or trays of glassware. The moment I reached for the button, the doors sprang open and a young man wearing a starched white uniform leaped out and smashed into me, both of us falling into a tangled heap on the plastic covered carpet. He apologized as much as he was blushing, and the others milling about took a welcome pause from their duties to double over in particularly abusive laughter. The young fellow helped me up, insisted on brushing me off and, despite my protestations, disappearing with my luggage. He returned a few moments later explaining in halting, over pronounced English, that I had nothing to worry about as my things would be taken to my quarters as soon as the paint dried. Until then, he suggested I accompany him on an errand he had to run. It was early; the sun was shining, and there was still time for a cup of coffee. How could I refuse?

I began to introduce myself, and he waved me off, saying, "I know. I know. You new 'Directore Sociale.' Si?"

"Yes, I guess I am." But how did he know that? Before I was able to inquire, he pulled me toward the gangway and we started down the very same stairs I had just climbed up a few moments before.

Sauntering into town, he was obviously in no hurry to return to the ship. I learned most cruise lines have in their employ at least one cadet seaman. The fellow is placed on board to learn the ways and wiles of becoming an officer on a luxury liner. Paulo, as he insisted I call him, was seventeen years old, small, slight, and possessed a charming European shyness in direct counterpoint to the pompous strutting of his white-clad superiors. Later on in the season, I saw these attributes attract the younger recently pubescent female passengers to him like flies to Venetian marzipan. While stopping for a drink at any number of outdoor cafes in the Caribbean and Mexico, I spotted him at another table sipping a soda with a sixteen-year-old vamp.

"I mean, like you know, this is really outrageous, you know?" she was telling him. "I mean like you're an officer and everything. I mean like my friends at Encino High would never believe this. You know? Like this is really 'rad.' Wow."

Not understanding a word of what any one of these sweet young things might have said, even though he studied English at his naval academy back in Genoa, he simply smiled and replied, "Maria Sue, you maka my spine freeze." Not able to maintain it, he would-break down giggling, his face reddening to a bright shade of Vatican carmine.

He worked in the engine room and was being trained in the operation of the steam turbines. Not a very pleasant position. The heat in the turbine bowels was overwhelming and the only device able to keep the sweat out of the engineers eyes were masks the veterans had fashioned out of sanitary napkins. Through long years of experimentation, they found sanitary napkins to be the only articles that had the absorbency to last an eight-hour shift. Being as Paulo was the last man in, so to speak, when the ship arrived at a major port it was his job to locate a drugstore and fetch enough boxes of the napkins to last the duration of the next cruise. Coincidentally, Fort Lauderdale was his first American port, so this was the first time he had run the errand, and I was the first "autentico" American on whom he was able to flex his English. He was so ingenuous; I avoided telling him I understood at best every other word of his conversation. Smiling and nodding, I went along with whatever he said. I tagged along as he marveled at the displays in the store windows, the walk/don't walk signs with actual outlines of human beings, and the surprising lack of public pissoirs.

Finding a large drug and variety store, I assured him this place would carry all the sanitary napkins he could ever possibly need. Once inside he could not believe the size of the place.

"Hey, as big as the town square in Genoa, no?"

"Possibly." I said, never having been to Genoa.

He began browsing about all the counters of hardware, toys, clothing, magazines and stereo equipment. A sleazy girlie magazine and a DVD player held his attention for equal amounts of time. Eventually he stumbled upon the pharmacist's alcove located in the rear of the store. Barely reaching the counter, which was of the raised variety so the pharmacist doubling as store manager could keep a keen eye out for shoplifters and the like, the young man piped up in halting English. "Please sir," he said, beginning to acquire a rosy hue, his large brown eyes looking up at the white-haired gentleman as though he were the Pope, "I would like twelve boxes of. . . of. . . ." Straining to remember the speech he was drilled on hours on end before arrival, he finally said, "Twelve boxes of ladies sanitary napkins."

Releasing a long sigh of relief, feeling for certain the worst was over. He looked at me confidently and smiled.

"Internal or external?" asked the pharmacist matter-of-factly.

"Ah. . . Ah. . .," he thought out loud, giving a uniquely Italian shoulder shrug and simultaneous pout, "you know." he concluded quickly, "the kind with the strings to go around the ears."

I heard a voice in my head laughing hysterically and saying, "Buckle your life jacket, Captain Ahab, it's going to be a bumpy cruise!"

THE CAPITANO

Captainos of cruise ships remain, even after casual scrutiny, a distinctly strange breed. Not only are they directly responsible for the safety and wellbeing of a few thousand people, but they man and supervise the engineering marvel that a luxury liner actually is. Granted there are Petty Officers directly below him responsible for the crew, the navigation, the engines, the hostelry, and the passengers, but should an emergency arise in any of the departments, it is the Captaino who is in direct command. Very often one will observe a Captaino emerging from the turbine bowels in grease-spattered overalls, having just dealt with a problem concerning any number of technical difficulties that perpetually arise with engines, air conditioning, plumbing, electrical generation, water desalinization, or waste disposal. They're the same problems any small town of one thousand or so could experience, the only difference being this town floats, and the Captaino reigns over it all. One does not assume commission of a ship fresh out of some "Academia di Maritimo" back in Italy. It takes years of experience.

Rarely are these gentlemen the suave, debonair matinee idol types, replete with graying temples and white hats that the advertising brochures would like you to believe. The Home Office hires models for those poses. If you were to see the Capitano of our ship wandering around in his civilian clothes, it would be difficult not to think he was a vacationing plumber from South Philly enjoying strike benefits pilfered from the till. In fact, one afternoon, while supervising the re-boarding of some five hundred passengers up a single gangway who were recently returned from a morning bus tour, a bald-headed, chubby fellow wearing white Bermuda shorts walked directly to the head of the line, chucking folks out of the way with his forearm muttering a gruff, "Scusa... scusa...," with each shove. Well, what is fair is fair, and rude and nervy are completely unacceptable. I quickly grabbed the guy by his shoulder and, with a well-intentioned but firm smile, told him he must wait in line like everyone else. This caused a ripple of applause to erupt from the passengers waiting and sweating in the immediate vicinity. I soon learned this recognition by the passengers saved my life or at least a broken jaw, as the chubby gent was known for his short temper as well as his title, Capitano Luigi Medici. Pounced on by attending sailors, I was hustled to one side as the Capitano was led up the gangway. Interference was run by the remaining sailors, jostling the passengers out of the way, leading their exalted leader up the gangway.

Our Captain was a husky Sicilian in his late fifties who had chalked up some forty years of sailing experience, most of them on cruise ships and a good deal on our ship. Home for a scant three months out of the year, he managed to raise a family of five sons and a daughter back in Italy. There was talk he had various other families throughout the world, an apartment house in Acapulco, and a condominium in Aruba, so he married the woman who collected the rents and kept the gardens trimmed, so what. As one of the Petty Officers once told me, "My wife, she gets a check from me every month for three thousand American dollars. She lives like a queen and she don't ask no questions." Punctuated in finality with a shrug of his shoulders and an, "Eh!"

Medici was about five feet four inches tall and just as wide. He had a seemingly jovial face, and, when not scowling while haranguing the crew or glowering at upstart Social Directors, his smile revealed a few gold caps on a collection of marvelously crooked teeth, none of which pointed in the same direction.

One morning I found myself walking quietly behind him as he cruised through a hallway. He took pleasure in sticking his head through an open cabin doorway while a passenger, having just tripped on the raised entryway portal, lay sprawled out on the carpet. Medici chided the unfortunate by helpfully reminding, "Hey lady! It is a ship. When you walk through the doors you gotta raisa you foots, huh?" He would then cavalierly help her up off the floor.

In addition, he went out of his way to admonish any passenger he thought slightly tinged with green or in any way afflicted with the *mal de mer*, advising, "Hey you Mister, you gotta the seasickness? Eata more pasta, ita fixa you right up. Okay?"

He then ambled off toward the Bridge, his hands swinging loosely by his sides, his thumbs rhythmically brushing his knees as he went. Meanwhile, I scraped the passengers up off the floor or directed the wobbly ones to the sickbay.

Master Medici, translating his title directly from the Italian, had affinities for three things in this world: tall, blonde women from the American West; antiques; and anything depicting the Milne character of Winnie-the-Pooh.

Each port seemed to produce a different tall, blonde, middle-aged woman from either Dallas or Tucson waiting for him on the dock. Dreadfully gracious Grand Dames, dressed as if competing in a Dolly Parton lookalike contest, they boarded with their designer luggage, accompanied him for a few days at sea, debarked early in the morning at the next port with a new one embarking later that same afternoon. It was all pleasantly convenient and never noticed by anyone. That is, never noticed by anyone not working on the ship.

An avid antique connoisseur, he had what was touted to be one of the most extensive collections of Mexican Santos, pre-Columbian figurines and religious paintings from the Colonial period this side of the National Gallery in Mexico City. In addition, as a man of Renaissance sensibilities, he collected every item he could find bearing the likeness of Winnie-the-Pooh or, as he preferred to call him, "Orsolino." A gathering of stuffed Winnies stood in his cabin descending in size from three feet tall to a few inches. His shelves were crammed with wind-up walking Winnies, assorted Winnie-the-Pooh story books in various languages, all of which he spoke and read, and ceramic planters with ivy growing from a pouch on Winnie's back or out of hole in his belly. He kept the manual, automatic, digital and pocket timepieces in a locked drawer in his desk. He charted the ship's course sitting in an official "Orsolino" director's chair, occasionally listening to a record he found in Caracas of Winnie singing playtime songs in Spanish. He knew them all by heart, humming along sometimes. For his personal use he had pillow cases, sheets, blankets, a comforter, electric toothbrush, and a bone china breakfast set, all portraying our Winnie happily going about his daily tasks.

One Christmas the Gran Chapeau, Mr. Sarducci, made Capitano a freestanding Winnie-the-Pooh cake, accented with fondant and marzipan. Standing two feet high, it had a bow tie sculpted from glacé pears dyed red, a date nose, spiced apple eyes and cute little toes molded from prunes stewed in an aspic. Unfortunately, during a lengthy and exasperating passage through the Panama Canal, Capitano left all his cabin portholes open. Entering his quarters and slamming the door after the upsetting day, he found that the overwhelming humidity had weakened Orsolino to such a degree that the little guy had ignominiously disintegrated into a craggy lump. The only vestiges of his former glory were the bulbous prune toes in aspic, wrinkling slightly. The Capitano weathered this disaster fairly well, the pride of his collection impervious to mercurial changes in global temperatures or shipboard temperament. Hanging above his bed in a gold leafed Baroque frame imported all the way from Italy just for the purpose was a three-by-four- foot Mola Winnie-the-Pooh. Molas are colorful hand embroidered layered appliqués, unique to the Cuna people inhabiting the San Blas Islands off the coast of Panama. For his birthday one year, the First Officer and all the stewards had chipped in and hired an obliging Cuna family to sew this huge masterpiece of native folk art, subject matter not distracting from its primitive beauty all that much.

Molas are about twelve inches square and usually depict aboriginal interpretations of birds, ducks and monkeys. The native family must have thought it strange indeed to be asked to create a bear, the closest thing resembling the creature they ever saw being a long finned dolphin or a fat dog standing like a man, wearing a vest, pants and a bow tie. They agreed, having come to expect such eccentricities from the strange people off the huge canoe visiting their tropical paradise every now and then. It took over six months to complete and, when the Capitano was presented with it, tears welled up in his eyes for the second time in his entire life, the first time being the day he received notice he was inducted into the Italian Navy.

When Capitano was entertaining lady friends aboard no one was allowed to notice. The responsibility of insuring this ridiculous command fell on me—for example, shoving staff members into broom closets while they were choking on their own laughter after he sauntered by with one of his lovelies. Obeying orders in general grew extremely difficult as it was impossible to miss this squat, charismatic gent ambling down the gangway off on one of his antique forays, stately blonde in a sequined cowgirl outfit, easily a head taller than he, following a few steps behind. Concerned with anonymity, he wore spotless white shoes, high white knee socks, white Bermuda shorts, a T-shirt with an ecstatic Winnie welcoming everyone to the forest, dark glasses, and a white sun visor with Winnie's face stamped on the brim with "Luigi" sewn across the top in yellow thread. Topping off the whole affair grew wisps of gray hair, defying the rose brilliantine, cavorting madly about his sunburned scalp.

"Hey kid," he once asked, yanking me aside on the gangway, smiling, his gold capped teeth glinting in the tropical sunlight, "You don't think anyone recognize me, huh?"

"Oh no, of course not, Capitano," I replied, hoping like hell he could not discern a blatant lie when he heard one.

"Ahhh, this is good!" he sighed, confirming my hopes. Setting off, he gave me a solid slap on the back of my head, squeezed the left side of my face between his thick thumb and forefinger, and added, "You a good boy. A bad liar, but a good boy. I like that, huh? Ciao."

Down the gangway he went, middle-aged wranglerette in obedient tow.

THE CHIEF PURSER, WOULD YOU LIKE TO ... DANCE?

Next in line in cruise ship hierarchy, not in rank but in who had the last word as to whether or not I remained a Social Director or galley slave, was the Chief Purser. Considered an officer, the Chief Purser is the hotel manager with a First, Second, and Third Purser his assistants. It is their job to manage all the affairs of running a floating grand hotel in the European tradition. Billing, ordering, maintenance, ship-to-shore communications, *espirit-de-corps* among the crew, and everything else such management entails were his sole responsibility, including asking hung-over staff members, myself more often than not, "Hey, how come you no sparkle this morning, huh?"

After bidding a fond farewell to two thousand passengers by ten-thirty in the morning, the pursers instantly begin supervising preparations for the next cruise. Stewards attack the cabins, re-making two thousand beds, replacing soap, towels, hangers, ashtrays, Bibles (a favorite souvenir), and matching the correct key with cabins after the fob mysteriously disappears, no doubt for a souvenir as well. Gardeners board to tend the hundreds of plants and trees growing throughout the ship, pruning, clipping, mowing, and watering. Crew members who have finished their contracts are loaded on buses to the airport for flights back to Portugal and Italy, and new arrivals are outfitted in their proper uniforms and are assigned berths. Feature length motion pictures are carried on in dozens of bulky thirty-five millimeter film cans (pre-dating video tapes by a few years), as are troupes of fresh performers, while some of the old vets are carried off.

Simultaneously, trucks fill the dock delivering stores for the next adventure. No mean task. Within hours seven tons of steaks and chops come aboard. Three thousand-five hundred pounds of chicken, duck, turkey, and goose, forty thousand fresh eggs (three thousand three hundred-thirty three dozen for those who are counting, with a few left over for pool games), a thousand pounds of coffee beans, thirty thousand pounds of crisp produce, a thousand gallons of fresh milk and cream along with four hundred gallons of ice cream supplementing the handmade varieties, and some twenty thousand pounds of dry stores (salt, pepper, ketchup, corn flakes, etc.).

In order to wash this all down properly, the boys supervise stowing twenty-seven thousand bottles of liquor, not including fifteen hundred gallons of bulk *vin ordinaries* brought on for the crew. Done with the precaution of a gold transfer at Fort Knox, armed with clipboards and wearing dark glasses, the pursers check off delivery of an international assortment of five thousand bottles of liquor; sixteen thousand bottles of beer, stout and ale; and sixteen hundred bottles of vintage champagnes and spumontes. Five thousand additional bottles of wine are also included, restocking the cellar containing choices spanning four decades of good years and one hundred different selections from France, Italy, Germany, Portugal, Spain, and California.

The crew had its own set of pursers. They supervised the loading of fresh water and lubricating fluids for the engines and machinery in addition to thousands of gallons of high-grade fuel, spare parts, light bulbs, you name it. The ship's philosophy, "If you might need it and it doesn't float along with the driftwood, you better bring it with you."

By five-thirty in the afternoon the ship is loaded with a full complement of two thousand new passengers, as many as two hundred replacement crewmen, provisions for three thousand, and is ready to sail for an exotic port.

Once the cruise begins, the pursers' duties commence in earnest. Our Chief Purser supervised the operation with aplomb and flair. A fair-haired Northern Italian who understood the responsibility of his position, he took every opportunity available to recreate his mind and body from the rigors of his stressful occupation.

When it came to women, the Chief Purser was convinced there was no such thing as an ugly woman, just a poor one. His technique for acquiring their company, however, was not limited to stalking the pool decks in a microscopic bikini as most of the Officers did. Instead, our suave hotel manager frequented the cocktail parties and lounges bedecked in the sartorial splendor of his meticulously starched and ironed white uniform, probably shattering like an eggshell if he as much as thought about bending over. One evening I noticed him walk up to a likely prospect, Dunhill cigarette held with insinuative delicacy between his thumb and forefinger, the hand holding it never falling below the midsection of his chest, he quietly murmured, "You know, you are the most beautiful woman on this ship. Would you like to—" he paused for dramatic impact, "—dance?" as he made a circular motion with the forefinger of his right hand, mincing the sensual lines of blue smoke rising between them like a spatula folding candied fruit into a batch of sweetened ricotta destined for a cannoli. More often than not, the answer was no. Undaunted, considering the rebuff merely an icebreaker, he moved in for the kill, his eyelids half closed, cooing, "Well then, you realize, how do you say in English, you maka my spine like a cube of ice. Tell me, would you like to come down to my cabino for a glass of 'especial' champagnia?" (always pronounced 'cham-paag-nia').

If this repost was met with still another parry, he laconically replied, "No? Very well. Have a most enjoyable evening." He would bow slightly and then, sighing remorsefully, would add, "Without me."

Not missing a beat, he skipped over to the next female, age or looks ignored, repeating the very same routine, even if the next woman in his path was traveling with his original quarry and heard every word of the well-rehearsed *"aria con amore, molto dulce"*. Do you want to dance, ice cube spine, and "especial" cham-paag-nia, word for word!

At first, a mortal man might consider such behavior foolish, if not bordering on the bizarre. At least I did. In view of the inescapable detail that, on any cruise, there could be five to six hundred unescorted women, including retired blue-haired ladies traveling together, secretaries and school teachers sharing cabins, and buxom young debs yearning for their parents to fall overboard and drown, one begins to see the logic behind the Chief Purser's approach. On a good night, he could cruise from ten to who-knows-how-many prospective women in an hour, so eventually he was bound to score. What drove everyone crazy is that he always did. Not merely once or twice a voyage. In fact, one night in the Officers Lounge, the Capitano himself, in a burst of uncharacteristic conviviality, threatened to put number tickets, like the ones found in a bakery, on Chief Purser's cabino door in an effort to keep the willing waiting in proper order. That is how well he did.

CRUISE DIRECTOR MARTY, OR JOEY, OR, JOHNNY OR LONNY

A Cruise Director is the person directly responsible for the entertainment and wellbeing of the passengers while cruising the oceans and ports making up a cruise ship's extensive international itinerary. Although a Cruise Director can hail from anywhere in the world, most claim their roots near Hollywood, near Broadway, or near Haymarket in England. One must use the term "near" for, considering the cumulative talents of these men, near is as close as they could ever hope to get to any of these entertainment Meccas as performers. Despite their constant efforts to improve, what with dance lessons, vocal coaching, and purchasing comedy material from hustlers in the parking lots of big city comedy clubs, they forever remain light years away from mediocre.

Of course, Cruise Directors always regard each other as the "best in the business." While serving on the entertainment staff, I heard the phrase bandied about as casually as Parmesan on a batch of hot pasta: "Oh Cruise Director so-and-so, aboard ship 'This-or-that', why, he's the best in the business!"

The question remains, what is that business? Show business? Not really. Ship performers work for a captive audience, none of whom has access to network television, radio, or even a daily newspaper. If not pleased with an evening's entertainment in the main showroom, they cannot skip over to another showplace down the street, that is, without getting their feet wet.

Well then, perhaps it is the cruise business. Again not really, as the entertainment staff has little say concerning advertising and none as far as booking, navigation, and choice of destinations. So exactly what is the business these men are convinced they are the best in? Who knows? Nevertheless, according to them, they did it better than anyone else, so it really didn't matter.

The Cruise Director on the T.S.S. Luna Sea was a middle-aged man named Marty Eberhardt whose last name unfortunately belied reality. Cruise Director duties were twofold. First, he was responsible for scheduling rehearsals and performances of the entertainers booked on the ship. Secondly, he gave "Travel Talks" in the showroom, simultaneously broadcast over the ship's closed circuit television and radio stations, his shining face and dulcet-toned voice beamed into each stateroom, bar, and public area. Every effort was made to insure no one escaped this carefully prepared program of facts and information concerning an upcoming port. In actuality, the travel talk is strictly an excuse Cruise Directors use to urge the easily impressionable passengers to frequent only those shops giving him the healthiest kickback while the ship is moored to the local wharf. One might say the shopkeepers are simply paying for advertising. *Subtlety* is not an operational word here; our Cruise Director peppered his talks with sage advice: "Make sure you don't buy any liquor from Joe's Cut Rate while you are in Saint Thomas, as most of the bottles are delivered to the ship all smashed and broken. Not all of them, but we have had some bad experiences with these people. If I were you I'd get all my stuff at Nick's primarily because of their extremely reliable delivery service."

This was our Cruise Director's way of saying Joe only coughs up three bucks for every four bottles of hooch delivered to the ship purchased by any of the two thousand or so passengers set free in that duty-free paradise. While Nick, on the other hand, bless his free enterprising heart, comes up with five dollars for every four bottles delivered, as well as an occasional U.S. twenty dollar gold coin. Nick, you see, understands the power of advertising.

During a stopover in Saint Thomas our Marty decided one liquor store was not paying enough for each box of four bottles purchased by our passengers and delivered to the ship. We met with the owner, a rather ominous gentleman, who looked like he'd cracked his fair share of skulls in his day. Marty pleasantly told the gent he now needed five dollars for each box delivered instead of the usual three. The guy looked at both of us for a moment and then said, "drop dead."

I figured he really meant it and would have no qualms about assisting us in attaining that goal. We left. The next Cruise Talk, Marty mentioned to a thousand or so adoring passengers that the service from this particular liquor store wasn't very reliable. When we hit the port, Marty asked me to accompany him as he took his "walk" in Saint Thomas. He met with a number of merchants and I watched as they stuffed fifties and hundred dollar bills in his top pocket. He then entered the liquor store with the threatening owner who just a week before, told us both to "drop dead." I mentioned to Marty this might not be a good idea, and he laughed.

We met with the store owner in his office and Marty ingenuously asked what the box tally was this cruise. The big guy, looking as dangerous as before, made a phone call. It seems the delivered box tally went from two hundred to twenty five. The guy hung up the phone and then growled, "Okay, you son-of-a-bitch, five dollars a box. Don't be seen on this island after 5 pm." He got up and lumbered out of the office.

"Pleasure doing business with you, too!" Marty called after him. As we got up to leave, Marty handed me a fifty dollar bill and said, "That's how business is done in Saint Thomas."

If rumors are to be believed, Cruise Directors use multiple offshore bank accounts, as it is the only safe haven keeping them one-step ahead of those pesky little nits from the Internal Revenue Service. The boys of the I.R.S. consider pinching a Cruise Director to be great sport, always bringing an extra battery for their calculators during an audit. Claiming citizenship from Monrovia to Rajasthan when caught, Cruise Directors are forced to come up with a conservative estimate of their yearly incomes. They really cannot do it. No one, including the Cruise Directors themselves, usually has any idea how much green stuff they finally cart home from kickbacks, payoffs, tips and gratuities, and certainly even a slighter idea as to where it all ends up. Considering most Cruise Directors drive away from the docks in Porsches and Mercedes, have condominiums in various parts of the world, and wear enough gold and assorted jewelry to make a Gypsy king envious, it is not hard to guess when all the cash, once burning holes in the pockets of unsuspecting tourists, finally cools down.

It was easy to spot our Cruise Director even though he tried staying submerged in his cabin for most of the season, surfacing only for meals and the evening show. Professionally attempting to keep his outfit vaguely nautical, it inadvertently assumed the enviable characteristics of an ensemble looking as if it were designed by a tenth generation madam from Havana, with a sense of humor. Lemon yellow or powder blue plastic shoes and belts (he felt white unduly common), cream colored trousers usually an inch too short (you see, salt air wreaks havoc on polyester), a gaudy shirt with epaulets unbuttoned well below his chest, and a yachting cap. Accessorizing were a few diamond pinkie-rings, a thin gold Swiss wristwatch, its face covered with diamonds and pea-sized gems where the numbers should be. There were enough gold chains, gold medals, and gold didlybobs hanging around a double-chinned neck, resting on an exposed belly, to make the gleeful Hindi elephant god, Ganesh, festooned for a joyous holiday, look like a bum. His favorite little bauble, which he wore every day, was a gold charm with his initials in chunky little diamonds, spelling out "ME" for Marty Eberhardt.

Marty wore all this splendiferous fribble, claiming it was given to him as "gifts" by shopkeepers on the islands. One certainly could not afford offending any one of them showing up in their shops one bright sunny day without it. Additionally, it was a dandy way to receive fresh tokens of appreciation, as few Cruise Directors, Marty leading the ranks, are beyond showing a shopkeeper a new gold chain or bauble recently given to him by a rival merchant with a directly offhand comment like, "Wasn't that nice of him, hhummmmm?"

Each evening Marty served as Master of Ceremonies in the showroom, warming up the audience with a few jokes, perhaps a song or two, or three. His routine began with the standard shipboard patter concerning passengers losing their way, not being able to get the key out of the door, or tripping in and out of their cabins due to the raised portals. It also included the inadvertent summoning the night steward at three in the morning, when all they thought they were doing was flicking on the light switch in the bathroom. This resulted in gales of laughter from those traveling for the first time. If a passenger booked a return journey, he heard the same hokum over again word for word and then asked me if Marty ever changed his routine. This is a most embarrassing question, especially when asked by a passenger last sailing with the ship five years ago. As he was our leader, or something along those lines, I defended him as best I could; assuring the curious voyager our Cruise Director certainly changed his material, it merely being a coincidence he heard the same jokes over again—when deep inside I knew I was talking about a man who never changed his socks until they began sticking to the inside of his shoes, so why should a standup routine be any different?

Every Cruise Director boasts a special forte, which he features in at least one evening's entertainment. Given the opportunity, he would gladly bill himself on as many nights possible. The Home Office, knowing all about Cruise Directors, strictly forbids this sort of thing. Our guy nevertheless, considered himself so multi-talented, he assured anyone concerned that dictums from the Home Office only applied to those marginally talented fellows possessing one specialty in their bag of tricks, while he was the master of many, right? Of course, I had to agree. I mean, why lose a job due to honesty? Who else but a tap dancer par excellence forgets a routine halfway through, stops, and begins the entire buck and wing from the top, claiming it was the drummer's fault. Now is that a trouper, I ask you? Certainly, Houdini had problems in his day, but a magician like our Cruise Director would have made the Master proud. When a pigeon had the audacity to die before being produced from the secret pockets in the lining of his plaid tuxedo jacket, Marty shook the bird around so professionally, feathers drifting to the floor below, the lifeless head hanging upside down, the audience supposedly never had the slightest idea the creature was dead. They thought it was part of the act.

Now, is that a talent? Finally, there was the singing. Marty admitted he had a hard time remembering words and staying on key, so he read the lyrics to numbers like "Indian Love Call" and "Some Enchanted Evening" with feeling from words he had written with a black marker on the stage floor under the mike stand earlier in the day. No one was ever any the wiser.

Validating his professional endeavors, our Cruise Director claimed to know more show business comics, on a more intimate level, than their own mothers. Modestly he admitted teaching David (Dave to his friends) Letterman and Stevie (sic) Martin all they knew: "But damnit to hell, I was tight with them before they hit the big time. I lent them money, gave them a place to stay, even handed them my best material when they were in a bind. A lot of thanks I've gotten for it. Hell, Letterman still owes me twenty bucks."

Making up for this miscarriage of show business justice, Marty showered his overlooked talents on any audience having to listen, every time he had the chance, which was each evening in the main showroom. Understand, most Cruise Directors consider their tenure aboard ship a temporary thing, the majority feeling they are simply waiting for the agent to call, having landed them a big part in an even bigger movie, the lead in a Broadway show, or in a replacement spot for any of the late night talk show hosts. Sadly though, for Marty, the call from the omniscient agent never comes, while his hair grows progressively greyer, the gut sags a little more over the belt, and the Vitamin E capsules, squashed open, enabling the smelly oil to be smeared over wrinkles and crow's-feet not there the morning before, becomes a way of life.

Early one evening while cruising the Caribbean, a young Social Director made the unforgivable mistake of cracking a joke while onstage during a lull in the horse racing festivities. Young and good looking, resembling a rock star who could be accepted at Oral Roberts University, this Social Director was hired after Marty spotted him ashore one morning cleverly insulting passersby from a dunk stool in a "Pitch 'Till You Dunk The Wise guy" arcade in a parking lot carnival. Maintaining an acerbic bombardment, he was not only juggling oranges but was playing the harmonica between jibes, perfect material for a Social Director. After telling Marty he was also a fair hand, or foot, with a unicycle, he was on board by the afternoon. The young Social Director's joke was harmless enough so there was no harm done, thinking Marty was still in his cabin tweezing hair from his nostrils, or spraying his toupee with Aqua Net in preparation for his duties as Master of Ceremonies.

To digress for a moment, the ship's policy was not to tip the crew or staff. The crew and staff got around this inconvenient policy by skimming from the cash brought in by horse racing, bingo, the tours, the casino, and the shop keepers in every port. For example, horse racing on our ship was scheduled before each evening's entertainment. The Home Office insisted the activity could only occur once or twice a cruise. Enterprising Marty, in cahoots with the greedy Chief Purser, managed to squeeze in a few extra races. Not only did the passengers get a kick out of the event, but so did the coffers of the staff and pursers, more on that in just a bit.

The actual horse race consisted of placing six brightly painted wooden horses and jockeys on the first space of a cloth spread out over the showroom's main stage. The cloth was latticed off into a "course" six lanes wide and ten spaces long. The buxom Ship's Secretary spun a dice cage containing four large dice while a volunteer from the audience peeked over her shoulder, keeping things legal, or at least looking so. With each spin the number showing up on each of the dice corresponded to one of the numbers on the six horses, and a muscular Deck Steward in a tight ship's T-shirt moved the horse forward one space. In other words, if one dice showed a four, another six, and coincidently two came up showing five, horse four moved one space, horse six one space, and horse five two spaces. This procedure continued until one of the horses crossed the finish line. It is the chore of the Social Director calling the race to stir the audience to a lunatic pitch. Not an easy task, considering most of our passengers had entered the stage in life preferring to be thought of as "sensible." Yet it is amazing how sensible gentry will scream and yell as though their fannies were on fire when a ranting Social Director assures them the louder they holler, the faster their little wooden horse will scamper down the course, aided by the roll of the dice. Incidentally, one has a tendency to cheer with a bit more abandon knowing that, for a two dollar bet, he might win anywhere from ten to a few hundred dollars. The purses were based on odds figured out by the pursers selling the tickets. We should all know what that could mean.

An age-old custom aboard sailing ships is splitting the profits of the cruise with the crew, a treat experiencing its heyday during the golden age of piracy. Each member of the crew, depending on his pre-determined share, received a percentage of the ship's on-board gross profits for that particular voyage. Modern day cruise ships are no different; piracy now manifests in tips, selling of shore tours, and gambling even though a large percentage of the money brought in by bingo, horse racing, shore tours, trap shooting, and cuts from the casino and duty free shops was actually returned to the passengers in prize money. With bingo pots going as high as twelve hundred dollars and purses for a horse race hitting an occasional six or seven hundred dollars, the bulk of the cash was harvested by the pursers and later distributed in this manner.

The pursers kept half the total for themselves and the other officers aboard. The Cruise Director received the other half. Supposedly, he was entitled to half that sum, dividing the remaining half into equal shares to be distributed among the members of the staff. Certain members receiving double or triple shares based on their responsibilities or their willingness to give in, or put out (our leader's sexual preference coming into play here).

Understand that when it comes time to dole out sums of money, numerous extenuating circumstances crop up, honesty usually being the most important. There is no way the Cruise Director could tell if the amount given to him by the pursers was indeed half the total garnered from the passengers during the course of that cruise. Marty's explanation of a light cut sounded like a child trying to defend his pulling out the cat's whiskers. Referring to the pursers, he would whine, "Well it's their ship and what they give us is what we get." Proceeding in the same vein, as a staff member, it was impossible to tell if the amount Marty finally decided to part with had anything to do with a fair share. Marty would snivel, "Hell you see, horse racing was up this cruise, but the tours and bingo did poorly."

There was always some combination of shipboard events on which to blame a light tip. Some payable events were always up, but more often than not, most were always down. One had to rely on our Cruise Director's mood on the morning he received his cut from the pursers. Hopefully, he had not opened a past due notice on one of his Porsches the day before leaving port.

The rewarding of shares was the only way in which a Cruise Director with dubious morality and tact could keep a rowdy staff in line. Shares given to the female staff members varied according to their willingness to comfort our leader late at night. As far as the male members of the staff were concerned, their shares hinged on how much of a competitive threat they posed.

Returning to our up-and-coming Social Director, who we left telling a joke on the main stage between horse races. Marty appeared as unexpectedly as a belch at a formal dinner. Pulling the Social Director aside and poking the boy in the chest with a delicately manicured forefinger, Marty smiled sweetly and said, "Hey, I tell the jokes around here."

"Oh you do?" replied the kid, still out of breath from calling the last race and excited from the laughter he received after telling his joke, "Who told you that one?"

When it came time to hand out the shares at the end of the cruise, the little brown envelope bearing the eager Social Director's name was decidedly lighter than the rest.

The Cruise Director could choose any woman on the ship who pleased him, unescorted or otherwise. The stories Marty related to me about his blitzkriegs were manifold, ranging from the mother who asked if she could video tape the festivities with her daughter as love interest to a transvestite who, after all was said and done, was not all that bad in the sack. Irrespective of these milestones in the history of sexual conquest, our Cruise Director attempted to maintain an air of down home respectability, traveling with his wife, Pinky, a few months out of every season,

Not actually a passenger and certainly not staff, Pinky tried assisting with socializing and mingling with passengers, handing out materials for masquerade night and other minor tasks that weren't too demanding. This is not to say Pinky was a dull sort, although one could say she would have a tough time making her way through a thin mist. Suffice it to say Pinky, a onetime cheerleader and baton-twirling champion, fell in love with Marty while on board celebrating her graduation from charm school. Unfortunately, she now suffered chronic hypertension, was prone to anxiety attacks, and gobbled Oxycontin like M & M's. In all sympathy, Pinky's problems were not without cause. You see, Marty encouraged his elfin-minded spouse to escort the all day tours of Acapulco, Caracas, or any large port, giving him and his assistant ample time to cruise the big hotels for an errant flight attendant or two. If they struck out, there was always time for a quick straightening out at a local brothel before Pinky returned from her day of shepherding various tours. When she returned from her tours, the responsibility required a double dose of Oxi just to be able to sit down and kick off her shoes.

Other than this infrequent lapse of good faith, Marty behaved like a saint while Pinky was on board. Within hours of her debarking, he zipped after the nubile Children's Counselors like a hummingbird in the throes of a sugar fit. Sauntering up to these buxom young women on a formal night, he bobbed and danced around them like a randy male pigeon in a public park. The girls blushed, rolled their eyes, and attempted to continue greeting passengers entering the ballroom for the Captain's cocktail party, ignoring as best they could Casanova's less then subtle advances.

He fancied young women wearing low-cut clinging gowns, braless certainly. Staring directly at their breasts, the voluptuous nipples causing sensuous ridges to form in the satin like gowns, cascading into wide vees like the ripples produced by the bow of the ship cruising through a calm sea, he hit on them with all the panache of a lonely bowling ball salesman at a national convention. His favorite opening line, "Hey sweetie. What is this I see? You get caught in a stiff breeze or something?"

Considering how much or how little they cared to preserve their positions or share, they rarely gave in, most telling him with a laugh to buzz off, or go take a good stiff shower. It is extremely difficult to intimidate college girls these days, especially those majoring in adolescent psychology.

The position of Cruise Director is not all sweetness and light. Some problems must be dealt with twenty-four hours a day. Passengers demanding to be married by the Capitano (something never done unless arrangements are made prior to sailing), passengers complaining about the rough seas, lack of sunshine, a surly steward, or a fly in the minestrone, were all commonplace. Additionally, a phenomenon occurs when a generally knowledgeable soul sets foot on a luxury liner. It is astonishing how certified pillars of society, doctors, lawyers, business executives, forget any vestige of shore-side common sense. Some of them devise questions defying a straight-faced answer: Does the crew sleep on board? Do these stairs go down? Do we have to declare anything we have consumed? My favorite: What time does the midnight buffet start? A valid inquiry really, as on our ship the midnight buffet began at 11:45.

Marty shunted most of these questions and problems off to our Assistant Cruise Director, who we will meet shortly. This gave our Cruise Director the time necessary to make out the schedules, a task requiring ten minutes on a busy day. He also had time to dwell on his travel talks, consisting of going over his records of the kickbacks received the last time the ship was in port and deciding how much of a mention a particular merchant deserved based on the generosity of his donation.

Yet he insisted he had no time to do very much of anything. He was constantly seen running throughout the ship, hurrying to get here or there, no one ever knowing where here or there was, usually one of the more secluded bars or the Officers Sun Deck. Conscious of maintaining his reputation as everyone's good buddy, he randomly sped through a passenger deck or public room, pointing his finger at a lucky soul, then waving his hand, palm facing himself as though he was an emissary from the Vatican, announcing, "Heyhellohowarlya" Pointing to another, "Hey, hellohowarlya?" and still another, Heyhello. howarya?" Including one more for good luck, "Heyhellohoware...you?"

Before anyone could answer, he was gone and as far out of sight as it was possible to get without vaulting over the side of the ship.

The late night gathering spot on our ship was called the Boboli Gardens Bar and Grill. It was given this name due to some potted plants hanging around and a life size replica of a statue in the Boboli Gardens in Florence. This was a rotund, naked gent happily astride a huge Galapagos tortoise. One memorable night in this bar, over a bottle of Italian red of no particular distinction (as he was buying), and a few hamburgers left over from the evening's deck party and barbecue, Marty, in a fit of candor, confided the following tip of the "business" to me. He prefaced his remarks with the fact that he does not reveal this privileged information to everyone, slurring the last syllable of his sentence, his head and torso slouching lower toward the small round table. There was little need to be concerned with appearances, as it was nearly three in the morning during a lengthy cruise when most of the retirees did so before ten o'clock.

"Before you come on board for the next season, kid," he began, "you should get into two habits: greeting everyone you see, and being friendly."

"How does one do this?" I inquired, letting him feel as though he were the Learned Theban and I his humble suppliant, never before realizing the art of being friendly was something one had to rehearse.

"Well," he continued, beginning to lisp slightly, "You go to a shopping mall on a crowded weekend or during a big sale, anyplace where there are a lot of people around."

There was a slight pause.

"And then?" I questioned, fearing if I did not keep up the conversation, he might fall asleep with his nose in the wine glass and drown.

"And then," he said, coming to life momentarily, "you jush find yourself a good shpot and shtart shmiling and say saying hello to everyone who passes. Don't matter who they are. That's the important thing, you gotta' do it to everyone."

How democratic, I thought.

"Is that it?" I inquired cautiously, fearing what else one had to do before they did it to you, all for the sake of the business,

"Dats it." he said triumphantly, emptying the last bit of vin ordinaire in his glass, sediment and all, shaking out the last drop, inadvertently finding its way onto his white pants, relaxing into a purple stain on his crotch. "Dats all there is to it. You do that before each season and someday you'll be the besht in the bishnish." He hiccupped, no doubt to-drive the point home,

Again with the best in the bish, business, I thought, wondering about all those curious sorts I have indeed passed in shopping malls and the like, smiling and saying hello as I walked by. Usually, I thought, because of the toupees lacquered over a bald top, pale complexions and in general a demeanor akin to Aschenbach in the late chapters of *Death in Venice*, they were simply dusty old sensitive souls on the prowl.

Next time it happens, I will certainly consider the following possibility. Perhaps, just perhaps, they are vacationing Cruise Directors keeping in professional mettle in preparation for their next cruise.

As everyone in the cruise business knows, best in it or worse, there will always be another voyage.

THE ASSISTANT CRUISE DIRECTOR AND HIS SOLID GOLD PENIS

Donny, a devilishly good looking fellow in his late thirties with thinning raven black hair and piercing lapis lazuli blue eyes, held the distinction of being the Assistant Cruise Director on the ship, before I was promoted to the position after his contract expired. There exists among the civilized people of the world a belief that behind every leader is an even greater assistant. Being realistic, hovering around every leader is an assistant quaking in salivating anticipation for the day he will assume the responsibilities of his obviously lightweight superior, the eternal assistant's creed being, "There but for the will of God and the Home Office."

Not so Donny. Although majoring in theatre at a marginally prestigious university somewhere in the back country of New England, he never became excited about it. He felt *Hamlet* was a pretty good play except it was filled with too many clichés. Erudite Renaissance man of the world that he was, he had heard them all before. After graduation, he took a summer job with the cruise line and had been sailing ever since. Unconcerned that his last promotion came some ten years ago when the Home Office promoted him from Social Director to Assistant, Donny remained positive that it was simply a matter of time until he was promoted to Cruise Director, on some ship, somewhere. How much time didn't really matter as long as he had three squares and a bed and that women continue to travel alone. If not alone, at least willing to take a dip in the three or foursome pond.

Considering the rigors of a life at sea, Donny was holding up remarkably well. Realizing he was in for the long haul and determined to wait it out, he softened his time with sex and booze, laced with liberal doses of more sex and more booze, with just an occasional dab of mega-vitamins and ginseng. His face was beginning to acquire that lived-in look in spite of the daily applications that the goo contained within a Vitamin E capsule had on his wrinkles, one of the many tricks he acquired from his mentor, Cruise Director Marty. He was convinced ginseng was an Oriental wonder root minimizing the wounds wrought by Father Time and his merciless scythe. When dealing with the most vital aspect of a man's personality, it was Donny's opinion that the hardening power of ginseng far outshone the whispered effects of powdered reindeer antler or the mythical renown of pulverized rhinoceros horn, all of which far, far, outshone the merits of the upstart snake oil remedies, Viagra or Cialis.

He shared all this with me this one fading afternoon on the pool deck over an iced light beer and a shot of tequila. We were relaxing between a ping-pong tournament and bingo.

"My boy," he said, liking to call me "my boy," thinking it gave him an air of sage believability, "take ginseng every day and you'll always be as hard as this shot glass," tapping the stout little glass on the table illustrating his point.

I wondered if the ginseng made you, well, as tall as the shot glass. I didn't dwell on the question, fearing if he insisted on showing me right here on the Trevi Deck, I would never be able to explain it to the Capitano, though he would probably understand. Completely.

The passengers loved Donny as he had all the makings of the quintessential All American Boy, ignoring the reality he was rapidly approaching his fortieth birthday. Playing the part for all it was worth, he made an effort to sprinkle his conversations with just enough "wow-wees" and "gee whizzes" to make a walker or wheelchair bound passenger grow suddenly obsessed with the idea he could toss his apparatus overboard and begin clog dancing. Luckily, none ever did.

When cavorting with the staff and crew, his demeanor changed radically. Every sentence he uttered was accented with a grunt, wink, or some sort of hand or body movement. If the Italians possessed a lexicon of a few hundred gestures concerning subjects of mainly a sexual nature, Donny possessed a few thousand, not including a few he used to elucidate his feelings and position on politics, weather, and the state of the universe in general. After chatting with Donny, especially while tucking away shots of tequila chased with light beers, it was obvious he could make either Victor Borge very proud, or someone with impaired hearing go insane. With Donny's status as "Cruise-Director-To-Be" as well as his access to jewelry at duty free prices, one would expect he owned a plethora of sparkling dangles and baubles. However, Donny, forever his own man. sported a single gold chain around his neck with a three dimensional twenty-four karat gold rendition of a penis and testicles hanging from it. I wondered at first if this midnight-haired paragon of the "Hail Fellow, Well Met" school of public relations was advertising his sexual preference. Perhaps he was boasting conquests, not unlike like the hunter who straps a dead moose to the hood of his truck and drives around his neighborhood for a few days after returning from a successful weekend in the woods. Successful for the hunter that is; the moose, I am sure, would debate the issue.

After getting to know Donny, I realized the opposite was true. Unlike the Chief Purser who had to ask women to spend the evening with him, Donny was never at a loss for feminine company. Some women invited him for a late night rendezvous to which, feigning flattery like a saint, he rarely refused to accept. As for the neck charm, Donny claimed it was a farewell gift from a couple he met during a cruise to Jamaica. Not only were the couple owners of a large chain of jewelry shops in Manhattan and Long Island, they were also extremely active in a number of discreet East Side swingers organizations. Soon after meeting Donny, they realized he was the perfect third for their anticipated shipboard *ménage a trois*. According to Donny, the couple's favorite musical accompaniment was the soundtrack from *The Sound of Music*, particularly the "My Favorite Things" number. Early one morning during the cigarette smoking stage of a pleasing session enjoyed by all, the husband of the duo asked Donny what his favorite thing was, claiming he would personally create a rendering of whatever it might be in solid gold. He wished to give Donny a token of a job well done, a suggestion causing the benefactor's wife to giggle in agreement.

Two weeks after the cruise returned to New York, the charm arrived at the dock delivered by a chauffeur in complete livery, driving a black Mercedes with darkened rear windows. I never asked Donny why he didn't choose raindrops on roses or whiskers on kittens.

This is not to say our Donny was an insensitive fellow. A multi-talented guy, he could probably excel at anything, as long as the challenge remained shipboard. For example, during the last afternoon of a cruise, Donny organized what is known as a "White Elephant Auction." During this activity, passengers could unload items acquired during the heat of a souvenir spending spree. Once back on board, they realized Aunt Jenny could probably care less about the shrunken head purchased for her from native tribesmen in Venezuela, or Uncle Ned, for heaven's sake, would not have room on the mantle for the pelican constructed out of coconut husks and clamshells. These goodies and many more like them were submitted to Donny, auctioned off, and the profits returned to the passenger who had the brilliant good taste to purchase the monstrosity in the first place. Obviously one man's trash is another man's treasure.

Donny, enterprising rascal that he was, scoured the ports for the most ludicrous items he could find, snatched them up for less than wholesale prices, and auctioned them off at many times their obvious or original worth. One season Donny went as far as getting his photo imprinted on kerchiefs, and his name on "fountain pens guaranteed to write in any language" claiming the proceeds went to the Retired Cruise Directors Home in Saint Petersburg, Florida. Such a purchase not only filled the need for a last minute souvenir, it also could be written off as a tax deduction, going as it was to support such a worthy charity. Hopefully, no one ever went looking for this noble retirement villa in Saint Petersburg, for it was not about to be built before Donny retired and, even then, you can be damn sure it would not be open to the public. Probably not in Saint Petersburg either.

Even so, our enterprising Assistant, realizing there was money to be made at these White Elephant Auctions, quickly decided someone with a minimum of artistic ability could easily reproduce the primitive art coming out of Haiti. This he found appealing.

"Hell, I saw the junk coming out of Haiti and knew I could do better," he said. "The next time the ship was in a civilized port, I picked up a set of watercolors at a toy store, tore up some brown paper grocery bags, crumpled them up and burned the edges with my Cartier lighter. Then I painted some weirdo scenes on them. You know the type, the ones that look like Haitians dancing around bonfires and other scenes of voodoo shit, like that. I signed them 'Donne,' auctioned them off for a minimum of twenty bucks apiece, and I made a mint." He motioned his hands like an umpire at a ball game declaring a runner safe. "I mean, I never said they came from Haiti, right? They looked like they did, so who the hell cares?" Snapping his thumb and midfinger, dashing into a thumbs up gesture, laughing puckishly.

At the conclusion of each season, Donny packed his bags, dusted off his photos and resumes, and headed for Hollywood, certain this was going to be his year.

At the beginning of the next season, perhaps a few months after he left with stars in his eyes, he returned. Not landing any acting assignments, he was filled with stories of all the near miss auditions he encountered and, of course, all the women he scored with. He repeated for anyone giving him the slightest cue his litany of complaints highlighting his misadventures in Los Angeles: the heat, the smog, the lack of a decent subway system, no egg creams, and the countless kooks he encountered while practicing being friendly in shopping malls. According to Donny, the only good thing Los Angeles had going for it was the accessibility of authentic Korean ginseng, copious amounts of which he purchased in preparation for another six months of cruising.

Inviting the staff down to his cabin for a bon voyage toast, he mused majestically while sitting cross-legged on his bunk wearing bikini underwear, a tight fitting European cut T-shirt, rolls and bulges a pinch more pronounced than the season before, and a loose fitting sky blue silk kimono decorated with exquisite hand embroidered tableaus of classical Tibetan pornography. "You know, there's an old saying that holds true for everything a man can encounter in life, I mean, women, jobs, anything." Pausing to create a dramatic moment, he added, "A good sailor seeks any port in a storm."

With that pronouncement, he licked a bit of salt from the back of his hand, knocked back a shot of tequila. chomped down on a quartered lemon section, and washed the whole sensation home with an entire can of light beer. He sat for a moment with his eyes closed, entranced. An eerie silence fell over the small cabin, broken when he issued forth a long and glorious belch, the likes of which, if sounded from the bridge of the fogbound Andrea Doria, would have saved her from her watery doom.

"That's right." he reiterated, relieved to the point of achieving a higher level of consciousness, "any port in a storm."

Sprinkling some additional salt on the back of his still-moistened hand, he prepared another lemon slice, reached for the bottle of tequila, and said, "My boy, cork another can of brew for me, will ya?"

Smiling like a man at peace with the world, he further prepared for another season as the Assistant Cruise Director.

THE SHIP'S DOCTOR, OR, A KISS IS JUST A KISS

As with any small town, the ship had a cadre of professional police officers, firefighters, and a suitable group of medical personnel. Headquartered in their own twenty-bed hospital situated on a lower deck, our medical facility had a fully functional operating room, dental and x-ray equipment, separate entrances for passengers and crew, two twenty-four hour nurses (both chain smokers), and a resident physician.

Our shipboard doctor, a tall, thin, blazingly patrician Milanese named Contini, approached his position with just enough dedication that enabled him to convince seasick passengers it was all in their heads, and malingering crewmen to feel the guilt of a generation of mothers, all without getting very involved. In his early sixties, it was impossible to guess his actual age, the only hint being gracefully graying temples, always combed with attentive precision and trimmed to perfection. Defying his years, his favorite avocation was strutting languidly about one of the upper decks wearing an extremely brief orange bikini. Competing with interrupting his magnificent tan was a huge gold Rolex watch strapped to his wrist. He considered it great sport to compete with the Chief Purser in seeing who could attract the attentions of the richest woman available. They both agreed unquestionably with the philosophy concerning the non-existence of ugly women, just poor ones.

During his hunt-and-sniff operations he was never seen without a small carton of milk from which he took little sips every now and then. I thought this in keeping with a man of the medical profession, until he offered me a taste one afternoon. Peeling me off the deck, realizing too late the carton contained pure unblended scotch with the slightest hint of half and half, he quietly offered the following advice: "The cream is very good for you, compari. It preserves the mucosa in the stomach. *Bene, molto bene.*"

He never said a thing about the scotch.

Our Doctor possessed an unbridled hatred for anything French due to wilting three years in a French Foreign Legion prison camp in Libya toward the end of World War II. "They even pointed a gun at me!" he would argue during heated conversations about the subject, thus proving the congenital barbarity of the French Nation.

"Well," I replied, "There *was* a war on, you know."

"Regardless, they had no right to point guns at me; I was a medical student from Milano. At the Milanese, you do not point guns. At Sicilians, *Ecco*, understandable, but not at a Milanese!"

When visiting his office as I often did, escaping the mid-afternoon heat and the pre-mealtime complaints (passengers having a tendency to grow cranky when denied food for more than an hour), I discussed life and politics with him, sipping espresso he brewed in an Erlenmeyer flask expropriated from the lab. He was convinced, by the way, that the greatest victory the Free World could glean was encouraging Italy to go Communist. That, he assured me, would sound the death knell for world Communism.

"After all," he concluded, "look what happened to the Fascists," feigning a spit for good measure.

During these little chats I would notice a neat pile of glass slides stacked on a corner of his austere desk. I wondered what they were for. The pile decidedly got lower a few days after debarking from any number of Mexican or Caribbean ports.

Three days after a wild night in Old San Juan with a few crew members, I sheepishly entered his office early one morning, much earlier than our usual meeting time. Before I was able to tell him what was bothering me, he inquired colorlessly, "The Caribe Bar, eh?"

"Yes." I mumbled, astonished he knew where we ended up, completely drunk and in the company of a few ladies never going to be candidates for sainthood, or even minor mission work.

"The others were here this morning. Ecco," he continued not looking up from his current issue of *Paris Match* magazine, handing me one of those glass slides, "bring it backa, first thing in the morning, eh?" He then began cursing under his breath in French at an editorial he would forever disagree with.

At dinner the day after a Wasserman test I took as a precautionary measure proved to be negative, he sent a bottle of spumante to our table with his compliments. I turned to the Captain's Table where he was dining and he gave me a high sign and winked. Somehow, I could not imagine my childhood physician, a pediatrician with a repulsive pencil thin moustache, all the neighborhood kids hated and labeled "Penicillin Blinski," ever doing the same.

A month or so before it became time for Contini to leave the ship to return to his duties as director of the largest hospital in Northern Italy, he invited a few of the staff up to his cabino for dinner. With the style and ease of a professional Gran Chapeau, he used an electric skillet to prepare a linguini with artichoke and garlic sauce that brought tears of joy to the staunchest disbelievers. Later on, after the others had left, we sipped Hennessy Paradis, talking politics to the wee hours of the morning. I had to refuse his offer of sending the Capitano a note in the early dispatch saying I was ill and unable to supervise the morning tour of Santo Domingo.

With dull orange rays of sunlight began peeking through the port holes, I begged his forgiveness, thanked him for his gracious hospitality, and prepared to leave. Walking me to the door, his arm slung around my shoulder, he pressed a sparkling new German steel hemostat in my hand and said, "They make, how do you say like a hipster, ah, good roach clips, man. Eh? *Buona notte compari!*"

A few days later, it seems a passenger concerned about a possible yeast infection visited the sick bay for an examination. Contini assured her there was no infection, but the woman insisted. To prove his point, with her feet still positioned in the sheepskin-covered stirrups, he assured her that if there was any infection at all he would never do what he was about to do. He then bent over and tenderly kissed her vagina.

For her sworn silence, the Home Office refunded the passenger's fare, and rewarded the woman with a first class cruise for two, anywhere in the world absolutely free. Contini was immediately thrown off the ship in Caracas. His return ticket to Milano was rescinded. He was on his own.

THE ENTERTAINERS, OR, ONE, TWO, THREE, KICK

Every so often a group of "too hip for the room" passengers would have their assistants ink a cruise into their oh-so-busy schedules. They were usually the trim mid-forties types who, after getting to know you a bit, would invite you down to their cabins to share a joint before cocktails. Invariably they would inquire about the evening's entertainment and I would tell them with honest pride we had a Spanish dancer, a comic, a juggling banjo playing unicyclist, a French Apache dance team, and perhaps a virtuoso harmonica player or accordionist. After listening patiently to the lineup, they would then inquire politely, with disinterest, "Are the bars on the ship open all evening?"

Understandably, the lineup didn't really have the caché of a command performance, but while our hoity-toity guests were off sipping their chilled rosé or Perrier and lime, a group of dedicated performers were working their fannies off, presenting a live variety show, the likes of which few have the opportunity to appreciate these days.

It's a shame really. The variety performer, no longer having many viable outlets for their talents shoreside, has to revert to doing their act on a tiny stage, swaying occasionally, with inadequate lighting, a less than perfect sound system, accompanied by a combo of talented musicians who couldn't swear they were sober for every performance, perhaps missing a cue or two.

Regardless of the Cruise Director's lavish introductions of the scheduled performers listing their accomplishments, such as million sellers during the sixties or seventies, Grammy nominations, appearances on late night talk shows, even resident gigs in Las Vegas or Atlantic City, it remained quite difficult to convince our passengers that a gig on a cruise ship was actually a well-paid professional venture. Many times a well-meaning passenger would saunter up to a singer or comedian relaxing during the day in one of the lounges or on the sun deck. They would extend their compliments by saying, "Hey you know, you are pretty good. You ought to do it professionally someday." The performer, thus flattered, would smile graciously and say thank you. Once the passenger rounded the nearest corner, our performer would then proceed to bang his or her head against a bulkhead or collapse into a sobbing heap on the deck. Sometimes both, depending on his or her individual constitution, or lack of it.

The performers could be categorized into three distinct groups. The "Hope-To-Be," the "Has-Been," and the "Never-were." The "Hope-To-Be" are a small group of young performers who considered a gig on a cruise ship as mere experience, a step up from performing at a dinner theatre. Perhaps the gig could advance their budding careers, though most probably it wouldn't. They take the job as the money is better than waiting tables and there was a bit of adventure involved. Most importantly, there was always possibility of some after-performance assignations or a surreptitious rendezvous or two.

The "Has-Beens," however, are performers resigned to their fate and consider working a cruise ship as exciting as an extended gig at a bingo hall on a Native American reservation. Unlike a cocky "Hope-To-Be," the "Has-Been," due to lean, bitter experience, is willing to recognize that a gig is where you find it or, more often than not, where it finds you. In the valiant tradition of the inveterate trouper, it doesn't matter if the front row is fast asleep, or even snoring, by the big finale, you keep smiling and sing your damn heart out. It beats being a white-gloved doorman at a retirement hotel on Miami Beach.

Oddly enough, many of the performers insisted on posting photos on the lobby display from those halcyon days when million-sellers were commonplace and national truck-and-bus tours were just another Spring and Summer chore that had to be endured. When it came time for their first performance, occasionally an audible gasp would rise from the audience realizing the changes Father Time had wrought.

If you ever asked yourself on a cozy evening in front of the fireplace, "whatever happened to Tandalaya, the gutsy belter who closed the *Dixie Drain Cleaner Hour* on Saturday nights," fret no more. She is probably working a cruise ship somewhere in the world and damn thankful for the opportunity,

The last category were the "Never-Were." A true "Never-Were" is generally a little too old, wise, and plump to be classified as a "Hope-To-Be." They ain't never, and they know it. Unfortunately, they feel they simply never had the lucky break that the "Has-Been" once had. They would continually remind anyone who cared to listen that they once auditioned with Imogene Coca for a gig on *Your Show of Shows* but lost out to that no-talent bum, Carl Reiner. The "Never-Were" couldn't honestly rationalize a gig on cruise ship as a paid vacation with meals. Vacation nothing. If he or she didn't work on the ship, they would starve. They have no steady residuals, no inheritance or trust funds, and could never afford investments. What was most unfortunate, they didn't even have a great memory of a show business accomplishment to get them through the dark times like a "Has-Been." Their dreams, unlike that of a "Hope-To-Be," are no longer out there shimmering in the misty future. For them the future has come and quickly evaporated. Their show business lives are here today, given life by the applause, and forgotten by morning.

The labels of my own invention notwithstanding, the cruise ship performer remains an extremely talented soul, not easily satisfied with selling insurance, teaching high school, or otherwise foregoing their dreams and becoming ordinary.

Periodically, a jaded passenger would make the ridiculously clichéd statement that a performer was a "frustrated" comic, singer, or even juggler. I always wondered if the passengers making these statements, usually dental hygienists sharing a cabin or the owner of a fast food franchise, ever dreamed of an interesting career while cleaning bicuspids or taking inventory of ketchup packets. Yet these same folks thought nothing of demeaning people actively pursuing their dreams, living their dreams, or reminiscing about how great it once was. Frustrated? I don't really think so.

The follow spot in the showroom illuminated a "fantastic vision" of humor, music and entertainment, right before the passenger's eyes, twice nightly. Problems arose when the artificial moonbeam illuminating the performance on stage blinded the artist to the slightest shimmer of reality.

Discounting talent, stature in their field, or dreams past, present, or future, once a performer stepped foot on board, in their minds, the planets decided to cease orbiting around the sun and chose the song and dance man instead. Life for the staff member assigned to their wellbeing became a nightmare. Pleading with the performer to attend the afternoon rehearsals, going over his or her charts with the band, and convincing the talent to just stay out of trouble was a daily chore. Regardless of a staff member's best intentions, performers still managed to occasionally bounce up to the bridge during a storm and encourage the Officer of the Deck to avoid any big waves during his show, or the randy comic who loved to impress teenagers by inviting a pretty one down to his cabin for a drink and a joint. Controlling these self-indulgent prima donnas became as difficult as Ulysses battling cyclops on his voyage to Ithaca.

The contracts of showroom performers came in four distinct categories. "Full Season Regulars" traveled and lived on the ship for the entire three-month season with the option to sign on for an additional three months. "Canal Pickups" were the Calypso tin barrel bands, limbo groups, and single acts like comics, magicians, and singers who boarded and debarked while the ship was passing through the Panama Canal. The action involved a rope ladder, a pilot boat, and lots of screaming and yelling. A bit less dramatic were the "Large Port Embarks & Debarks." These included shift-changing cruise staff, talent, band members, and disc jockeys along with their equipment. Included in this mix were staff and performers who had to end their contracts early due to chronic seasickness, chronic drunkenness, or after attacking a fellow performer, an officer, or the Captain himself, and then being rewarded with an extended stay in the ship's brig. Finally there were the "Emergency Debarks." A particular instance of that variety involved a social director who had lunch in Mazatlán. En route to our final port, the fellow became violently ill and we had to immediately schedule a Medi-Vac flight for him back to Los Angeles. Hospitalized on arrival, he was diagnosed with sepsis after human fecal matter was discovered in his blood stream. Seems a broken sewer pipe in the kitchen of Señior Frogs in Mazatlan had infected a small piece of lettuce that probably fell on the floor, and ended up back in his, and only his, Caesar salad. Granted, "emergency debarks" were not a common occurrence amongst the cruise staff and performers, but we were careful to avoid most of the restaurants in Mazatlán after that, particularly those serving Caesar salads.

MR. MYRON COHEN

Most of the performers booked on the ship came from talent office in New York. Occasionally a corporation would book the entire ship as a thank-you for its star personnel. Minolta was one of these companies. In addition to requesting special dinners and events, they also booked world famous comedian Myron Cohen for two performances during their seven days at sea. This really surprised me as I remembered Cohen to be an avuncular older man, soft spoken and elegant, who we used to watch on Sunday nights on *The Ed Sullivan Show*. The quintessential "old school" comedian. He didn't seem to be an appropriate act for a group of aggressive high-earning corporate sales people from a major corporation. Nevertheless, we welcomed him on board with respect and awe.

I was assigned to his welfare and comfort while he was with us, which wasn't a difficult order. He was a pleasure, simply requesting room service for most of his meals, and a few extra towels. Prior to our first rehearsal one afternoon, I was sent to his cabin to request his presence. I knocked on his door, he answered wearing a brocade bathrobe and matching velvet slippers with the initials MC embroidered in gold on the tops. He opened the door slightly, and I told him through the crack, it was time to rehearse. He listened nicely, and then said, "No, thank you." and gently closed the door.

No? No, thank you? I thought to myself, how does a performer do his thing without a rehearsal? What about the lights? What about any sound cues? What about the entrances and exits? Oh, my god!

I rushed back to the showroom and nervously told the Cruise Director running the rehearsal that I had just asked Myron to attend the rehearsal and he said, "No." and closed the door in my face.

"Well," said the Cruise Director with a shrug, "No is no." He continued the rehearsal with the dance team and a virtuoso harmonica player.

Later that evening I was sent back to Myron's room to tell him the show was ready to begin. He opened the door slightly again, this time clad in the nice robe, with a tuxedo underneath.

"Mr. Cohen," I said excitedly, "It's time, sir. Shall we go? The show is just about to start!"

He listened politely and then said, "How old are you young man?" the question threw me for a moment, but regaining my composure in a heartbeat, I answered, "Twenty-seven."

He nodded approvingly, somewhat impressed, I would like to think, and then he continued, "I've been in show business about forty years longer than you have been on this planet. I have never missed my entrance." He gently closed the door in my face once again.

Feeling faint, I ran back to the showroom and told the Cruise Director that Myron refuses to leave his cabin!

"Okay, just calm down and start the show." He handed me the mic, and I started warming up the house. A few corny jokes, a few mentions of Minolta thrown in to sweeten the pot, met with thunderous cheers, whoops and applause. When it was time for Myron's introduction, I looked at the Cruise Director, who was leaning against an offstage flat, and made a rolling motion with his finger, signifying to speed things up, so I did.

"Ladies and gentlemen, it gives me great pleasure to introduce the one, the only, Mr. Myron Cohen!" I just stood there like a lox, not knowing what to do next.

A nano-second later the spotlights ballyhoo swept to the double doors at the entrance to the theatre in the back of the room. The lights shimmered on the closed doors for a moment, before bursting open. In walks Mr. Myron Cohen resplendent in a tuxedo with a spotless white dinner jacket. He slowly walked down the aisle smiling and nodding modestly to the cheering audience, youthfully hopped up the steps, and walked center stage. I suppose he was able to see the relief in my face, as he extended his hand for the microphone, shook my hand with the other, then leaned over and whispered in my ear, "Never missed an entrance." He winked at me and then delivered sixty minutes of killer material, leaving the young, aggressively hip audience rolling in the aisles.

A few days later he was scheduled to disembark while we were passing through the Panama Canal. His bags were brought to the open double door hatchway in anticipation of being lowered to the bobbing pilot boat precariously tied up alongside. I was sent to get him from his cabin. He came with me this time, and we walked to the entry doors, with the rope ladder attached to curved stainless steel rails like one would see on the deep end of a swimming pool.

Myron took one look at the rope ladder, glanced slightly out of the open doors seeing the bobbing pilot boat below, then looked at me and said, "No, thank-you," this time shaking his head in finality. He then turned and gently walked back to his cabin, went back inside, and quietly closed the door. He remained ensconced in his cabin until we docked at San Juan. When it was time to disembark once again, he approached the gangway and made sure nothing was moving. Before stepping out on the ramp, he looked at me and winked, and stuffed a crisp twenty dollar bill in my hand. Elegant, old school, and funny as hell. Ladies and gentlemen, Mr. Myron Cohen.

ROWENA – JUST A SINGER FROM A SMOKEY CAFÉ

Rowena was a pert torch singer with a husky voice, short straight black hair, very pale complexion, and a penchant for bright red lipstick twenty-four hours a day. She sang primarily Garland and Minnelli hits with a few bluesy gospel numbers to change things a bit. While on stage she wore man-tailored tuxedos exclusively, varying the shades between black and morning gray. She traveled with a thin, strung out piano player who doubled as her conductor, and two cherubic young fellows she called her "dressers." The four of them shared a cabin which, per their request, came with two single beds.

Late afternoons of performance night the boys could be seen scurrying about the ship organizing and preparing Rowena's din-din: a club sandwich on whole wheat toast, no bacon, a bowl of vegetable soup, no alphabets, a chilled bottle of Mumm's, and a quarter gram of Lebanese hashish. The boys brought this last item on board themselves, realizing that the kitchen might have some difficulty supplying this pleasurable, though illegal, commodity. They had a hard enough time securing an ample amount of Rowena's requested vintage of Mumm's. Her menu was served at four on every performance night, with either a red rose or a white carnation in a bud vase as decoration.

One evening, a free-for-all erupted when, instead of the rose or carnation (after all, she did give them a choice), a drooping yellow gladiola stem was crammed into the tiny silver bud vase. Heads were threatened with rolling and tears flowed, as Rowena shrieked the obvious,

"Without the proper flower, my outfit isn't complete!" she pouted. "A limp damn gladiola will fucking ruin 'Old Man River' and make a laughing stock out of 'Over The Rainbow!'

Rowena was able to go on as scheduled after I came to the rescue with a playfully articulate (as well as expensive) bottle of Dom Perignon and our house trombone player came up with another gram of Lebanese Red. The two dressers, taking Rowena's ranting and raving to heart, were driven to the edge of simultaneous anxiety attacks. They decided to take refuge in one of our darker, more obscure lounges, weeping around the piano bar while getting soused on a Pink Lady and a Sloe Gin Fizz. One was overheard to lament, "Mary, for sure, that last time we were in Caracas, I should have never allowed Ro to talk me into getting *Slave Labor* tattooed on my ass."

"That was definitely a mistake, honey." sighed the other.

Rowena received a standing ovation for her performance that evening, sans rose, carnation, or even a limp gladiola pinned to her lapel.

KENNY KINGSTON – PSYCHIC TO THE STARS

Kenny Kingston, "Psychic To The Stars," was a popular act appearing on our ship regularly. His promo bio claimed past clients included John Wayne, Harry S. Truman, Dwight D. Eisenhower, Lucille Ball, Rex Harrison, Marilyn Monroe, Greta Garbo and, more recently, Whoopi Goldberg.

Traveling with his mother, this showbiz psychic claimed to be in his mid-sixties though, in reality, mid-seventies night be a bit more accurate. He favored dressing in pastel pinks, yellows and oranges—"sun colors," as he called them—though he insisted he wasn't a devotee of a popular guru who espoused the same color scheme for his followers during that time. His blond toupée, jutting out about half an inch from the back of his head, went well with his rose-tinted eyeglasses.

Kenny opened his show by reverently commanding the audience to grab the hand of the person sitting next to them, whether they knew each other or not, and join in a rousing rendition of "You Gotta Have Heart." He stressed singing with feeling, as it invited all the good spirits out of the cosmos and into our very own showroom. Bounding into the audience, resembling a lamb dyed pastel colors for an Easter pageant, he would choose a passenger at random for a "reading."

Having the somewhat embarrassed audience member rise, he would ask their name and where they were from, while positioning himself behind the subject, placing his fingertips on their temples, massaging gently. Simultaneously he would relate what the spirits, newly arrived from the cosmos, were telling him about the passenger. Coincidently, if the passenger had a Spanish surname, he would ask if they had a "Juan" somewhere in their family tree. A Jewish surname would be asked about a "David" somewhere in the great beyond, an Italian name a "Maria," of course. If their answer was positive he would move forward asking if the Juan, David, or Maria were still alive, and what they did for a living and if they got along with the passenger. Basically he had the passenger do his act for him. If they answered in the negative, he would pivot immediately by frowning and sadly informing the subject the spirits were suggesting losing just a little weight, dumping a current lover who is up to no good, and feeling free to spend a little of their savings on redecorating their kitchen.

After divulging all the spirits' information, be it good or bad, he ended with an upbeat tip, "Tonight is a great night for the casino!"

Encouraging the audience to applaud the spirits, not himself, as if the attending vibes were actually back-up singers for his showband, called Kenny and the Good Spirits, he would then slip the passenger a large white button emblazoned with, *I (Heart) My Good Spirits!* on the front, and Kenny's name and 800 number printed on the back. He called the buttons "Psychic Kenny Love Buttons."

When cruising the halls, Kenny enjoyed walking up to folks, grabbing them wherever convenient, and whispering, "Great aura! I see a fantastic aura around you today. Take advantage of it!" as he continued bouncing down the hall.

One afternoon while I was sitting at a poolside bar he startled me by grabbing my thigh and giving me the "great aura" rap. Almost choking on my cooling gin and tonic, I thanked him politely. What else does one say when told he has a "great aura"? I suppose if he told me my aura was bad, I'd have reason to be concerned. But good aura or bad, I was relieved when he let go of my thigh, fearing any number of things, primarily losing circulation to my lower leg, to say nothing of what a casual passerby might think.

One morning in the casino, after unceremoniously dumping a few fifty dollar trays in the dollar slots, he sauntered over to a stately woman feeding a five dollar slot. "I see a very secure aura around you. Secure. Securities, banking, umm, are you associated with banking in some way? An heiress perhaps?"

"I wish, sweetheart," replied the flattered woman, "but I've been on Social Security for years!"

"Well, perhaps in a former life!" he smiled, slipping her a Psychic Kenny Love Button, and skipped out on to the glaringly bright pool deck without looking back.

One evening just after embarkation Kenny rushed up to me and asked if I were the Cruise Director. I told him I was actually the First Officer but I would be happy to help him out. He told me the talent booker in New York told him I could get him two free passes for his mother and himself for the evening tour of Acapulco featuring the Twirling Aztec Flyers or "Voladores." No problem, I told him, we have passes for the performers, just ask the Cruise Director on any night you have free while we are in Acapulco. He thanked me and, with mother in tow, trundled off to the casino.

The next afternoon, just before tea, he came up to me again and had the very same request, comps to the Flying Aztec show in Acapulco. Positive I wasn't experiencing a tropical version of Déjà vu, I repeated what I told him the night before. All he had to do was ask the Cruise Director on the day we tied up in Acapulco, and there wouldn't be problem.

Smiling coyly, he purred, "You really have a superb aura, you know that don't you?"

"Yes Kenny, I've heard." I didn't say he was the one who informed me of my good fortune the afternoon before.

"Well remember, you gotta have heart." He winked, handed me a button, and made a bee-line for the colorful macarons and assorted French pastries displayed in tiers on the tea trolleys. He was a vision in light yellow shirt, pale pink Bermudas, high white knee socks, and white patent leather penny loafers with shiny dimes where the pennies should have been.

By the end of his run, I was the proud owner of over a dozen Psychic Kenny Love Buttons.

Late one evening I found him and his mother wandering aimlessly through the hall on a lower deck. "Kenny, what's going on? Can I help you with anything?" I asked.

"I can't find our goddamned room! What's the story with this bullshit room numbering?" he said, waving his room key fob in my face.

Shocked just a bit by his uncharacteristic salty language, I gently explained how to read the room key. The first number is the deck, first letter stands for fore or aft and the numbers following were the actual room numbers. Still trying to lighten the situation, I added, "Kenny, you of all people," I joked, "Can't you just hold the key to your forehead and ask the spirits?"

"Fuck off cutie pie," he growled, and added rather pedantically, "That's my act, okay?"

He turned and schlepped his mother down the hall.

IZZY THE COMIC

Many years ago, prior to my flight to the big city seeking fame, fortune, and an apartment without a tub in the kitchen, my dear old dad took me aside one sunny afternoon and imparted three snippets of wisdom to me: Don't get mixed up with sleazy broads, keep your nose clean, and be wary of anyone sounding like a Rabbi from a Reformed congregation in the suburbs.

Time and life being what they are, I have to admit my father and I had differing opinions as to meaning of "sleazy" and I always kept my nose clean, facilitated by carrying two handkerchiefs at all times. Unfortunately, I never met anyone sounding like a Rabbi from the suburbs, a rather esoteric description and certainly not anyone who ever traveled in my immediate circles. That is, until I met a stand-up comic named Izzy (not his real name), booked as a regular performer for the entire season at sea.

Born and raised in Brooklyn, New York during the late thirties, Izzy somehow developed an accent that was west of Oxford, east of Harvard, splashing around in the mid-Atlantic on a raft of pickle barrels. On stage he sounded like a Dead End Kid lost in a delicatessen. The moment he stepped off stage, one would be hard pressed to think he wasn't a member of the Royal family. Impossible to prune even the slightest Royal twig from his family tree, he was, nevertheless, a very special person.

Izzy had a long running role on an even longer running Broadway show years ago. Because of his brief claim to fame, he billed himself as "The Lighthearted Funster from the Great White Way." When pressed for the name of the show he was in, he skirted around the subject; as it turned out the show was actually *The Diary of Anne Frank* which, as we all know, wasn't famous for being a laugh-riot sensation.

This is not to suggest Izzy was not a talented comic. Without exaggeration his comic ability bordered on genius, as the crabbiest audience member would be convulsing with laugher by the time he concluded his evening set.

I learned something very important about show business from Izzy. It seems our lighting control board was located on a console behind the piano on our little stage. After introducing an act, the emcee, yours truly more often than not, retreated to the position behind the piano, created a bit of a ballyhoo with the lights available, and the act would enter the stage from either the right of the left of the backstage area. While the talent worked, the emcee would just sit on a small stool, in direct line of sight with the audience, waiting for the "Big Finish," and then adjust the lights accordingly before jumping back center stage, thanking the preceding act for a great show, and then introducing the following performer.

This one particular evening I noticed Izzy shooting curious glances at me throughout his act. He killed as usual, but after the show he corralled me in one of the lounges and, in no uncertain terms, recited the riot act concerning being in full view of the audience and not laughing during his set.

"The audience can see you, and if you don't laugh during my act, neither will they! It doesn't matter if you have heard the jokes before, just laugh, damn it!" He then uncharacteristically stormed out of the bar in a snit.

Lesson learned. The next evening, I laughed to the point of tears at every one of his somewhat tired jokes, and the audience responded appropriately. Izzy shot me a few glances during his set, while cresting a laugh, but this time he added a wry smile and nodded his head ever so slightly.

Practicing what he preached, adding to his fawning good manners with the passengers and his Charlton-Heston-playing-god diction, while waiting in the wings, he doubled as a one man laugh track when any of the staff, particularly the Cruise Director, attempted to crack a joke on stage. A loud booming roar here, an ecstatic chuckle there, each one different and just loud enough to prime the rows of passengers nearest the stage to start laughing, which cued the remainder of the audience to join in as well. While flipping through all his laughter gymnastics, he never cracked a smile. Usually he just continued working on a crossword puzzle, shining his shoes with a bar towel, or practicing rolling his hat from his head down his arm and into his waiting hand. The trick always worked backstage, but never once during his performance, until the very last attempt while taking his bow, accompanied by a rim shot and crescendo by the band. The audience would roar and cheer in delight.

Despite his valiant efforts to keep in shape, spending his days working out in the gym, or pacing around the Promenade Deck for hours, it was painful to see him gasping for breath and hyperventilating after a performance. He would weave off the stage with only enough energy to collapse into a chair and double over, forcing his head between his knees to avoid fainting, but never missed the final bows with all the other performers. It was Pagliacci-esque, if you will, resembling, as he did, an aging court jester forever cracking jokes and making people laugh. He had no choice due to bills and rent that had to be paid ashore, and while he was able, he had no intention of going gentle into that good night.

Certainly he was to be congratulated for plying his trade so late in life. Not only did he enjoy it, he had a magic ability to melt the coldest audience into a laughing heap with a mere gesture or a few words. Yet every night after his set he would hobble off stage as though he were a pilgrim returning from Fatima uncured. When running the follow spot from the rear of the house, you would hear the audience scream and applaud their approval of his hysterical act. If you were waiting backstage, hearing Izzy's rasping and wheezing would rend your heart in two. If you asked if he needed any help, he would wave you off gasping, "I'm fine. I'm fine. Don't worry about it, just let me know when it's time for the curtain calls, okay?"

From outward appearances, Izzy had no vices. He looked forward to long walks while in port, visiting libraries, art museums or cathedrals. He drank an occasional glass of wine, but never smoked or chased women, although he was prone to give one-man standing ovations to Pilar, our resident Spanish dancer and singer. After losing her husband, who was once part of her act, she continued entertaining with her stirring renditions of "Eres Tu" and "La Paloma Blanca" while mincing about the stage like an adorable poodle in spiked heels. Izzy treated her like a diva from Barcelona, applauding wildly and shouting the appropriate "Brava! Brava!" after each of her performances. During early evening they could be found slowly strolling arm in arm on one of the deserted upper decks taking a bit of air. Pilar rarely exposed her peaches and cream complexion to the light of day, fearing the sun would damage her third generation Castilian complexion, even if two of those three generations hailed from Bayonne, New Jersey.

Unlike the staff who returned from a day in an American port loaded down with buckets of KFC, jars of peanut butter, grape jelly, and who knows what else. Izzy boarded with cases of canned dog food, kitty tuna, and two fifty pound sacks of dry pet meal, one for dogs and one for cats. He held an abiding love for animals, especially those diseased downtrodden strays and rejects wandering around the docks and piers of every port where we tied up. Partially blind, limping mongrels with protruding ribs, cats with mangy oil-splotched coats, some sneezing with running noses, all waited patiently for Izzy's arrival. Bounding down the gangway, he brought the cans of food, boxes of liver treats, doggie bones and a plethora of nibbles, kibbles, and assorted yummies for these hungry discarded denizens of the docks. Kneeling down like Saint Francis in Bermuda shorts, he would be surrounded in minutes by these onetime pets and companions running and limping from all corners of the busy docks. Izzy fed each one, even by hand if necessary. Once they had their fill, appreciatively licking their paws or rubbing up against their benefactor, Izzy packed up the remaining food and headed back to the ship.

A short time later, you could see Izzy bounding down the gangway setting off on one of his marathon walks along the esplanades lined with palms and bougainvillea. As the crowded tour busses from the ship sped by, Izzy would wave and throw kisses.

BABETTE AND ROBAIRE - LES DANSE STYLISTS PARISIAN

To hear Babette and Robaire wax poetically about their quaint village was to realize all the beauty of a spring morning just south of the Alps on the French Riviera: "Ah *mon ami*, to be back in Saint Simeon in the spring. The carpets of lavender, the warm sunshine, the pink cheeks of the baby children, *c'est magnifique!*" But it wasn't the Alps; Saint Simeon remains a small fishing village on the Saint Lawrence Seaway and, other than Babette and Robaire, the town's only claim to fame was *Le Festivale Du Smelt*, or Smelt Festival, held every July. French Canadians from this small fishing hamlet in Quebec, Babette and Robaire held the distinction of winning a local ballroom dance competition fresh out of high school. According to their nightly introductory patter, the pair went on to win the Canadian National Championships two years running. This leads one to ask the fervent question, "where does an award winning dance team go from there?"

Dancing since their late teens on cruise ships sailing all over the world, they truly dazzled passengers nightly with their flamboyant but Gallic interpretations of tangos, waltzes, and assorted ballroom classics. In addition, they hosted Champagne Fêtes during which members of the audience chose a dance and whom they wished to dance it with, and the winners received a bottle of bubbly for their noble efforts. Babette was the more popular choice over Robaire, though one evening an elderly gentleman with thinning hair, looking as though it was recently darkened with shoe polish, requested Robaire's company for a waltz. Blushing, Robaire respectfully declined, but whispered to the ingenuous gent that he would be available for a private lesson tomorrow afternoon.

During the days, the pair graciously agreed to give lessons to anyone yearning to learn the latest steps as well as pay a small remuneration for the service. Hip-Hop lessons were the most popular, along with an occasional request for the Cha-Cha-Cha. Babette always added the third "cha" to the title, as well as pronouncing it, "Le Sha-Sha-Sha," adding a bit of charm Françoise, non?

Babette still had her looks, nothing short of every high school boy's cheerleader fantasy, with a small ever-present red gossamer scarf tied in a bow around her neck. She was a vivacious dream girl with muscular dancers legs and body, relaxing ever so gently into middle age. Bruising more often nowadays, she discovered the calming effects Xanax and a bit of oxycodone during a stopover in Grenada. Since then she purchased a few hundred of each every time the ship hit Grenada and had an ample supply for the next few weeks of cruising.

Bruises and "medicine" notwithstanding, Babette spent her free time flitting about the decks chirping and chatting with every one about anything crossing her mind, or theirs. Mostly hers.

Robaire, in odd contrast, was a taciturn young man, a cool polar opposite to his wife and her incessant vapid chit-chat. His chosen garb for performances were tight-fitting one-piece ballroom dance costumes, stunning the audience with their bright colors and intricate sequin patterns, a few of the sequins having fallen off long ago. It didn't seem to matter that, in his early forties, his once-hourglass figure had begun to gather at the waist and hips. Rather than resemble the handsome young man on the top of a wedding cake, as he liked to think he looked, his appearance of late had taken on the line of a Bosc pear. Unconcerned, his only other exercise beyond dancing consisted of collecting preserved butterflies and pressed tropical flowers, none of which he barbarically chased down himself with a catch net and a pair of tweezers but which were purchased from assorted catalogues. He mounted them all in numerous scrapbooks with specialized non-acidic pages. Robaire had an affinity for frumpy wool peasant smocks with shawl collars. He wore them with proper English desert boots whenever up and about the ship, even when cruising the humid tropics.

Billing themselves as world-class performers, neither of Les Danse Stylists Parisian had ever been to France, let alone Paris, though they once performed on the S.S. France many years ago. For some odd reason they both took a sense of pride in bragging they had never attended a performance of a ballet. They were sure, however, the dancing must have been first-rate considering all the fuss that people, especially the Montreal types, make about the performances.

Our passengers swooned over this couple for no other reason than their unmistakably French accents, embellished every chance they had with the charming catch phrase, "Ah, how do you say in your language?" No one seemed to care that their back country French Canadian accents were to Paris what Brooklynese was to the English of Buckingham Palace. Nevertheless, as long as our dance team continued to sound like younger versions of Yves Montand and Simone Signoret, the passengers were suitably charmed, the Home Office was thrilled, and Babette and Robaire remained overjoyed at being gainfully employed.

Periodically, Robaire visited our spa for a massage by one of the hefty women who ran the concession. We learned he insisted on wearing his undershorts during the entire process, including having a lengthy sauna before and after the procedure. Later we joked with him about his unnecessary modesty and he defended his actions by saying, "Well, my friends, how do you say, it's only proper, *n'est ce pas*? I mean after all, Helga the masseuse is a friend, you know. It's not like she is a complete stranger or sister in hospital, now is it?"

We could never figure out the logic behind that one. According to him it's only acceptable for strangers or nurses to see you naked. Really?

Changing backstage during production numbers one evening, the Cruise Director mischievously brought to my attention both Babette and Robaire had predilections for bright red underwear.

We couldn't figure out that one either, but, then again, perhaps it was none of our business.

LINDY SHORE & VIVIAN AVALON, WE'RE A CLOSING ACT, PERIOD!

Lindy and Vivian Shore were a husband and wife singing team. She sang, he played the piano and sang along. They used their individual professional names fearing that Lindy and Vivian Dunkleman just didn't have that particularly show business ring to it. Moreover, each had made a modest impact in the business in his and her own way, so they were intent on preserving their image for their shrinking coterie of loyal fans.

The "Inimitable Lindy Shore," a cuff-tucking Tin Pan Alley composer and arranger, owned a set of perfectly capped teeth that bulged a bit when he grinned, looking like Chicklets. He accompanied Viv on the ship's Baby Grand piano while she sang her showstoppers from that netherworld of musical hits from the late fifties to this very day. Following a few of her numbers, Lindy would share the limelight. He styled his act after various Vegas lounge acts, but rather than scat improvised lyrics to the usual jazz classics, he took his act one step further, taking his material from his versions of hits from *Les Misérables* or *Wicked*. Sporting a pencil thin moustache, diamond pinky ring, and white patent leather loafers without socks, he pounded on the piano like a demon, especially when Viv was "rolling," having the audience "right in the palm of her hand." He became so possessed while playing the piano, his smartly groomed toupée occasionally tilted to one side, well in view of the audience. Unfazed, he was able to straighten the wayfaring hairpiece with his left hand, while continually pounding the ivories with his right. The audience would chuckle politely. Seeing this done for the first time, I was really impressed by his musical dexterity, but then as the sliding and straightening of the hair piece occurred on a regular basis, at least once every show, I realized it was part of the act. When the audience finally noticed the creeping coif, embarrassed audience chuckling turned to uproarious laughter when Lindy quipped, "That's right folks, at my age the rug gets sent out with my shorts!" The audience howled in recognition.

Vivian—Viv to her friends—was a large, imposing woman standing about a foot taller than hubby Lindy. She had a weakness for long false eyelashes that pecked little mascaraed dots below her eyebrows when they fluttered during the long notes. She wore svelte rhinestone-encrusted gowns cut very low in the front and even lower in the back. The entire unit sparkled madly in the follow spot beams whether she was moving or not. She didn't seem to notice her back had begun to sag a little, especially over the seams of her form-fitting outfit. During the day she could be seen chatting with passengers throughout the ship. She was always seen delicately holding, pinky extended, a vodka and lemonade, wearing black leather gauchos and a stiff brimmed hat with red chi-chi balls dangling all around, resembling a gently swaying Charo mingling at a fiesta.

Among variety entertainers there is a definite self-insisted pecking order as to where in the show the act performs. No one wants to open and everyone wants to close. Lindy and Viv were no exceptions.

"We headline at Branson and Tahoe, when are you kids going to get with it?" they would argue with the highest of dudgeon. Fine. If there was one quality our Cruise Director possessed in bushels it was the ability to deal with performers just as temperamental as he was. Besides that, flattered at being considered a "kid," he would take the path of least resistance and graciously acquiesce to let them close. He also commanded the usher to leave the back doors to the showroom open during their act. Some folks had a tendency to file out during their performance and the light flashing into the room from doors opening and closing could prove to be a bit distracting. Undaunted, their finale consisted of a spirited international medley of *Arriverderci Roma, Hava Nagila, When Irish Eyes Are Smiling*, and finally a pulse-quickening rendition of *La Bamba*, encouraging the remaining members of the audience to stand and clap along. The standing and clapping would magically turn into a spontaneous standing-ovation every night, which the pair modestly acknowledged as they bowed.

A few years later my mother told me a "big" act from the cruise ships performed in their Sunrise, Florida condo showroom the preceding Saturday night. It turned out to be the none other than the "Inimitable" Lindy Shore and Vivian Avalon! They were the last act, and received a standing ovation. The usher who volunteered for a free ticket guarded the door to backstage and just so happened to be part of my mother's weekly mah-jongg group. My duly attending father and hyper excited mother were secretly given access to the backstage area after the show. My mom cornered Lindy and Viv just on their way out. Lindy was carrying Vivian's heavy rhinestone-encrusted gowns as she always changed into something fresh for the second act. He was also struggling with the charts for the house combo, pulled along in a small rolling suitcase. Undaunted, mom said she told Vivian I was the Cruise Director on a ship they performed on a few years ago. Viv politely claimed she remembered me, sent her regards, as well as agreeing to sign my mother's one sheet program with an eyebrow pencil mom had in her purse. Unfortunately, they just had to refuse my mother's invitation to come back to her condo for coffee and cake, and sped off into the humid night in an Uber driven by an eighty year old.

THE TOURS, THE DRUNKS, AND EVEN MORE COMPLAINTS, OR, YOU DON'T HAVE TO BE DRUNK TO ENJOY A TOUR, BUT IT HELPS

One of the essential experiences to be had while enjoying a stay amid the opulence of an international cruise is the diversion offered by a shore tour. Unfortunately, the ports can only be considered diversions, as one spends but a few short hours in any one of them, overnight at best. As any seasoned traveler will tell you, it is extremely difficult to get a genuine feeling for a country, its customs, and its people, by visiting for such a brief period of time. For many tourists it takes a few hours just to figure out the exchange rate of a dollar, as well as locating the center of town, if there is one. Unfortunately, most passengers find it too confusing to seek the major points of interest, the museums, natural wonders, hot night spots or even a bordello or two—sanctioned by the local health department, of course.

To remedy this confusing situation, and understanding that most passengers book passage for the cruise itself and not necessarily the ports of call, ship companies have devised the shore tour. Designed to meet the interests of the casual traveler as well as the intrepid explorers among the manifest, the Home Office goes out of its way to fashion a few hours ashore that are at once easy and comfortable, yet informative and moderately stimulating. No politics, no opinion, just speed, safety, and a dash of beauty. If at all possible air conditioned Mercedes motor coaches and a small sample of the local brew, be it rum, tequila, mescal, or curacao, are provided. Occasionally there was a spicy concoction offered called *Leche De Tigre* or Milk of the Tiger. Though there was no telling what the components of that fiery libation were, you could be sure the principle ingredient was not milk.

Another phenomenon of cruise ship tours is that passengers loved to follow the local tour guide like obedient ducklings. The tour guide was always bounding ahead of them while waving a small official pennant and quacking about this or that to anyone who could keep up. Most passengers could care less about trying to figure out what he was saying in heavily accented English and simply looked forward to the free drink that awaited them before being loaded back on the humming, air conditioned coaches. (More on the free drinks in just a bit.)

In spite of our preparations and concerns, there were always complaints. The convention of B'nai B'rith members from Massapequa, Long Island, New York was not very pleased with the cheerful tour guide pointing out and, then waving to, a group of picnicking Nazi ex-pats in a public park in Maracaibo. There was the housewife from Michigan who, luxuriant in bouffant hairdo and oversized, light sensitive sunglasses, the bottom corner of one lens engraved not with an initial or tennis racket but with a sketch of her Class-A motor home, fretted one afternoon as we made ready to sail from Venezuela.

"If the equator was only a few miles from Caracas, you should have at least organized a tour to go see it. I mean, how many of us are going to be in Caracas ever again?"

I assured her we did have a tour to the site but, along with the famous mountain climbing cable car in Caracas, it was closed for renovations. This explanation, though questionable in veracity, satisfied her for the moment, giving me enough time to reflect on the old saying, "A little knowledge is a very dangerous thing."

Prior to booking any tour we warned passengers as best we cared to (knowing full well we received a small kickback for each tour sold) that, although there was not all that much to be appreciated in this particular port, a morning tour was still an excellent way to get an idea of what was to be seen. Then after spotting an interesting beach, market place, or cathedral, you could always catch a cab and return to the site in the afternoon, fortified with a hearty lunch on board, and perhaps a short nap, and still be back in time for a few fresh petit fours prepared for high tea.

We were aided in our efforts by the local tour operators who understood that most Americans, especially those taking hermetically sealed air conditioned bus tours of the tropics, could occasionally be hard to please. To counter this concern, copious amounts of indigenous drinks were offered at every stop in never ending amounts. Tequila, mescal, and Margaritas flowed in the Mexican ports, rum punch laced with nutmeg streamed out the Lesser Antilles. Orange Curacao, naturally enough, gushed from Curacao and Grenada, and rum Cokes or Cuba Libres, their title depending on the shop keeper's opinion of Castro at the time, surged from every bar, key, cay or atoll.

The staff always touted the drinks at each stop as the best in the world, beside the fact they were free and bottomless, more or less. Most of the shops serving all these generous free drinks were jewelry stores and souvenir stands owned by the brother-in-law of the tour operator, or a cousin of the bus driver, or more often than not had a deal with the Cruise Director for a percentage of the sales any batch of tourists made during their visit to the shop. Their operating creed: "Get a rich American drunk, and he will buy anything."

That was true, evidenced by the boxes of seashell encrusted crucifixes, stuffed bull frogs posed as Mariachi bands complete with sombreros, serapes and little wooden guitars, and various other touristy kitsch a sober person, tourist or otherwise, would never even consider if not under the influence of a refreshing beverage. Our philosophy was get any passenger drunk, rich or not, and they would probably not have a complaint when ambling off the tour bus and back to the ship. If they did, it would not be blamed on us. A husky, ruddy-faced alumnus from the University of Alabama, for example, on board for his twentieth class reunion, was a perfect case. Fanning himself with his snakeskin banded Stetson while wiping the soles of his high heeled unborn kid cowboy boots on the gangway before entering the ship, he announced, "Hell, them Mayan boys sure had a hell-of-a-lot of nerve building those ruins so far from the ship!"

Frequently the extravagant amounts of booze served to our passengers worked against all our good intentions, as during our "Fiesta Folklorico," a dinner and show held on the palm-laden oceanfront back patio of one of the larger hotels in Acapulco. Transporting three or four hundred of the willing, five to a cab, to the hotel didn't really pose any problems. The facilities at the hotel were certainly adequate for all the passengers as well as a few interlopers from the hotel itself and the neighboring establishments. While waiting for the buffet and festivities to begin, the passengers were unofficially entertained by shirtless teenagers on the beach juggling machetes or taking swigs of gasoline, and then igniting it as they spit it out, causing a huge plume of fire to light up the balmy night. During their impromptu performances they would have younger cohorts work the guests at the tables by the edge of the beachside patio for tips, and perhaps a sale of a serape or woven blanket they carried thrown over their shoulders. If they dared to take one step up on to the patio, they would be immediately swatted on the head by an attentive waiter or busboy, so they stayed clear.

The ticket included an authentic buffet of Pacific Coast Mexican delights which would easily impress any Mayan King. Platters and bowls overflowing with various sorts of ceviche (a pickled fish dish consisting of raw chunks of marlin, shark, or grouper marinated in fresh lime juice with chopped cilantro, tomatoes, onions, and garlic) as well as whole broiled fish, juicy steaks, chicken and pork creations, all slathered with piquant moles, a luxurious dark sauce prepared from slow cooking unsweetened chocolate. There was a surprising lack of what most Americans feel is "traditional Mexican" fare such as tacos, burritos, and enchiladas. These dishes are popular primarily in Northern parts of the country and differ greatly from what is proudly prepared on the Pacific coast. There was, nevertheless, an older woman grating and kneading masa on a stone metate and pressing fresh tortillas, which she grilled right on a little stone oven sitting next to her on the patio. For desert there were flans (egg custards) floating in a dark ultra-sweet caramel sauce, as well as pastries, sweet cakes, and a plethora of chilled tropical fruits, mangos, guavas, papaya, melons and more, all peeled and skewered on sticks to be eaten like Popsicles. All these delights crammed festively decorated buffet tables orchestrated by gently thumping waves, under a darkening sky streaked with pink over an undulating Pacific just beginning to sparkle with silver moonlight.

Most of the passengers were oblivious to their romantic surroundings and were more concerned with loading their plates with mounds of delicious goodies from the buffet. While filling a few wrinkles in their stomachs with this repast, the passengers were entertained with a lavish floor show. The extravaganza featured debonair vaqueros on horseback doing rope tricks right there on the stage as well as gorgeous senoritas in white flowing dresses with red roses accenting their long, jet-black hair. They performed every national dance imaginable and then modeled, in a gracious parade, all the ornate costumes from the various regions and states of Mexico. Music for the show was provided by a fifteen piece Mariachi band.

The crowning glory of the evening's entertainment, as I learned on one of the first tours I escorted, was that no real Mexican fiesta, large or small, was complete without a cockfight.

That's right, a cockfight. Now, there is no way in creation an American audience will tolerate cruelty to animals in any shape manner or form. Hearing the cockfight announced, I simply lowered my head on the table and bid a hasty prayer to the Cruise Director in the sky, pleading for a simple earthquake or moderate tsunami, anything He could muster on short notice that would prevent the next act from happening. It had been a long day and I knew I would not be able to deal with the torrent of grievances streaming from hundreds of self-righteously indignant, hysterically horrified passengers that I would allow the barbarity of two pugnacious fryers to claw it out on the dance floor.

I looked up when I heard spirited "oles" and "give 'em a left" emanating from the crowd, and saw the fighting cocks were actually two little people in chicken suits, ritualistically fighting it out to the accompaniment of an up-tempo ditty of Mayan flutes and drums. Thanks to the continual flow of Margaritas filling the glasses of the righteous from the moment they stepped from their taxis, and the fact it was actually people in chicken suits smacking each other where convenient, the passengers' righteous indignation quickly evaporated. People hitting each other, after all, is civilized. Thankfully, the hosts of the fiesta separated the feisty little combatants before any gory damage was done.

The critical summation of the evening's festivities general among most of the more sensitive of the passengers was, "What a great finale to a great show! Now where is that pretty little senorita with the Margaritas?" Those less erudite were unconscious, leaning back in their chairs, breathing through their mouths.

With the ending of the show our troubles began. Although there was little difficulty in getting passengers from the ship to the hotel, returning them back to the ship was another story. The primary reason for this was most of our folks, at least those still able to walk, were shellacked to a brilliant sheen, leaving us with a task not unlike herding drunken alley cats. The welling of patriotism arising from Americans abroad, as well as being thoroughly polluted, is astounding. We were able to identify our charges from the dispersing crowd as the ones clinging to each other for support, while singing fuzzy renditions of "America the Beautiful" or "Dixie."

The cab drivers, paid by the head, not the trip, insisted on full loads and full loads only, five people, no more, and certainly no less. Making matters worse, each cab refused to budge until the one in front of the line was filled with, you guessed it, "*cinco personas.*" The cabbies must have had a terrific union.

The passengers, many traveling as couples or in small groups, some married for fifty years or more, refused to be separated for the five minute dash back to the ship. To insure getting all the passengers aboard before sailing, we were forced to plead, beg, and entice the truly stubborn ones with promises ranging from free drinks on board to souvenir key chains. We would try anything, in fact, that would entice a cranky passenger into a cab and away from leaning against a palm tree in a snit, and moving along.

Crafty folks who realized that they had us by the seams of our starched white shorts reverted to blackmail. "We will be happy to split up for the ride back, but only if you promise a ship's tie for my husband when we get back."

"We'll give you two ties, get in the cab!"

"Red ones?"

"Red, blue, pink, any color you want. Just get in the cab. Please."

"But Gladys, I think those ties are ugly."

"Shut-up Murray, we need a present for your brother Max!"

With that snippet of undeniable logic, one of them climbed into the waiting cab and the other into the cab directly behind it, and everyone was happy, including brother-in-law Max, though he was yet to find out.

Staff always took the last cab back to the ship after scouring the hotel from floor to floor, not forgetting the pool decks, patios, verandas, and of course the beach. If any passengers were left behind, one of the staff would be eviscerated and thrown to the sharks, and nothing was worth that.

Wrapping up Fiesta Folklorico was done by memory, as we were modestly inebriated ourselves, in addition to balancing stacks of leftovers in Styrofoam containers the hotel management showered on us. The Styrofoam containers were filled to overflowing with chips and guacamole, arroz con pollo, ceviche, pork moles, and who knows what else? It wasn't that we were rabid aficionados of Mexican food all that much, it was more as a welcome respite from the seven course continental cuisine served "French Service" in the main dining room night after night. They also bet, rightfully so, the more treats they showered on us now, the more passengers we would encourage to attend Fiesta Folklorico the next time the ship was in port. They were absolutely correct.

During our final sortie down the beach one balmy evening we came across a woman attempting to bury herself in the sand, claiming, when the tide rolled in, it was going to kidnap her back to Los Angeles, and she didn't want to go. At least not yet. As we approached, she began throwing handfuls of damp sand our way, which we easily fended off, successfully defending our wiggling stacks of Styrofoam containers. Dragging her out of her self-imposed foxhole as modestly as possible (at least I know I was modest about it; I can't vouch for the others), we brushed her off a bit and then dragged her, kicking and screaming, to the hotel entrance, stuffed her into the last cab, and we were all driven back to the hotel. Thankfully she was lulled to sleep by the bumpy road and our ride back was thankfully uneventful.

We caught the ship just prior to raising the gangway, carrying our snoring charge into the reception area and gently laying her down on a sofa. We breathed a collective sigh of relief as the ship's horn blared and were sailing off into Acapulco Bay. About this time we thought it would be a good idea to ask her what her cabin number was and then carefully load her up on a luggage cart to have a steward or two roll her back to her cabin. We couldn't allow her to remain spread eagle on a sofa on a public deck, murmuring something about Room 914, until someone came by to claim her. We assured her there was no Room 914 on the ship, as the numbering only went up to 500. She was adamant, insisting she was in Room 914, and furthermore her husband was a big guy who loved "kicking ass and taking names," so we had all better watch out! With that ominous threat, she issued a melodious belch and began dozing off once again. Prior to docking in dreamland we roused her long enough to inquire if she remembered her cabin number. Concentrating on my tie tack, she gurgled, "It's not a cabin, it's a room, you asshole! Room 914 of the Acapulco Princess Hotel and if you don't like that, you can sit on it."

With that, her head flopped down on a sofa cushion as she docked in dreamland.

Her words hung in the air like a death sentence. The entire staff realized simultaneously that she was not one of ours. We stood there for a moment with our sombreros askew, our lives in the balance. One of our more experienced Social Directors suggested we just throw her overboard before they secured the outer bulkhead doors and be done with it. Who would know? I fondly realized there was a reason this guy was in his mid-fifties and still a Social Director. I suggested perhaps looking for some ID and checking it against the passenger manifest might be a more prudent idea. Everyone agreed. Not finding any ID we decided to take her at her word. We knew we had to act very fast; if not, she would be our guest for a very long time as we were not docking for at least six days and were headed for a passage of the Panama Canal, with the next stop being Martinique.

Rushing to the Bridge, the Officer of the Day laughed when we told him he had to turn the ship around, quickly. He laughed even harder when we told him why. "You are all, how do you say in English, 'Geese that are cooked.'" Dismissing us with a flick of his hand, he returned to his cup of espresso and well-thumbed version of Italian *Penthouse*.

Fortunately for us, like an archangel from on high, the Harbor Pilot was still on the Bridge and heard everything. Smiling, he suggested he might be able to help as his Pilot Boat was still tied up alongside the ship. Whenever an official of the Mexican Government, especially the maritime officers, suggest they "might" be able to do something, it means they definitely can do anything as long as they are supplied with enough bottles of Johnnie Walker Black.

Flying down to the Quartermaster's office/cabin, we roused the sleeping officer from his bed. After we pinned a few crisp twenties to the hem of his Virgin Mary statue, he lumbered into a back room. Moments later he returned, crossing himself, handed us a few bottles, and told to get the hell out of his cabin as it was the middle of the night.

We ran for our shipboard lives back to the welcome deck just in time to see the Harbor Pilot approach our lady friend, who awoke at his touch and drowsily purred, "Oh, Fernando, you were terrific again tonight, baby. But tomorrow you just have to give me two towels for my chaise lounge, okay lambkins?"

"*Si Senora*," the Harbor Pilot replied debonairly, carefully tucking the bottles of whiskey under his arm. He elegantly extended his hand and led his wobbling charge toward the open hatch, yawing wide into the thick darkness. Somehow—don't ask me how—he got her down the precarious rope ladder, into the bobbing pilot boat, and they were off to the Acapulco Princess, Room 914. At least, we hoped they were.

Lying two hours south of Puerto Vallarta by boat in the state of Jalisco is a tiny cove adorned with thousands of swaying palm trees looking as if it belongs somewhere in the South Pacific. Called Yelapa, the tiny village of little palm-thatched cottages, at least during the years we visited, boasted one electric generator, available for emergencies only. Kerosene lamps were the lighting of choice; a river served as the launderette; and there was even a paved road, albeit five hours away by horseback and a bit longer by mule-driven wagon. If artist Paul Gauguin had known of it, he might have spent some of his time there rather than schlepping all the way out to Tahiti.

But this was years ago and things have changed drastically since then. The Mexican government, taking full advantage of its rustic charm and tropical beauty, constructed high rise apartments and hotels and added numerous other modern conveniences like electricity and running water. Nevertheless, in the old days, it was a tour available on our ship.

We pushed a tour to this unique little paradise for hardy souls only. The tour consisted of an all-day excursion to the cove on a rickety old wooden motor yacht that had actually belonged to John Wayne before he traded it in for a reconditioned minesweeper. When it wasn't ferrying zinc oxide-smeared tourists out for a day of rustic tropical fun, the boat served as the cove's only regular link with the outside world. A minor complication which we conveniently forgot to mention in the glowing description in our tour brochure was that the tiny cove lacked any sort of pier for visiting boats to tie up. Staff believed the locals refused to build a landing pier just to make our lives as difficult as possible. Actually, it seems the reason had to do with the position of the cove and the severity of the swells coming directly off the Pacific, though I'm told a small concrete and iron pier exists now, a luxury we could only dream about at the time.

Compounding our difficulties was the hospitality of the wooden yacht's crew. The moment our passengers stepped on board in Vallarta, the crew began plying our passengers with Margaritas ladled out from a large reconstituted steel drum. For those not acquainted with the potency of a lovely Margarita, one only needs to know it is a tasty tropical libation consisting of quarts of tequila and a few squeezes of lime with the remaining fruit thrown in for good measure, and then a bottle or two of Triple Sec. Finally, a block or two of ice are thrown into the cauldron to chill everything down. The drink is deceivingly mild like a tasty limeade and pleasantly refreshing until you have had two or three, and then you realize that the only way to reach the cove is jumping from the yacht into a waiting dugout canoe bobbing in the waves alongside our antique steamer. The canoes were guided by frail old men clinging to large stern rudders while their tattered straw hats and wispy grey beards occasionally flew about, obscuring their failing vision. The dugout, with ten or so passengers clinging to the sides for dear life, lurched and surfed though the foamy three-to-five foot waves and eventually made it to the pristine beach with a resounding thud.

With all due respect, after spending two hours or so bucking and weaving through high Pacific swells on the ride down from Puerto Vallarta on a rickety old yacht without the benefit of stabilizers like our cruise ship had, the prospect of having to surf to shore on a small dugout canoe was quite daunting—especially since passengers would be sharing space with a few sacks of mail, some jerry cans of kerosene, or perhaps a goat or a caged rooster (all necessary for ballast). This didn't sit very well with some of our haughty passengers. In fact, many would decide, with a seasick belch, to take the yacht back to Vallarta and forget the whole thing.

That was never going to happen, as one of us would have had to accompany the grumpy passengers back to the ship, leaving one less staff member to assist in wrangling our herd of wild passengers running amok in this tropical Eden. We did our best, therefore, to convince the pouting passengers not to return to the ship and at least give the charming little cove a chance. Backing up our arguments, we would wax poetic claiming they would never have the opportunity of surfing onto a beach in a dugout canoe, so why not try it just this once? One thing about cruise ship passengers must be their sense of adventure, their willingness to try something at least once, or perhaps just consider to do so.

That was all the time we needed. Before being able to conclude that, yes, their lives would be in grave danger by just setting foot in that bobbing little canoe, we lifted or pushed the screaming skeptic into the dugout. Clutching the gunwales of the unsteady craft in white-knuckled fear, they were off, skipping across the bounding main. It was amazing, really, that once an otherwise petrified passenger was zipping toward the beach at a blinding speed, he or she rarely screamed at all.

Once ashore, having weathered the usual inquiries if the canoes were Coast Guard certified, and if not, why not, we were able to re-direct their concerns by serving a surprisingly elaborate buffet lunch. It was brought over in numerous ice chests by the kitchen staff in their spotless white uniforms. They used the very same canoes that were used to bring the passengers ashore, and no one or anything ever fell overboard. We knew there was a charming thatched-roofed restaurant right there on the beach serving a cornucopia of local delicacies: a meat of some sort, stuffed and roasted in an armadillo shell, little roasted parrots on a skewer, or chunks of turtle in a piquant chocolate mole, reminiscent in taste and texture to my mother's pot roast. But, rather than give our folks the opportunity to become righteously indignant of the local *table d'hôtel*—armadillos and turtles were zoo animals after all—we served them a portable picnic version of what they would have had on the ship, with unlimited chilled vin rose or Pacifico beer and, for the time being, everyone was content.

Meanwhile, the staff gorged themselves on chunky turtle stew, assorted types of grilled whole fish, or iguana in a red sauce or a dark brown mole. We were in heaven and figured what self-righteous animal lovers didn't know couldn't possibly hurt them.

Tired swayback horses were available for rent, leisurely sauntering up a narrow mountain trail, through rather dense tropical rain forest and then into a small village, proudly centered around a small church. The edifice had four walls, a floor and an altar, but no roof or ceiling whatsoever, in deference I suppose to the tropical heat. We came to rest at a waterfall spouting out of the mountainside some fifteen hundred feet above us and cascading into a sparkling clear pool below. If there were no passengers with us, off came the tennis shorts and into the pool we jumped to cavort and carry on like crazy people. The horses, bored and certainly not impressed with our nakedness, just lapped up the cool water and ignored us. When pluckier passengers in Abercrombie and Fitch outfits decided to chance the sojourn up the mountain, we still jumped into the natural pool but maintained a modicum of modesty, keeping our tennis shorts on. Most folks were content to wander around on the beach, inspecting tide pools or snoozing in one of the many hammocks strung between every available palm tree in the tropical crescent.

By day's end most passengers were sunburned to a crisp or saddle sore or both. They were all very eager to line up on the beach, prepared to endure the never-ending waves in the canoe ride back to the old wooden yacht. This was an orderly enough procedure; on good days it was reminiscent of the evacuation from Dunkirk, punctuated only by an errant mosquito or a diving sea gull relieving itself. However, many folks, seeing a staff member for the first time in hours (as we spent most of the day well out of sight skinny-dipping in the mountain waterfall), leaped at the opportunity to complain about most everything. Their gripes covered hermit crabs in the outhouses being almost as bad as the lack of flush toilets and running water in general; no electric outlets for hair dryers; toes skewered with sea urchin spines; and horses refusing to gallop in slow motion in the surf as you see in all the beer commercials on television. Unable to do very much about the litany of complaints, we did supply Band-Aids® and a spritz of Bactine® for the toes impaled by the sea urchin spines and urged them to see the ship's doctor on their return to the ship. We were sure to pack the more vociferous moaners and groaners on the first canoes back to the yacht, feeling, correctly, out of earshot, out of mind. At least, for the moment.

In general, the tours went off without a hitch, though every so often a minor catastrophe would rear its lovely head and we simply had to deal with it. For example, one time in Cabo San Lucas an elderly gent traveling alone boarded a docking tender belonging to another ship. He discovered his mistake after returning to what he thought was his cabin after teatime. Entering the unlocked door he found a pair of cavorting newlyweds deeply entwined into what honeymooners usually do, and it wasn't washing out a pair of socks. We picked him up at the next port, chipper and none the worse for wear. In fact, he really enjoyed telling us in intimate detail what he saw.

On another occasion we assigned a new Social Director named Clara-Jo, a recreation and religion major on leave from Bob Jones University in Tulsa, Oklahoma, to escort a sailboat tour out of Saint Thomas. We had a few spring break college boys sailing with us, and when they realized Clara-Jo—who was cuter than a bug's nose, by the way—would be the tour guide, they fell over themselves in a rush to sign up. Once underway the boys drank a bit too much of the complimentary rum punch, grew a little tipsy and, when the craft came about suddenly after anchoring, tumbled, flippity, flop, splash, into Magens Bay. Answering the call of, "Man Overboard!" Clara-Jo rushed to the rail to find the boys swimming around and cavorting like tadpoles. On noticing her concern, the guys quickly assured her they were okay and invited her in to join them, as the water was fine. She refused professionally, claiming she was, after all, working, as well as having forgotten her bathing suit.

"No problem baby-cakes!" they yelled back, "use ours!"

Two pairs of sopping wet surf shorts, a Speedo, and a jock strap come flying over the rail, landing in drenching splats on the teak deck.

For the remainder of her contract she requested escort duty for every boat tour scheduled anywhere in the Caribbean. Hell, things like this just never happened in Tulsa. Bless her heart.

In Caracas, Venezuela the local tour guides would point with pride to the National Sloth. This was the slow-moving, three-toed variety familiar to zoo-goers, here residing comfortably in the open on a tree in the plaza. Caracas was a study in contrasts; the spiffy government buildings rose above a landscape strewn with ramshackle abodes where the people lived. Despite the warm climate, all visiting women were commanded to have their shoulders covered, and the men had to be wearing long trousers—no Bermuda shorts allowed in the hallowed area where the National Sloth dwelled. These conservative mandates apparently applied only to tourists, not the National Sloth, who decided to relieve himself all over one of the guest's silk Tommy Bahama sport shirt. The passenger was beside himself in self-righteous pique and naturally threatened to sue the Venezuelan Government for damages. The local tour guides, trying to calm things down a bit, suggested the passenger had no right to be standing beneath such a hallowed national mascot wearing such an ugly shirt.

It was when our besotted passenger threatened to throw a stone at the National Sloth that things became truly serious. We saved him from what would have been a lengthy prison sentence by promising him that the Chief Purser had a fund for just such an emergency and would gladly reimburse him for the damaged shirt once everyone was safely back on board. Hearing that, and noticing the Capital Police in black berets carrying assorted machine guns currently cordoning off the area (thinking with experience that the ruckus might be a diversionary tactic for a coup), he quickly cooled his temper.

You may think it strange that someone would be disposed to cause a riot simply because a national pet decided to answer Nature's call all over his sport shirt. Yet many passengers were willing to risk even more for the sake of being allowed to go on any particular tour. A middle-aged fellow ingenuously asked me on the dock in Saint Thomas if he could go on the scuba diving tour even though he didn't know how to swim. Amazed at his request simply because drowning might be an issue, I told him I would get back to him on that one.

By this time in my career, I had learned to accept any request made by a passenger with the self-control of a Hindi Mystic. Let's face it, no one appreciates an honest question answered with hysterical uncontrolled laughter. Taking the absurdity of this situation to an even higher level, when I jokingly told the operator of the scuba diving tour about my passenger's bizarre request, he nonchalantly replied, "Sure. Why the hell not? Most of the punters who I take on the tour have never even had their heads under water. And you want to know something else? I haven't lost very many at all!"

Considering the risk that some passengers were willing to take for a marginal adventure, it never occurred to me what others were willing to do for the sake of a buck.

Another example we heard about later: the enterprising muleteers in Haiti who, once they had our passengers high atop the mountain entrance of Henri Christophe's Citadelle fortress three thousand feet above sea level, would refuse to lead them back down the mountain. We were told they would gladly change their minds if, as a token of good will and appreciation, each passenger came up with a "tip-in-advance" of ten dollars U.S. It took us a long time until we heard the last of that one, even though we reimbursed every guest for the unexpected ransom demand.

While on the subject of hustling tourists for a few bucks here and there, it's hard to forget a young Social Director we hired as an emergency replacement for a Social Director who had to be airlifted home suffering from coral poisoning after stepping barefooted on a spiny sea urchin in Magens Bay. This left an important opening in the ranks that had to be filled immediately.

The Home Office flew in a replacement Social Director who arrived in Puerto Vallarta and who, by the time we reached Acapulco a few days later, had fully acclimated to life on board. He certainly endeared himself to many of the passengers, and that was most important. One morning, seeing how the passengers eagerly took to the tour busses, he decided to organize a tour of his own. Not inquiring if such an endeavor was sanctioned by the ship, the Home Office, or even the local constabulary (who, if you recall, we bribed with gallons of booze every time we were in port to insure all things going smoothly), he made his plans. He hired a local mini-bus one afternoon and filled it with innocent fun-seekers he had met on the ship. They sped off for an area that was then jungle and swamps just southeast of Acapulco called Puerto Marquez. It is from this very same cove that pirate ships once anchored in drooling anticipation of ships of the Spanish merchant fleet en route to Acapulco laden with silks, spices, and other goodies from Asia and the South Pacific. If the merchandise was not stolen by the pirates, it was then taken overland by wagons, loaded on other ships on the Atlantic side, and sent to fill the coffers or Queen Isabella and King Ferdinand back in sunny Spain.

Bordering this infamous bay is a paradise of dense tropical jungles and humid swamps. It is home to huge cypress trees, numerous varieties of palms, and at least as many species of graceful egrets, white herons, colorful parrots and macaws, chattering monkeys, and assorted other jungle denizens too numerous to mention.

Our enterprising young Social Director devised a tour consisting of squeezing groups of eager passengers into shallow draft longboats and having locals pole them through these very same swamps. Randomly pointing out what he thought were dandy points of interest, or at least by stretching the imagination just a bit, could be. He announced, with authority, "To your left ladies and gentlemen, you will see the exact location where Academy Award® winner Humphrey Bogart kissed another Academy Award® winner, Ms. Katharine Hepburn, in the climactic scene in *The African Queen*. On your right, if you look closely, you can see where Johnny Weissmuller single handedly turned back a herd of stampeding elephants with a single yodel." In point of fact, neither *The African Queen* nor *Tarzan* was shot anywhere near these areas, but the tourists were none the wiser.

What he didn't bargain for was a pack of bb-gun wielding kids somehow getting wind of a flock of rich *touristas* poling through what they considered their personal swamp. At an obscure bend in the river, they held up each canoe as it passed, liberating every camera, wristwatch, gold chain, wallet, purse, and anything else they thought of value. As one could imagine, our usually docile passengers were enraged with this unexpected feature of the tour, authentic though it might have been.

"Crap like this would never happen at Disneyland!" concluded one disgruntled victim.

The Social Director, confident of being keel-hauled by the Capitano for even thinking he could pull off a stunt like this, stuffed all the wayfarers back on the mini-bus and then disappeared. Even his next of kin never came by to pick up his belongings he'd left in his cabin. It is possible he was in cahoots with the bb-gun toting delinquents and is now living fat and sassy off the proceeds fenced to the local Mafiosi, or he could be ignominiously stuffed into a garbage can resting on the bottom of the swamp, his presence not all that appreciated by the enterprising young pirates. No one will ever know. The ship even filed a missing person report with the local police force and they turned up nothing.

I came to learn that no matter the intricacy of the pains we took to insure an interesting half day or full day excursion ashore, someone would always find something to complain about, all of them beginning their rants with an innocuous enough sounding statement like, "Excuse me sonny boy, can I talk to you for a second?"

A case in point involved a glass bottom boat excursion over a huge coral reef lying just off Saint Kitts in the Caribbean.

As we were cruising to the reef, a well-fed middle aged woman wearing a wild Hawaiian shirt that practically reached her knees waddled over to me and demanded, "Why isn't this water blue?"

"I beg your pardon," I said, thinking I didn't hear her correctly.

"I said," the color rising in her face, "why isn't this water blue?" motioning toward the sea shimmering in the sunlight as though it were contained in a punch bowl of Baccarat crystal so bright and clear that with little effort you could actually count the scales on the schools of fish swimming around below.

"Well madam," I said, in halting desperation, "it must be the reflection from the clouds."

"That's no answer!" she cackled, "What kind of answer is that? When I was on Princess Cruises, the water was always a brilliant shade of ultramarine blue. Much bluer than this!"

"Well," I said, beginning to sense that old familiar dread, "if it will make you any happier, as soon as we return to the ship I'll ask the Capitano about it," knowing he would free-kick me over the side if I as much as mentioned anything as bizarre as this to him.

"A lot of good that will do! What can he do about it?"

"Nothing." I admitted, vanquished.

"Of course nothing!" she cackled back like a cantankerous parrot, "You wanna know something? I'm never going to sail with your company again. I mean, why should I waste my time coming to the Caribbean if your water isn't blue? You know, last year I took a trip around the world, so rest assured, next year I'm going somewhere else!"

"Bon Voyage," I thought to myself, not daring to say it out loud, as this boiling fussbudget turned in a huff and stomped off toward the lunch buffet.

Briefly pondering her question, I came to the conclusion she was absolutely correct. There is positively no reason to come to the Caribbean if the water isn't going to be blue.

Hearing the entire conversation, the Head Steward who came along to cater the tour handed me a gallon jug of rum punch liberally spiced with freshly ground nutmeg. I quickly downed a few hearty quaffs of the tasty brew. Then a few more. Maybe even one or two additional after that, just for good luck. In no time at all, gazing out like a zombie on the undulating sea, I came to the foggy conclusion that yes, the cranky lady was right, the water didn't look all that blue. By that time, I just didn't care.

THE REVOLUTION IN GRENADA, OR, I'LL GIVE YOU THREE KEY CHAINS FOR THE HOSTAGES... YOU CAN KEEP THEIR CAMERAS...

Grenada (pronounced *gren-A-da*, not *GRA-naada*) is a charming island republic considered part of the British Windward Islands. It is nestled comfortably in the cerulean blue Caribbean Sea just northeast of Venezuela and due south of Martinique. Their quaint little circular port, too shallow for our cruise ship, made the use of the ship's tenders—smaller boats necessary for bringing the passengers ashore. Arriving at the capitol, Saint Georges, you must humbly motor boat past Fort Georges, a huge stone fortress built by the English centuries ago to protect their priceless spice trade. The Fort still guards the harbor entrance with antiquated cannon peeking out from ivy covered gun ports. The guns still protect in working absentia a myriad of private yachts and small commercial sailing vessels bobbing peaceably at anchor within the circular harbor, or "Careenage," as it is called today.

Within moments of stepping on to the cobblestone streets, you are pleasantly transported to an eighteenth century colonial English village. Venerable Georgian buildings plastered in candy-colored pastel shades surrounding the harbor, as well as popping out from the flourishing green hillsides like marzipan fruits adorning a holiday treat. Larger steel hulled commercial vessels and barges without the luxury of a fleet of small tenders like we had on our ship must use the harbor on the opposite side of the island as the "Careenage" is barely twenty feet deep even at high tide—way too risky for the deep draft tankers and supply vessels to attempt a moorage. This is certainly not a bad thing, as it preserves the pristine nature of this charming port. Brightly colored wooden dories with English Seagull outboards and *Water Taxi* scrawled on the outer gunwales in fire-engine red paint crisscrossed the cove, merrily putt-putting along as they went.

The docks and adjoining cobblestone streets, bathed in the warm scents of cinnamon and nutmeg, makes one feel as though one is stepping into the kitchen of a favorite aunt on a holiday baking day. Colorfully dressed local women and girls cram the sidewalks hawking hand-processed spices stuffed into discarded bottles and jars found all over the island. Old catsup or beer bottles were the favorites, along with an occasional square chutney or steak sauce bottle. They were all re-cycled into spice containers, sealed with a fat twig, a discarded cork, or a clump of straw bound tightly together with a colorful ribbon.

Spice is, and always has been, the chief and only export of the island. Hence, when referring to this clump of remote Caribbean islands the early colonists and exploiters called them "The Spice Islands." Even though the bright, almost equatorial sun bears down mercilessly, the aromas and scents of cinnamon, nutmeg, mace, saffron, vanilla, bay, cloves, cocoa, and numerous other aromatic flavorings, barks, pollens and leaves are hustled by hefty women buzzing all over the docks, their wares carried in huge baskets balanced on their heads, or set up on rickety tables lining the streets.

Walking by, you are constantly harangued with alluring variations of, "Hey you, Big Man! You buy your spice from Nancy, now!" and into my hand she would thrust a small piece of thin discarded cardboard, with her name laboriously printed on it with a dull pencil. "Just so, you remember me now, Nancy at the dock!" she would call, raising her voice above the mushrooming crescendos of steel band music and conga drum combos roiling out from the wide open French doors of every little bar or café, lining the streets.

Women not having the monopoly in free enterprise, shirtless and barefooted teenage boys moved about the crowds balancing a block of glistening ice on their heads, selling strips of sugar cane, or sweating bottles of Caribe beer precariously balanced on top. Younger entrepreneurs, not yet having the neck muscles or coordination to balance blocks of ice on their heads, would set up shop under a shady coconut palm, displaying hundreds of pink-hued conch shells of all shapes and sizes, and urge anyone close enough to hear, "Hey mon, this conch shell now. Biggest in de 'eyelands. For you just two dollar U.S. Come on mon!! What say you now?"

Among the more enterprising set, it was popular to run up to an unsuspecting tourist, or myself, and quickly cram a large English penny in to my hand, with the hopefully convincing pitch, "Okay Mon, I just give you a big English coin, now you give me a big American coin like a silver dollar. Half dollar? How about a quarter dollar mon? Okay, okay what a deal I give you, one thin dime Mon. Don't make a man beg now!"

Before agreeing on a deal with this little con artist, a scared look crossed his face, and he darted up an alley. I looked around and a tall sartorial constable, wearing a white pith helmet, red tunic with gold buttons and braid, bright Royal Blue trousers with a wide yellow stripe running down each leg and black spit shinned boots, with what must have been metal taps announcing his approach on the cobblestones. He smiled as he walked by and touched the brim of his pith helmet with an ominous looking billy club as a friendly salute. I was told in this part of the Caribbean, because of some sort of colonial interpretation of the law, any lawbreaker, especially teenagers, were always considered guilty until proven innocent, rather than the other way around. I could understand why the kid ran for the hills as soon as he heard the rhythmic cadence of the policeman's stacked heels. It would not be at all surprising to see a sweating, overweight Colonial in a white suit arrive in a horse-drawn carriage in the midst of all this colorful cacophony, sweating nervously while fanning himself with a palm frond, complaining about the gout and the damned drums, "What do they mean, Winslow, what do they mean?"

Grenada was one port the staff particularly enjoyed. Scheduled to be there for only a few hours, some of the entertainers and crew would seek out the nearest apothecary and stock up on English Quaaludes, available over the counter at ridiculously low prices. So low, I was told, and considering the street value back home, many dreamed of financing trips to Europe or a new car after they returned. The going price at the time was about thirty-six dollars U.S. for a bottle of one hundred pills with a street value in New York or Los Angeles of over five dollars per pill. So there was, to coin a phrase, "gold in them thar pills." Oxycontin, Ativan, Xanax, Darvon, Trazadone, and many other pharmaceuticals were available for a pittance without a prescription. Many of the staff and crew took advantage of the prices while on board, hoping to peddle leftovers to friends and neighbors once they arrived back in the United States, England, or Italy.

Marijuana, though still illegal in most of the world, was also available, though not purchased over the counter or directly from any sort of dealer we ever saw. Every time we arrived in Grenada, a fellow traveler on the staff was assigned to place a shoebox containing a new pair of trendy tennis shoes on a specified palm stump, just beyond the tree line of the specified beach. Before the last launch returned to the ship, one of us ran back to the stump to retrieve the shoe box, now stuffed and crammed to overflowing with the finest marijuana a pair of sneakers could buy. It was tied with a string, with a card that usually read, "Pleasure doing business with you, Mon!"

Rather than run the risk of raising the suspicions of any law abiding passengers, we didn't enter the ship by the main gangway, but took the crew entrance instead. This led us through the galleys and kitchens. On the way were sure to deposit a healthy handful into a few plastic bags purloined from the kitchen, then stuff a bag into each of the officers' cubby holes. The Head Chef got one, as did the Chief Purser, the Chief Engineer, the ship's doctor, the Staff Captain, and of course, the Capitano himself. On days the Master Baker was given his stash, it was always fun to note the colors and layer count in the seven-layer cakes that evening; they occasionally ran to nine or ten layers, and were undoubtedly more vibrant and colorful. After the "passing out" ceremony there was still enough herb remaining to split up into hefty portions for ourselves. Late one evening, down in our private quarters, we generated so much smoke the Fire Warden on his rounds noticed the odor and activated the smoke alarms. We ran him down and calmed his fears with a bag of weed, and the fire alarms were quickly silenced. The next morning he reported a humming bird from the island short-circuited the system. He was able to repair it easily. Nothing more had to be explained.

Getting back to Grenada the following week, we regularly offered a tour of the island called "The Queen's Drive," touted as the very same tour Queen Elizabeth took when she visited the island back in the late seventies. Cramming five tourists, clad in Hawaiian shirts and colorful Bermuda shorts, plus a hefty driver, into a tiny English Ford was no easy task, but we promised a free spiced rum punch at every stop, so the participants were encouraged to cooperate.

The driver scooted all over the verdant isle pointing out, if he felt like it, the sugar cane mill, the nutmeg and mace factory, the Governor's Mansion, the public schools, the brothels (one for locals, one for tourists), the ruins of a few colonial era churches, and a venerable cemetery overlooking the harbor with graves dating back to the seventeenth century. There were epitaphs in English, French, or Dutch, depending on who was exploiting the islands treasure of spices during any particular period in history.

The commentary given with the tour was not exactly standard Grey Line patter. One could be considered lucky if Malcolm or Reginald pointed briefly to a shack with a rusted tin roof with the wonderfully informative commentary, "Look there Mon. Sugar mill, 'veddy big, 'veddy old." Any further inquiries were met with, "Can't talk now Mon. Must concentrate on highway here." A reassuring concern, considering the "highway" he was referring to consisted of one lane of dirt intermittently dotted with tired clods of well-worn macadam and crushed stone pavement. This was frequently shared with an errant flock of goats or a road crew with machetes taking a breather from their exhausting efforts of trying to keep the surrounding jungle from laying claim to any more of the road than it already had.

I always noticed how the local people looked at the cabs stuffed with tourists as we sped by. Our folks were convinced the stares were in anticipation of a hijacking, or something worse, and using the innocent hostages for some sort of wicked island debauchery. In reality, they were simply poor workers looking with wonder and awe at these overfed, pink faced people getting over excited at the prospect of snapping photos of a banana thicket or a nutmeg tree. To these guys, such subjects must have held as much fascination as we might have with a fire hydrant. A memorable experience which always made the passengers squeal with delight was when the car, on a road last paved in 1946, sped past a goat urinating on a palm tree. Your guess is as good as mine as to why a subject like this might have been so appealing.

The real fun began when a disgruntled passenger from Iowa demanded we go back to the site of the goat and palm tree as she had forgotten to remove her lens cover. Reginald, our driver, always one to have his way with words, would reply, "I 'tink we stop soon for de rum punch and nutmeg soon, you forget about the peein' goat 'den!"

That was the end of the conversation. Mrs. Iowa, sulking in the back seat, shot a glance at me that would have clabbered sweet cream. I gave her a commiserating shrug and looked forward to the rum punch rest stop, hoping this time there were no hermit crabs or friendly little field mice scampering about the souvenir stand.

En route to Grenada from Curacao one spring, news was wired to the ship that some "unrest" in the form of an actual revolution was taking place on the island. Our Radio Operator, a lovable but rumpled middle aged subject of the Queen, named Nigel, who had given up good posture around the same time he foreswore brushing his teeth, made no attempt to gloss over any of the reports he was receiving. He announced the events of the day over the public address system between sips of his gin and lime and puffs of his ever present Balkan Sobranie hanging askew from his tortoise shell cigarette holder. The news spread like a pandemic through the entire ship, rumors blooming into ridiculous proportions. Passengers on the verge of hysteria accosted hiding staff members with bits of erroneous information, begging affirmation. Would we indeed dock on an island in turmoil? Could the ship be seized and, if so, who would re-book the connecting flights? Was Castro instigating the insurrection? Would their lives be in danger? Did we plan on altering the itinerary to Saint Lucia instead, entitling everyone to refunds? Many of the entertainment staff were feverishly sending telegrams to their favorite apothecary for reasons not necessary to discuss.

Regardless of all this understated panic, it seems the revolution did not amount to very much. The revolutionaries did manage to arouse the Prime Minister from his afternoon beauty rest and place him under arrest. The PM's True Blue Defense Force barracks was surrounded, and the hundred or so soldiers quickly surrendered to their cousins and friends staging the coup. Simultaneously, government ministers were roused from their beds and taken to the shaded garden of the local jail where tea and biscuits were served promptly at ten. The fire station in town quickly ran up a white flag of surrender. It was actually a white undershirt borrowed from one of the resident firefighters. During the ten-hour uprising (it began at 5 a.m. and was over by 3 p.m.) the island's radio station had been seized by the revolutionaries and broadcast popular reggae and calypso tunes. The broadcasts were only interrupted for special announcements such as, "Will the citizens keeping animals on Mount Royal please come up and feed them" as well as, "Will whoever borrowed the keys to the police wagon, please return them."

So this was the Grenadian Revolution. Prior to the embarkation of the tours, the Cruise Director pulled me aside and whispered, "Listen, in case there is any trouble, I have decided that you will be in charge of negotiating for hostages, or whatever."

"Whatever?" I replied incredulously, inquisitive lad that I am.

"Shhhhh, quiet down!" he continued, "We can't alarm the passengers. Now don't worry about a thing, I'll call Snowball Jackpot

Bingo for you this afternoon and make sure you are on the last launch back to the ship. Oh yeah," he reminded himself, "be sure to count all the cabs as they leave the dock, and make damn sure the same number return. Okay?"

"Are you fucking crazy?" I said in no uncertain terms.

"Now look here young man," he said sternly, not all that pleased with my choice of adjective. "The Captain and I both feel you are the best man for the job. Now, we will both be on the bridge, or at least somewhere on the ship in case anything happens. So, you have nothing to worry about.

"Can I bring some of the staff with me?"

"No, they have been confined to the ship as I need them to help me get ready for Carnivale Night."

Fabulous, I thought. It's always nice to know your cohorts are indispensable.

"Hey, wait a minute!" I called, catching up to him before he could conveniently lose himself in the crowd of passengers waiting to plod down the gangway into the bobbing tenders. "I mean, what if hostages are taken? Just what the hell am I supposed to do then?"

"Quiet," he said through his teeth, attempting to stay calm, "Look," he said placing his arm on my shoulder as he began to walk me back to the gangway, "How bright can any of these revolutionaries be?" making air quotes with his fingers, "I mean, living in all this heat and all," he said, playfully punching my arm. I didn't laugh, I didn't even smile, I don't think he appreciated my stoicism. "Look," he said, growing serious once again, "just bring along an extra handful of souvenir key chains. They're genuine pewter, you know, made by Ginori in Italy. Trust me, you won't have any problems." With those reassuring words he slipped in to his cabin and slammed the door.

Gosh, I thought, hearing him bolt the door from the inside, to think he would actually be willing to call Snowball Jackpot Bingo for me, while I was off ransoming hostage passengers with pewter key chains. What a guy!

I climbed down the gangway hoping for the best, my pockets, by the way, brimming with key chains.

The day on the island was uneventful. All the tours returned and the shoebox was collected from the tree stump as scheduled.

Surprisingly enough, after closing down the disco that evening around three in the morning and considering the events of the day, I wasn't the least bit ready to turn in. I made my way up to the Bridge, which had a late a late night serenity about it. The room was basically dark except for a few lamps glowing red and ethereal green lights glowing up from the radar screens. This enabled the Bridge crew to easily see the full expanse of the moonlit sea rolling out before them. I glanced down at the main radar screen and saw the little blip that represented the ship in the center of the screen heading for what seemed to be a huge iceberg in the middle of the Caribbean Sea. Concerned, I called the Officer of the Bridge over and showed him the screen, genuinely concerned about an impending collision.

He looked at the screen, chuckled just a little bit, licked his finger, wiped up the white smudge on the screen and massaged it into his gums, and said, "Problema evitato, vecchio mio! Problem averted, old friend!" and he waved me off with a quiet giggle. I asked if he knew about the palm stump on the beach in Grenada. He laughed and said of course they did, but the Bridge staff had reliable sources in Caracas. He winked, turned away, and began scanning the horizon with the huge pair of night vision binoculars he wore around his neck.

I figured it was time for me to return to my cabin.

THE CROUPIER, OR, WHEREVER THERE'S CASH, SOMEONE WILL FIGURE OUT HOW TO STEAL IT...

All ships sail with a casino of some sort, some large, some small. They consist of slot machines and various electronic games of chance, which included electronic Twenty One and Baccarat. This eliminated the need to hire an excessive number of dealers and attendants. Our ship sailed with a Lead Croupier and a younger fellow who served as his assistant. Both were trained and hired from the Home Office in Monte Carlo. The casino was open twenty hours a day, giving the attendants a few hours to service the machines without any players present.

The Lead Croupier was a good looking red-headed young man from Ireland. His assistant, also from Ireland, was a black-haired fellow with bright green eyes. They were extremely popular among the women on board, both passengers and staff, young and old, with their lilting accents and charming touch of the Blarney. They were both particularly diplomatic when, at least once every cruise, they would claim, a "punter" would come up to the cashiers cage and say, "Okay, so I just lost twenty dollars in the slot machines. Do you give it back to me, or what?"

The Lead Croupier carried all the keys to the machines and the coin safes, which he stored in the ship's vault. His assistant was mainly responsible for maintaining and cleaning the machines and vacuuming the casino during his late night and early morning shift. If a problem with a payout or a jammed machine occurred during his watch, he would make an official note, with copies, to be presented to the Lead Croupier in the morning.

What was particularly nice about the Lead Coupier was that he knew which slots were ready to pop. When a member of the staff sauntered in escaping the noon day sun and the rampaging passengers, he would point out the machine with a discreet motion of his chin, silently mouthing the number of the machine. A hundred dollar investment would eventually yield a five hundred dollar jackpot. He never accepted a tip of any sort, even though we always tried to stuff a twenty or two into one of his pockets. He would just smile and say in his musical Irish lilt, "Just buy us a Guinness next time we are in a civilized port."

We were rarely able to take him up on his offer, as every time we hit a large port like Los Angeles, Miami, San Juan, or Caracas for more than a few hours, he would disappear into town and not return until just before embarkation. Invariably he would be loaded down with suit bags with extremely impressive labels and assorted colorful shoeboxes. Needless to say, he dressed like a prince. He had various styles of Christian Louboutin shoes, even tennis shoes, all with the trademark red soles. His closet was full of so many custom-made suits, some with vests, some without; he never wore the same suit twice while managing the casino. Always prompt and on time, he was never without a diamond encrusted gold watch—Rolex, Patek Philippe, and Bulgari among his favorites.

To say the least we were all in awe, thinking we must have chosen the wrong professions, or he was on the receiving end of a very old money trust fund or two. Here was a friendly young guy with bright red hair, a lilting brogue and a twinkle in his eye, who bragged he never went to university. We even drilled his assistant to find out what exactly was going on, and the kid claimed he had no idea as he wasn't allowed to tag along on his superior's shore side jaunts, but loved it when the croupier occasionally told him which machine was ready to pay off. We didn't let on we were enamored with the guy for the same reason.

After a usual wild night in Old San Juan for most of us, the Lead Croupier returned to the ship the next afternoon. His right hand was in a plaster cast from the tips of his fingers to his elbow. He wasn't carrying any packages this time, and after boarding made his way directly to his cabin. Late in the evening, around two or three, many of the staff and officers would make their way to the ship's bakery. A table would be set up loaded with an assortment of beautiful layer cakes, as well as a variety of pies and tarts, all missing a slice or two. They were available for any of the officers or entertainment staff to enjoy. Dining room policy insisted that any cake or pie with just one slice missing was no longer appropriate for passenger consumption, and would be thrown to the sharks by dawn. Prior to that, it was open season on the goodies for anyone needing a slice and a cuppa. It was a great way to wind down from a grueling day.

The first evening, or actually early morning, after getting his arm wrapped in plaster, the Lead Croupier forlornly shuffled into the bakery. After getting a snack and a cup of espresso, both balanced precariously on his left forearm, he made his way to the large round communal table, attempting to sit as far away from us as possible. It wasn't going to happen. We all rushed the guy and pleaded with him to tell us what the hell happened. He thought about it for a minute and then mumbled.

"The bloody bastards broke my fuckin' thumb! On my fuckin' right hand, mind you! My god damn counting hand, for the love of Christ!"

"Who?" we inquired.

"The bloody goons from Monte Carlo! The bastards were waiting for me on the dock."

"Why?" we all nervously inquired, thinking we were next, due to our frequenting the "hot" machines at his behest.

He assured us winning a jackpot was not an issue; the machines still registered our hundred dollar preliminary investments. It was simply a mathematical calculation. Our level of awe grew to unfathomable heights, as well as welcome relief. He went on to explain the machines we had in our casino, though filled with electronic bells and whistles, were actually old fashioned analog coin-only machines. Because of that, there was an empty coffee can of sorts in each machine that had to be placed in the center of a circle painted on the inside base of each machine. The cans received the coins as they were deposited through the slots. The coin hit a lever on its way into the can, and was then registered and counted. Move the can a few centimeters to the right or left and some of the coins would hit the rim of the can and tumble to the base of the machine. Not having hit the counting lever, there was no record of it being deposited, but the coin would activate the reels on its way down, so no one was any the wiser. When a winning combo of reels spun into place, a separate funnel filled with coins would drop the appropriate winnings into the tray below with a joyful clinking and clatter. No tokens, no electronic receipts; on entering the casino the passengers would exchange their paper money at the croupier's cage at the entrance and be given sparkling clean coins in exchange. The Assistant Croupier was also in charge of "cleaning" coins before distribution.

Once a day or so, when alone in the casino, the Lead Croupier would reload the win funnels and empty the coffee cans brimming with "legal" coins as well as sweep the coins that didn't make it into the can into an official looking canvas bank bag. His personal skim, if you will. He would later exchange the canvas bags filled with coins for paper money in different local banks at every port. If asked by a curious bank employee about the sacks of coins, he would be honest and say he ran the casino on the ship, and they couldn't travel with all the weight. Once receiving the bundles of paper money, he had to get rid of them as well, so he went shopping.

The powers that be in Monte Carlo soon realized the count was coming in short, cruise after cruise. To remedy the situation, the Home Office arranged for an "accountant" with a ball/peen hammer in his brief case and a few husky assistants to be waiting for our Lead Croupier on the dock adjacent to Old Town, our favorite haunt during layovers in Puerto Rico. Somehow the Lead Croupier ended up with a broken thumb and a few crushed knuckles on his right hand as a little reminder every night when he had to tally the days count. For the twenty-eight days is took us to visit the Caribbean, transit the Panama Canal and finally reach Los Angeles, he had to service a few hundred machines and count hundreds in cash with crushed knuckles and a broken thumb.

We tried to ease his pain by innocently mentioning he was lucky they didn't kill him. To which he replied, "Well lads, I fear that might be next."

He disembarked quickly and quietly from a rear gangway early on a misty morning after we had tied up at our terminal in Los Angeles. His arm still in a cast, he wore a pair of red-soled tennis shoes and carried a single suit bag slung over his shoulder. He breezed through U.S. Customs with their drug sniffing beagles without any problems. Before leaving, he gave his assistant first pass at all the luxury items he had to abandon in his cabin, including a few of the gold watches, the remainder of the loot to be given to the room stewards. No one heard from our red headed Lead Croupier from Ireland ever again.

By two in the afternoon a new guy, this one from France, arrived and introduced himself to the assistant, who was now sporting a gold Rolex. They both began preparing to open the casino once the ship sailed well south of San Diego, eventually surrounded by friendly Mexican waters.

OF BELLA FICA'S, BUSY ASSES, AND WOMEN WHO HAD CARS OF THEIR OWN

When the ship docked at a home port, be it Los Angeles, San Juan, Miami, or New York, one could always count on seeing a covey of those whom the crew and officers referred to as *Bella Ficas* waiting in well-dressed little bundles of designer outfits decorating the bustling, somewhat inhospitable dock.

The term *Bella Fica*, we came to understand, was actually a somewhat vulgar Italian expression, not to be confused with the good luck amulet of a thumb thrust between an index and middle finger, known as a *fica*. As a side note, while touring the ruins of Pompeii in Southern Italy, the elderly tour guide made all the women in the group cover their eyes, before unlocking a little door on a living room wall, revealing some extremely pornographic and ribald paintings. If you are easily offended, PLEASE STOP READING NOW! If not, *Bella Fica* is Italian slang meaning *Beautiful Pussy*.

Some of the sailors and officers even wore gold versions of the fist and thumb charm around their necks along with assorted squiggly red horns of various lengths and crucifixes with Jesus in high relief suspended from a variety of anchor chain linked necklaces. One Portuguese deckhand had Da Vinci's Last Supper as a medallion in three-dimensional solid gold relief hanging from two chains around his neck, with a red *fica* charm dangling from either end. It was supposed to protect you from the "evil eye." Regardless of the literal colloquial translation, we used the term as a rather sincere form of endearment and affection. Admittedly, there might have been just a wee bit of sarcasm involved with the label, but you had to accept that as part of our overabundant testosterone-infused charm.

While vacationing on our ship, these women—school teachers from the suburbs or secretaries from high-rise law firms—were always more than eager to find a cheerful sailor to write home about. Standing on the dock, alone, they would meet the ship on a cold winter morning, yearning to relive their moment in Camelot. A staff member, officer, or crewman, treating them like royalty while on the ship, was expected to act in the same manner a few weeks later, as usually promised in fleeting moments of passion. Oh, do times and feelings change.

Even after what we considered a short seven day cruise, new worlds were created as far as shipboard loves were concerned. Besides, when the ship was finally moored and the embarkation and Customs inspections had begun, one was preoccupied with bidding *arrivederci* to the *Bella Fica* of that particular cruise, avoiding the *Bella Fica* waiting for you on the dock, while at the same time keeping a sharp eye out for that very special *Molto Bella Fica* who not only had a car but a convenient nearby apartment, as well. Usually this special someone was a woman you had genuine feelings for and had met on still another cruise. You would rendezvous at a clandestine location well away from the ship, climb into her car, and be off for a shore-side whirl. If all went well, you would be back on the ship moments before sailing.

Occasionally a *Bella Fica* would get a surprise nibble from someone on the staff or crew, especially after twenty-eight day itineraries, when the average age of the passengers was sixty-seven. Yet the majority of these women waited, antsy with anticipation for that marvelous two legged adventurer to come sailing home through the mists and into her welcoming arms. As the sun rose and the day waned, layers of chic clothing were peeled off, revealing new combinations underneath. But just like an onion, peel away too much, and when you finally reach the center, only tears remain.

Among the staff and crew an unwritten law existed concerning the *Bella Ficas*: if an impatient Bella asked where someone in particular was, or when they were getting off the ship, either you did not know the guy, or he left much earlier, or he was debarked with rickets in Caracas. While doing the innocent act, the object of the woman's passion was sneaking off the ship for an anticipated rendezvous by way of the galley exit hidden behind sacks of crew mail and pallets of fresh vegetables in wet burlap bags.

After a lonely arrival day of unrequited waiting, perhaps resting on a crate of carrots destined for the hold of the ship, the *Bella Fica* slowly came to the realization the man she was able to order about with abandon a few weeks earlier was simply doing his job back then, and doing it quite well. At five o'clock the ship's horns would let loose with their ear shattering blasts, the confetti and streamers flew, and our *Bella Fica* finally understood her day of anxious anticipation and dreaming was all for naught. Invariably, she would finally leave, never to return.

With each cruise, however, two or three new Bellas appeared on the dock taking her place. Guccied and De La Rentaed to the teeth, swathed in Versace, and daintily avoiding any puddles so as not to damage their red-soled Louboutin pumps, they would eagerly await their moment of recognition, running in slow motion toward a long sensual embrace. The dreamy reunion, like their fantasies, rarely materialized.

The Busy Asses were the secretaries and paper shufflers who worked for the Home Office. They descended on the ship when it docked and for the entire morning and afternoon scurried about with a manifest that just had to be delivered, or a Bon Voyage fruit basket, or something else of dire importance to no one but themselves. Not to suggest their attitudes were snooty or anything as complex as that, but I had to admit they acted as if all of naval history hinged on their completing their vital task of delivering the beer manifest to a quartermaster or a flower arrangement to Mr. and Mrs. Maldemer.

One afternoon a comely stereotypical Busy Ass, afflicted with a hopeless case of California Surf Bunny shallow, sallied up to our youngest Social Director, who was assigned to greet new passengers and check boarding passes on the gangway. Possessing a body like Barbie and the personality of a Dixie Cup, she had no qualms about asking our young Social Director if he would be so kind as to pick up a quart of turtle oil lotion for her the next time the ship called on Mazatlan.

Our Social Director, having honed his debonair technique a bit by now, inquired half in jest, "What will you give me in return?"

"My body." she purred, smiling coyly, yet with more sincerity than Shirley Temple playing Heidi.

"Oh really?" he gagged his voice cracking a few octaves, "why don't you meet me in my cabin, D-Deck number 420, when I get off at four-thirty, and we'll see what we can do about that, okay?" He dug into his pocket and nervously handed her his room key.

"Okay." she chirped, snapping away the key, and she was off to deliver the party hat manifest to the Third Purser.

When four-thirty chimed, the Social Director, hyperventilating with excitement, walked very quickly down to his cabin, but slow enough so as not to arouse suspicion from the pursers or staff. It seems gangway rendezvous are quite common, and extremely frowned upon as conduct unbecoming an officer or member of the entertainment staff. Reaching his cabin he noticed the door just slightly ajar, but he took a deep breath and entered.

She was sitting cross legged and enticingly nude on his bunk, intoning the lyrics and swaying alluringly back and forth to a tune by the Beach Boys coming from the ships music system. Looking up as he entered, her long eyelashes danced as she sighed, "Wow, like this is my favorite nostalgic song, you know?"

Vaguely acknowledging what she just said, the Social Director tore off his polyester uniform and leaped into the bed with her. There wasn't any time to be wasted on preliminaries, as the ship sailed in thirty minutes.

During the ensuing festivities, she halted abruptly, looked straight into the panting Social Directors eyes, and asked soberly, "Are you clean?"

Obviously she didn't want to give an impression that she was without a single scruple, or worse yet, get infected by something nasty.

By five minutes to five she was gone, and for some odd reason never seen on the dock again. It was a good thing too, her absence not being missed by our randy Social Director one bit. He never purchased the bottle of turtle oil as he had promised, even though we visited Mazatlan, the port of its origin, many times since that spontaneously combustible afternoon.

Later on in the season our young damsel's mother who, as fate would have it, turned out to be in charge of the hiring and firing of all the Busy Asses, was heard inquiring about the staff,

"Were you the one who promised my daughter the quart of turtle oil?"

Fearing shotgun reprisals, or worse, for the slightest knowledge of the escapade, we all replied, "Daughter? Turtle oil? Who?"

Our choral performance of denial so exquisite it would have given chills to the leader of the Mormon Tabernacle Choir. Momma, however, did not seem the least bit vindictive, and the story ended there. Who knows—perhaps in a port, long, long ago and far, far away—her very daughter may have been conceived after a torrid assignation with a willing Social Director. Let's face it, beach, ski, and tennis are not the only type of bums existing in our wicked, wicked world.

Finally, there were those angelic, wonderful women who owned cars. For a young man working on a cruise ship, the time spent in a home port, if only a few short hours, became as precious as gold or being allowed to sleep in until noon. Our schedule of docking at ten and sailing at five never varied.

To see these special women glide through the gates, be they in Porsches or Volkswagens, was more stimulating then the sweet sound of a buxom young high school teacher clicking down the hall in high heels. The golden girls in their silver coaches whisked you away for an errand or two, a lunch not including gloved French Service or pasta, usually just a burger and fries, and then off to her apartment. Once there you could kick off your shoes, sip a beer out of a bottle, and watch a few minutes of a football game on her widescreen tv before attentions turned to other things.

The dash back to the ship was always a last minute scramble: underwear and socks stuffed into the pockets of your orange rain parka, shoes untied, laughing uncontrollably at the stop signs passed, red lights ignored. Accelerating over the Vincent Thomas suspension bridge, already beginning to mist over, you would strain like hell to see if the ship was steaming out of port under the bridge, and hoping like hell it wasn't. After a few hurried kisses and promises to write that were never kept, I would leap on the occasionally lifting gangway with seconds to spare, with an acrobatic dexterity that even surprised myself. I was clutching fresh dry cleaning, a paper sack filled with home baked goodies, bottles of vitamin C and E, toothpaste, crunchy peanut butter, maybe a bucket of extra crispy fried chicken, a Sunday *New York Times*, and a month's accumulation of shoreside bills and junk mail. Occasionally the gently swinging gangway, like a carnival ride, would swing one way or the other, causing some of the precious booty to come flying out of the sack, crashing on the dock or splashing into the roiling water below, to the delight of the dive bombing sea gulls.

Meanwhile the ship blasted its horns, the bow thrusters would engage, pushing the huge ship sideways into the channel, the main engines would rumble to life, and we sailed ahead for another seven, ten, fourteen or twenty-eight day cruise. After a while, the length of the cruises didn't really matter that much, as the days of the week lost all their meaning. It was strictly a matter of how many days we were going to be out of Los Angeles, New York, San Juan, or Miami, and how many days it would be until we returned.

As we sailed down the harbor channel toward the open sea, the sun was always setting in a blaze of pastel orange and red like a painting by Maxfield Parrish while the chimes calling the passengers to first sitting in the dining rooms sounded promptly at six-thirty without fail. Even though symphonic sunsets occurred almost every evening while we steamed out of port, with pods of dolphins leaping playfully on either side of the bow, I always wondered why the seatings in the dining room were never adjusted to accommodate viewing these astounding evening nocturnes. The dinner chimes for first and second sitting sounded every night like clockwork, ignoring what was happening outside our little nautical world.

OF CHERRY BOYS, RELIGIOUS GIRLS, AND WOMEN WHO WEAR THEIR BOOTS TO BED...OR, TWENTY DOLLARS, GETS YOU TWENTY MINUTES...

When human beings gather for any length of time in any confined space for any reason, sex will sooner or later rear its lovely head. Applying this axiom to the world of cruise ships, volumes have resulted concerning the trials and tribulations of this favored aspect of human behavior. There is something about being far away from home that encourages randy activity. Ignoring the fact that, while traveling wherever you are is someone else's home, one tends to indulge in activities of a more earthy nature that one would never think of pursuing back home in Peoria.

The indigenous populations of the various ports and cities visited by the ship were well aware that otherwise sedate and conservative tourists tend to discard any vestige of dignity when enticed by a dangling pasty, not unlike a red cape flashed before a salivating bull, and the locals go out of their way to make whoring and wenching as acceptable as possible. In other words, they want to get laid. Although brothels are yet to gain broad acceptance throughout the length and breadth of the American heartland, except for Nevada, they are extremely common from Tijuana to Caracas. Called "strip tease bars" and even "private clubs," their entrepreneurs realize the futility of such euphemisms and plainly christen their brothels with beguiling, yet obvious names like "The Beehive" or "La Colmena" in El Salvador or "Happy Fields" nee "Campo Alegre" on Curacao, allegedly run and supervised by the Shell Oil Company for the edification and enjoyment of their workers, as well as for anyone else desiring a drink, or maybe a little something extra.

Stories about shipboard trysts have become part of our culture thanks to popular television sitcoms that extoll the adventures of the lovelorn on ships happily sailing the world's deep blue seas. Many people feel, what with popular encouragement portrayed in episodic adventures of boy chasing girl, and girl chasing boy and everyone getting what they want, more or less, in the end, including a cheerful wave from the Captain and crew before the final credits, that this is what to expect when booking a cruise on a luxury liner.

Nothing could be further from the truth. I have yet to come across a captain smiling and waving his official approval to a passenger having the good fortune to score while on his ship. The Captain of our ship, for one, liked to believe this sort of peasant routing never took place on his ship—which is not to say it didn't take place in his cabino, but that is not the point here. As the Chief Purser brought to my attention, on any ship of respectable size one could expect at least a few thousand or more women traveling alone—or, as it says in the Social Director's manual, *signora non accompagnata* (unescorted women). While all were not of the age to court and spark, many were. Coupled with the reality of our ship being maintained and operated by a male crew of a thousand or so engineers, officers, stewards, bellboys, cooks, bakers, pool boys, photographers, and shopkeepers—all far from home and longing for some feminine attention and understanding—an explosive situation was usually the result.

The Home Office insisted that every woman traveling alone had to be asked to dance at least once during the course of the cruise. Sounds like a good combo, no? Hundreds of women looking for adventure, or at least a dance, and hundreds of young, randy lads looking for whatever they could get. Knowing all about the frisky nature of his passengers and crew, the Captain went out of his way to muck things up with strict rules concerning the deportment of his boys with the women, single or otherwise, traveling on his ship. Sinning of the flesh was officially not allowed.

Unofficially, it was another story but, for the record, the rules of engagement were as follows:

First, the sailors—the fellows who ran the engines and all things mechanical, including cooks, technicians, carpenters, plumbers and anyone else working below decks and not in immediate contact with passengers—were sternly forbidden to be seen on any public deck for any reason other than a hasty repair, and always under the watchful eye of a superior officer. This scratched a few hundred of the eligible gents from the running or the chasing and left about twenty or so eligible males to service the hordes of wild, saturnalian females on board, albeit some with blue hair. The remaining officers and members of the cruise staff were not without their rules as well. Officers reserved first "dibs" on any woman striking their fancy. If a staff member sought the affections of a young woman and an officer decided he liked her as well, that was the end of the pursuit as far as the staff member was concerned. This did not mean the officers were free to roam the decks as they willed. If a male passenger decided he felt a certain pitter-pattering in his heart for the same popular female passenger who was driving everyone else crazy, then the officer was flat out of luck. A purser or chief engineer would have a difficult time surviving a complaint made to the Home Office by a ruffled full-fare buckaroo concerning the loss of the love of his life by the suave advances of a continental gentleman in a starched white uniform employed by the Italian Merchant Marine.

Despite all the rules and strictures of diplomacy, life for an eligible male employed by the ship ran a close second to what a hungry fox might experience finding himself locked in a henhouse. There was never a dearth of young ladies about the decks, happy to comfort and caress, after a drink, or less. In fact, there was an unofficial contest among the cruise staff to see who could have sex with the most women in a twenty-four hour period. The big winner claimed four. I never won the contest, though I did come in second a few times.

In fact, my favorite ploy, admittedly taught to me by our Assistant Cruise Director, was as follows. Dance one dance with a comely suspect, offer to buy her a drink. While sipping, mention as sincerely as a puppy that you could get in to all sorts of trouble if a superior officer caught you speaking with a woman as attractive as she was. To remedy the situation, the following query always worked:

"What are you drinking?"

Regardless of what she said, you replied, "My steward can get us anything we want, so why don't we split from this nursing home. You go first and wait for me on deck. In a few minutes I'll meet you, and we can go down to my cabin together." Here came the best line of all: "I'd really like to get you know you better."

In all my years of cruising, the routine never failed, and I've never been able to figure out the reason.

Why then, would anyone who only had to buy a drink here, or dance a dance there, before retiring to a roll in his private cabin, even consider stuffing himself into a dilapidated taxi at any time of the day or night, filled with six to who-knows-how-many drunken shipmates, and zoom off to a brothel on the outskirts of town? Call it male bonding, call it what you will, I never gave much thought as to why we did it; descending on the establishment like a band of modern day pirates attacking an innocent seaside village, we just did.

Perhaps it was for the adventure, the camaraderie, or for the unlucky ones, the ignominious status of having to endure the long line in front of the sick bay a few days later for a mega-dose of antibiotics. Bad luck notwithstanding, every port had a favorite brothel and it was simply a matter of time before we sent the morning tour on its way or introduced the acts for the evening show, and off we went, day or night, screaming, yelling, and carousing like residents of an asylum making a break for freedom.

One is not born with the ability to cast discretion to the wind and descend into the nether world of cheap beer and expensive women, or expensive beer and cheap women, depending on one's individual taste. It's an acquired talent. When reading about brothels and running amok in literature, a neophyte to the real world might consider such references as something of fantasy, smug in ones middle class security, that nothing like that ever actually happens in real life. Boy, was I ever in for an abrupt awakening.

It was thanks to an air conditioning malfunction causing an unscheduled call to Cozumel on the Yucatan Peninsula. Waiting for the technicians to be flown in, the Cruise Director gave us all the night off, as he *mea culpa*'ed himself black and blue, agreeing to take care of the extra rounds of bingo, schedule another feature in the movie theatre, and run the hastily set up deck party and barbecue. He obviously had a rendezvous planned he didn't want any of us to know about. We did our best in assuring passengers that we were docking for extremely minor repairs, urging them to remain on board. In order to make sure our folks stayed put, we began circulating a nifty rumor claiming the village was a onetime home to a modest leper colony. Hopefully, this would discourage the diehards from scampering ashore and getting lost, or worse, before we sailed.

Once the passengers were safely occupied, we skipped down the gangway heading for the small village to see what there was to be seen. Not able to see very much as the streets were barely lit and very dark, we did manage to find an obliging cabbie who eagerly took us to his favorite brothel, calling cards and post cards for the place lining his window visors. We later found out he received a bit of a kickback for every able bodied gent he brought to the place. Live and let live, why not?

Our party consisted of the following stalwarts: Nigel, the radio operator, with his ever-present shoreside hibiscus tucked with dapper abandon behind his right ear; two of the ship's photographers, cranky, working class Brits who, when not completely drunk, were working very hard to get so; Tim, our meek Fire Control Officer, who we took along because we figured he'd be good for a few laughs; the young Social Director, Ricky, who, as mentioned earlier, looked like a virginal rock star if there was such a creature; and finally Donny, our inimitable Assistant Cruise Director, his gold penis and testicles charm dangling innocently around his neck, as though it were a crucifix.

Our cab driver introduced himself as Carlos and his pride and joy was a Chevrolet from the late seventies, showing at once signs of devoted care and abject neglect. Rusting through various points on the body, the spread of oxidation was retarded somewhat by the application of several coats of hand brushed enamel, or a smear of grey bondo. Small round reflectors lined most of the body where the chrome once was, as well as a few STP stickers here and there patching a hole or simply applied for decoration. On the roof of the car sat an old taxi sign, shattered on one end, revealing a dull yellow bulb shedding ample light to the surviving lettering on the sign spelling out "axi."

Artistically written on the front fender in extremely ornate lettering were the words, *El Carretero de Diablo*, translating roughly to "The Devil's Charioteer." I realized this was merely the name of the car, but began to seriously wonder if the name referred to guy who would be driving it. Undaunted, we piled in, and the cab roared off into the humid night.

The interior looked more like the interior of a funeral home in Mexico City than the inside of Chevy from the early seventies. Chi-chi balls in Mexico's national colors green, white and red lined the windows, and a small, very plastic chandelier with a flickering red light dangled from the socket where the dome light should have been. Photos of favorite saints and assorted virgins hung from the coat hooks in handmade frames of flat ice cream sticks painted pink, decorated with bits of coral and tiny sea shells. Topping it off, a thick scent of roses enveloped you as you entered, making you feel as though you had just inadvertently plowed your way into a blob of rose-flavored gelatin.

Quickly settling in, Nigel and Donny took the front seat with Carlos, with the two photographers, Tim, Ricky, and me squeezed into the back. Not half as cramped as it sounds; in another life, the car must have really been a taxi because the back of the front seat was equipped with fold down jump seats, only one of which still worked. Ricky sat on that one, Tim gingerly balancing on the transversal bump trying to avoid the photographer's knees while knocking down the portraits of the virgins or bumping into the jostling chandelier with its flickering red light.

"Gaw," muttered one of the photographers, "What a grotty pen and ink. (Translation: stink) Why it smells like a bloody 'oar 'ouse in 'ere!"

"You mean we gotta pay good 'bees and honey' (money) to ride a 'jam jar' (car) that's got a stink like a bloomin' 'orse and cart'? (fart) Bloody cheek, that's what this is!" groused the other.

"Nigel, what the hell are they talking about?" asked Donny, trying in vain to fan away a bit of the thickly scented air from the immediate vicinity of his nose.

"It's Cockney rhyming slang, seems like they're a bit upset with the rather ripe odors. Can't say I blame them actually, what?"

"Hey Carlos, my man, can't you get any more speed out of this thing?" called Donny from his seat by the permanently open window. "Get some fresh air in here, you know what I mean?"

"Okay. Okay, no problem," and he pressed his foot against the gas pedal. The engine roared, but we didn't go any faster.

While driving down a battered street hugging the coastline, our driver spoke up diplomatically. "Señors, I am Carlos. Tonight I hope to 'eserve as your guide. But, before we go to the house of the ladies, please be my guest." He produces a heavy brown jug, corked with a crisp knot of straw.

"What is it?" I inquired.

"Drink. Drink. You like," urged Carlos like a doting aunt. "You like!" Lifting the straw stopper from the spout of the jug with his teeth, while keeping the other on the wheel, he handed it to me. You only live once I thought, so closing my eyes, I took healthy swig. It didn't taste bad at all. Then I swallowed, and it still didn't taste bad. Comparable to a musky tequila with a charcoal finish.

"What is this Carlos? It tastes great." I said

"Mucho gusto, mi amigo." said Carlos, bowing his head modestly, "It's a mescal, I make myself. You like?"

"Homemade mescal, is it?" cut in Nigel, "Pass it along then lad, pass it along."

I did, and he took an unbelievably long quaff that probably would have drowned anyone else, the wilting hibiscus behind his ear dropping and spinning gently to the backseat behind him.

"Aaaaahhhh!" sighed Nigel in appreciation, his eyes widening like planets and watering with pleasure.

"That's Tiger's Milk, lads, *La Leche de Tigre*!"

"Si, señor." said Carlos proudly, knowing authentic *Leche De Tigre* included a healthy spritz of tabasco, but he wasn't about to temper Nigel's appreciation of his brew. Nigel passed the heavy jug to Ricky. "Here you go my boyo, grow some hair on your chest."

"Gee." giggled Ricky nervously, shooting us all a quick glance before taking a quick swallow. "Damn, that's hot stuff!" he said, choking just a bit and shaking his head, causing us all to laugh.

Laughing as well, he handed the jug to Tim who was trying his hardest to seem inconspicuous.

"Here you go Timmy my boy!" said Nigel, grabbing the bottle away from Ricky and shoving it into Tim's protesting hands. Grasping the bottle with his fingertips as though he were holding a dead cat, he looked around at us, and you might say we were staring back at him as unsympathetically as possible crammed as we were in this tiny car barreling down a very dark highway.

"Well," squeaked Tim, "I suppose a little sip wouldn't hurt."

"Come on then, stop mucking about!" said Nigel, his patience wearing thin.

"Here goes." said Tim with a nervous smile, and he took a swig, and then another.

"He like, eh?" said Carlos as he pried the jug out of Tim's hands and handed it to Donny.

Donny, unceremoniously wiped the spout with his sleeve, before downing a few gulps.

"Not bad." he managed to comment, after catching his breath, "But I've had better." He handed the jug to one of the photographers.

The first photographer took a sociable swallow, exhaled hotly, and then passed the jug to his cohort, the one who earlier made a disparaging remark about one of Carlos' sisters. He grabbed the jug and started drinking in large gulps.

"Oh, by the way amigo," Carlos mentioned innocently, "don't choke on any of the *cusano rojos* in the bottom of the jug. If you swallow one of the little red worms, you may lose your mind."

"Arrraghh." gagged the nervy photographer, showering everyone in the car with a fine spray of the stuff.

"But don't worry señor," said Carlos, smiling like a panther, "I don't think you have much mind to lose."

We all started laughing, appreciating Carlos' well placed bon mot. Score two points for Mr. Carlos.

The ride was rather uneventful after that, except for the occupants beginning to sway toward mutiny as the cramped conditions, rose perfume, and Carlos' driving technique that must have been learned from the "Proceed through the countryside as though you are being chased" school of driving instruction. All these extenuating factors began to get on everyone's nerves. Carlos assured us in the Yucatan it was all perfectly legal to pass on blind curves, provided you beeped your horn. In addition, you weren't breaking any laws if you accidentally flattened an errant armadillo, jack rabbit, or snacking vulture hopping about on the roadway. As long as you didn't cause an accident with another car or truck, damage the highway, or otherwise impede the flow of traffic, you could drive as you pleased.

We were in no condition to argue, the mescal making itself known. The only real complaint was made by Donny, naturally, when he slammed his knee into the dashboard after a near miss on a browsing skunk. This caused the glove compartment to pop open resulting in two bottles of fresh mescal to come dropping out like bombs from the belly of a B-52. One bottle scored a direct hit on Donny's left knee, the other one smashing onto the instep of his sandaled foot. Neither of the bottles was damaged so we told Carlos to ignore Donny's threatened lawsuits from the Mexican Supreme Court in Cozumel, as if there was even one there.

After careening over what seemed to be three quarters of the Yucatan Peninsula, hitting nary a cactus but wreaking havoc on the small critter population, we finally arrived at the parking area of our garishly lit destination, glowing in flashing red and green neon. Crawling out of the car, I was sure to check on the grill of the old Chevy, tied on to the chassis with a rope, to see if there were any furry or feathered remains dripping from it. There were none. I breathed easier, relieved we did not cause the death of any of the local fauna who may have ventured out for an evening's constitutional only to become a yummy roadkill snack for a vulture.

With the sense of feeling slowly returning to our legs, we were immediately surrounded with herds of mustachioed men wearing huge sombreros, and carrying guitars of at least ten different sizes and shapes. Each pleaded in varying degrees of fractured English,

"Combo? Combo for hire, Señors?"

"Hey, my freng', you like the Mariachi? For you 'berry 'berry cheap!"

"You like the music with your ladies? Very cheap, guaranteed!"

Barely able to focus on the groups of pleading musicians, let alone what they were talking about, Carlos was quick to shoo then away, quietly promising to talk with them a bit later. Besides that, he told us the girls preferred rap and hip-hop anyway, and would probably be our "dates" for free if we gave them an iPhone with ample room for digital downloads.

"Damn, I wish I knew that! I have a suitcase filled with outdated phones they would have loved!" moaned Donny, smacking himself in the head, yet again.

"Bet the wanker has a mirrored ceiling as well," smirked one of the photographers. Giggling and jostling each other, our group of stalwarts followed Carlos up a stone pathway leading to a building, our feet crunching on the carcasses of hundreds of electrocuted insects who inadvertently careened into the glaring neon sign with the name of the place, "El Convento" or "The Convent," flashing and crackling above it all.

The front of the structure was festooned with thick clumps of banana trees off to the right and left. Center was an ominous looking wrought iron door shaped like the entrance to a dungeon. Hanging precariously from a rusty bracket was an ancient enameled metal sign claiming the place was approved by Duncan Hines, as well as accepting an international assortment of credit cards.

Reaching the portal, Carlos waited until we quieted down a bit before solemnly knocking three times. A small opening in the door slid open slicing a sharp beam of light out into the darkness, blocked out by a pair of eyes a moment later.

"Si?" came a deep, ominous voice from behind the eyes.

"*Buenos noches. Es Carlos*" said out host, surprisingly as deeply and mysteriously as the pair of eyes. After surveying our motley crew, the eyes disappeared and the little opening clinked shut. I wondered what the eyes thought of us, as I can't say we looked like a collection of live ones, though I'm sure the criteria for entry was not based on appearance, but rather the anticipation of being able to drop lots of cash.

By now, Donny had unbuttoned his shirt well passed his navel, and was adjusting his chains and charms so the solid gold penis and testicles pendant was front and center. Nigel, having picked a fresh hibiscus, was smiling broadly, the flower tucked securely behind his ear, his ample belly hanging over his belt. Ricky was blushing hotly, his hands jammed as far into his pockets as possible. Tim was searching his beaded Navajo coin purse for the correct change to purchase a prophylactic or two from a tatty assortment which an indigenous woman in a colorful serape had displayed in a semi-circle on the ground near the entrance of the establishment. Her inventory included a small assortment of two-to-the-box Chicklets, cheap plastic combs, and tin key chains with movable charms depicting an assortment of people, animals, and a number of internationally famous politicians doing it to each other in a number of creative ways. The two photographers were off relieving themselves by the banana trees, taking what they called a "snake's hiss (piss)." Standing with this crew, I was trying to look blasé, giving the impression I really didn't know these guys, but just came along for the ride. My thoughts were quickly interrupted when the little speakeasy peephole zipped open once again and the same deep voice as before intoned form behind the dark eyes, "Carlos. Si."

The heavy iron door slowly creaked open.

"All righty, then." Donny cackled, licking his lips and snapping his fingers like maracas.

"Well, here goes," said Ricky with a very nervous smile.

"Cripes," questioned Tim, struggling to read the fine print on the condom wrappers he had just purchased. "Do you think you can use these things more than once?"

"Well old boy, once more unto the fray!" said Nigel, but before I was able to reply, I realized he was not talking to me, but to his crotch.

The two photographers were muttering just this side of incomprehensibility. The only phrases I was able to catch had something to do with "cobblers awls" (balls) "eight day clocks" (cocks), and "Donald Ducks." Your guess is as good as mine as to what "Donald Ducks" rhymes with.

So, reminiscent of the children of Hamlin obediently following the mesmerizing tune of the piper, we entered in to a long darkened hallway, lit with a bare light bulb, as the huge iron door slammed behind us with a surprising slam and echo.

Tacked to the wall, in the glow of the light bulb, was an early portent of things to come, a large poster of a yawning lion with the caption, *En Nuestro Negocio, El Cliente Es Rey*—translating to "In Our Business, The Customer Is King," a reassuring sentiment if nothing else, considering someone had blackened out a few of the lion's teeth, drew stitch marks on his forehead, and drew in a black eye. After all, Carlos had assured us this was a "classy" place. I just hoped we both shared the same meaning of "classy."

From the dark hallway we entered into a courtyard alive with the revelry of a Bosch painting with a decidedly Spanish influence. Carlos gave a brief history of the place before setting us free to run amok. Called "El Convento," the building was originally built during the Colonial Period as an actual convent for a missioneric order of nuns from Spain. Rather than dealing with the bacchanalian locals who felt they had absolutely no need for any sort of redemption, the nuns decided to seek a flock more attuned to their message and checked out of this outpost long ago. The sisters who currently occupied the Convento's walls were a smidge more successful in getting their message across, charnel though it be. Such is the way of the world.

A splashing multi-tiered fountain stood center with a full bar bustling with activity surrounding it. Clumps of banana trees with clusters of ripening fruit hung down, travelers palms spread out east and west, resplendent birds of paradise, as well as huge three and four tiered spider plants, colorful bougainvillea and lush ferns filled every possible crook and corner. Blooming orchids were resplendent in the humidity and swayed sensually from the arched balconies surrounding the bustling courtyard below. Small rooms opened out onto the terraced walkway above, each with an arched iron door like at the entry. A few of the doorways had slinky, scantily clad young women, alluringly leaning and gracing the doorjambs, like panthers anticipating a hunt. Ornate Spanish pillars stood every few meters supporting the surrounding balcony, each entwined with tangled greenery, accented here and there with flaccid red, yellow, and orange hibiscus flowers. The entire patio was delicately scented with night-blooming jasmine and an occasional whiff of supple gardenia blossoms.

A heavily made up woman in her late forties ran the brightly lit and well-appointed bar. She poured the drinks and issued orders to a flock of skinny drone-like fellows who scurried about with trays of beers and assorted snacks and refreshments.

In a dark nook opposite the bar was a compact tattoo parlor presided over by a villainous looking gentleman with a long drooping moustache. He wore an athletic styled undershirt splotched with purple stains revealing a jumbled collection of tattoos covering his hirsute arms, shoulders, and particularly furry back. Thinking this might be as good a place as any to get a tattoo, I wandered over and watched as the hairy guy prepared to execute his art on a shirtless young customer. The subject had decided to get the name of his love of the evening engraved forever on his skinny bicep. She was proudly and approvingly draped over his shoulder, anticipating the tip she was going to receive from the tattoo artist for bringing him a willing customer. Her name was going to be illuminated with vines, flowers, and a butterfly. The boy sat with his arm resting on the tattooist's table while the subject of this evening's devotion cradled his dizzy head in her ample bosom, Pieta style.

Breathing on the needle, then wiping it thoroughly on his undershirt, he dipped it daintily into a vial of indigo ink, and then went to work with a crackling buzz. I'm sure he changed his undershirt at least once a week, but even so, I decided I could do without a souvenir tattoo.

While I was reaching this astute conclusion, my shipmates were taken to a large table directly in front of a small stage. The stage was a platform, actually, with roughhewn boards nailed over discarded fruit crates. As the girls grinded their bumps, one of their spiked heels frequently lodged between a gap in the boards, causing the dancer to lose her balance and wiggle a bit. None ever toppled over, but when a fall looked even slightly imminent, thunderous cheers and "olés" arose from the appreciative but not very attentive audience. Complementing the action on stage was a small combo consisting of a snare drum and cymbal, a trumpet, and cheap electric piano. To hear this orchestra crank our Ravel's "Bolero" while the girls slithered and gyrated on stage was an example of the exotic arts at their best.

Seated at odd sized tables throughout the courtyard were gentlemen of all ages, ranging from their late teens on up. All were dressed nicely, meticulously manicured pencil thin moustaches on a few, neatly combed wavy hair on most, with some showing elegant streaks of gray, perhaps a bit of balding. Obviously, not the habitué of slimy under life.

I had expected to see shocked middle aged men hiding their faces, wearing high black socks held up with garters, baggy white boxer shorts and singlet undershirts, with small black oblongs blocking out their eyes disguising their true identities from prying divorce lawyers. At least, that's how the guys looked in the *Modern Detective* magazines cramming the big wooden rack in the corner drugstore when I was a kid. The customers in this establishment seemed to be paragons of their communities, out for a night on the town without their wives. No one averted his eyes or covered his head with his jacket when our eyes met. Each man was a sultan of his individually rented harem for the evening, and everyone was happy. No telling what the wives, supposedly languishing back on the hacienda, felt about the situation, but there was no doubt they had figured out a way to extract payment in kind from their philandering spouses—one could be sure of that.

No sooner had we sat down, then our table was mobbed by a bevy of heavily made up and perfumed women. Big ones, little ones, young and old, exotic dark skinned beauties with almond shaped eyes, to voluptuous Earth Mother types, having crossed the line to overweight years ago. They all jockeyed for a position of notice, laps being the most popular, while others hung around your neck or sat on the table in front of you with their legs spread open just wide enough to be enticing, though not reveling anything not yet paid for. Hands and fingers from who-knows-where, let alone who, began fondling anything on your body easily accessible and there for fair game, hair, ears, shirt collars, fingers, jewelry and even belt buckles and zippers by the more entertaining of the bunch. None spoke English very well, but all took a turn of moistly whispering in your ear, "Buy me a beer good lookin'" and "You like? You like?" You got an ample bosom pushed into your face regardless of which direction you turned. Considering all the questioning and possibilities, it was almost impossible to form an educated opinion.

Amid all this posturing and hoochie-koochie existed a definite protocol. Agreeing to buy one of the ladies a drink, the others scattered almost immediately for better prospects. Buy drinks for a dozen girls and twelve hung around, but generally the purchase of a drink served as a preliminary process of elimination.

After a few minutes the original gaggle thinned out to a dozen or so girls intent on scoring at our table, not quenching a thirst. A male morale booster like no other, gales of laughter arose if you as much as winked at one of them, or made the least suggestive yet insignificant gesture like scratching your head or mindlessly flicking your nose.

Donny was a big hit with his penis charm affectionately referred to by all the girls as "La Paloma" or "The Dove." Many tried to finger it, the bolder ones trying to lick it suggestively. Donny kept a watchful grip on the chain and charm, convinced that, in a moment of weakness, one of the ladies might attempt to snatch it away.

When the drinks arrived, I thought I was the only one who noticed that the girls were given empty glasses with their bottles of beer. After sipping from their bottles, they spit the beer into the empty glass. Though puzzled as to why they did this, it didn't seem to bother anyone else except Donny. Detecting this strange behavior around the same time I did, he was first to question it.

"Hey, what the hell are you doing?" he demanded of one of the girls mid-spit.

Smiling with a warmth that could melt concrete, she replied innocently, "You no want me to get drunky-drunky and pukey-pukey, do you, mi amore?"

Before he was able to answer, I interjected, "There's no arguing with that, is there? I mean it's not like she ordered a bottle of Dom, is it?"

Not entirely convinced, I was relieved nevertheless seeing Donny decide to withdraw his righteous protest over the "sipping and spitting." They were working girls after all, professionals at that, all things considered, and the evening was just beginning.

Ricky sat on the other side of the table glowing a deep shade of beet red. I seriously wondered if he would ever return to his fair complexioned self again, especially after his treatment by the ladies of the place. Most of the girls were older than he, obviously by experience, if not by age. They intuitively sensed he was new to this sort of thing, as far as enjoyable sinning was concerned. Each time any of the ladies passed, she planted a huge swampy kiss on his burning cheeks, leaving big red lipstick smears, saying, "When you ready Cherry Boy, you go with me. Okay?"

Nodding like esteemed older sisters, they acted as though they were trying to convince a shy younger brother; as long as he bought his first date a hamburger, there was nothing wrong with expecting hot steamy sex in return.

Nigel was presiding over a rowdy bunch of large women, his retinue reminiscent of an intimate gathering after the sacking of Troy. Shaking bottles of beer, one in each hand, he would pop the lids with his teeth, showering the ladies and himself with cascades of white foam. Laughing and hooting hysterically, they merrily decided to lick each other dry.

The two photographers, supporting themselves by leaning against a wall near the bar, were talking up two young women who were obviously twins.

Tim sat at the table courteously, facing us with his back to the stage, wondering out loud why they had not brought him the glass of skim milk he had ordered at least ten minutes ago. Few girls showed any interest in him except for one sitting modestly by his side. She kept her hands folded on the table, gazing directly into his eyes whenever they happened to look her way, which was not often. Eventually it dawned on him to buy her a glass of milk as well. She acquiesced as shyly as a fox.

Meanwhile, a stripper working the makeshift stage a few feet from our table was now down to a G-string and two tasseled pasties. She dipped a hand into the crotch of the G-string and, with a few ecstatic gyrations, produced a cherry red Tootsie Roll pop, no telling where it had been stored. She smelled it sensually and swooned, licked it sensually and swooned again, and then twirling the sweet sucker like a top, she sent it flying to the table directly down in front of a surprised Tim. The crowd went wild. She then popped off one of the pasties with ease and threw it to a cheering table toward the back of the room. Unfortunately, she seemed to develop a bit of difficulty removing the other one. In spite of her valiant efforts, accented with an assortment of saucy pouts and gyrations, she positively could not get the right pasty to pop off as easily as the left one had. She then knelt down in her hands and knees and positioned herself so the pasty, and her breast, dangled directly over Tim, who was still sitting with his back to the stage. The drummer began a drum roll, and the crowd began to cheer. Tim, thinking an insect was buzzing around his head, made few swipes at the annoyance with hand, the drummer ringing out rim-shots with each unsuccessful pass. The stripper, no newcomer to show business, realizing how this was pleasing the crowd, persisted. Jiggling the fringes of the pasty just above Tim's head and ears, she brushed them about just enough to be annoying. Tim, not one to be intimidated by a fly, took a broad swipe blindly behind himself, at the suspected bugger, his hand landing solidly on the stripper's right breast. Another rim-shot rang out, this time accompanied by an explosive cymbal crash. Turning quickly, finally realizing what was going on behind him, he recoiled in shock and fell over backward in his chair, landing on the stone floor with a crunch.

The patrons of the place began cheering as though Tim had just thrust a beribboned pick in to a sweating bull's neck. Flustered practically into disintegration, Tim recovered quickly, placing his chair in an upright position, and sat down, pretending nothing had happened, even though the stripper was now slapping his head with both breasts, accompanied with cymbal crashes on each pass, the remaining tassel fringes flying in the wind.

Donny leaned over and screamed something in Tim's ear, "Are you kidding!" he replied in amazement.

"Just do it, asshole!" yelled Donny, who then returned to entwining tongues with one of the young ladies who, after nipping at his ear to regain his attention, was now massaging his bare chest with her free hand. No telling where her other hand was, let alone what it was doing.

A bottle of beer flew out from the darkness and landed with a foamy splat just short of the stage as the young lady who chose Tim as her date for the evening pulled him near, reassuringly whispered something in his ear, and then mimed sensually licking her finger. She nodded and urged Tim to do the same

The decibel level was now a deafening roar with some patrons standing on the tables and dancing along with the driving music.

Tim, on the verge of wetting himself, something he had not done since his early toilet training, followed his comely escort's advice and tepidly licked his finger. The stripper bounced her gyrating breast down for another pass as the crowd chanted some sort of soccer cheer, "Bonga chia, chia, chia, bonga chia, chia CHA!" while the trio played with such maniacal abandon, the beer bottles remaining on some of the tables were jiggling about and doing fandangos as well.

Tim, standing on a chair for better leverage, slipped his properly moistened finger between the pasty and the seething breast, and, ZAP! It popped off the ample breast like a bottle cap on a hot bottle of beer. The crowd's shriek was deafening. The band exploded with a loud flourish and multiple crescendos. The stripper leaped a foot above the stage shaking her entire body in orgasmic abandon, beads of sweat shooting off her glistening body like electrified missiles, perfectly illuminated by the strategically placed back lighting, illuminated for the finale.

Dangling the paper and glitter coated pasty from his finger, Tim slid back into his chair in shock. His cute escort congratulated him with a big hug and a shower of kisses. The exhausted stripper took her bows, graciously acknowledging Tim by tossing yet another bulbous cherry red Tootsie Roll pop retrieved from the crotch of the same G-string, at the same time retrieving pieces of her costume strewn about the stage earlier in her act.

As the place began calming down, another stripper began her routine to a scratchy version of "La Paloma Blanca." I noticed Nigel sandwiched between three zaftig Amazons stumbling and swerving for the stone staircase at the rear of the court yard. Laughing and pleasantly incoherent, Nigel was being carried up the stairs shouting, "Hail to thee sweet maidens of Mexico, descendants of the noble Maya! I am the returned spirit of Montezuma, come to sweep you away to the golden Chichen Itza in the sky!" With that, he threw the wilting hibiscus tucked behind his ear earlier out onto the bustling patio area below.

The two photographers, nowhere to be seen, had no doubt gone up the stairway earlier, or had fallen asleep underneath; no way of telling for sure.

Donny had narrowed his field to a pair of nubile beauties and was haggling over the price, trying to play one against the other. Unfortunately, they were just as clever as Donny, insisting on twenty dollars apiece, claiming one for fifteen and two for twenty-five was in no way a terrific deal.

Ricky patiently nursed his original bottle of beer, his face and forehead a pastiche of lipstick lip tracings. It seems every woman passing by landed a big sloppy one somewhere on his face, accompanied with the alluring whisper, "Ready now, Cherry Boy?" Surprising no one, he eventually grabbed the hand of one of kissing beauties and returned the favor sensually on her lips. Hand in hand, they disappeared up the staircase.

Tim was engaged in an animated conversation with the lady who instructed him on the proper way to remove the stubborn pasty. She was smiling coyly, nodding her head in knowing agreement, probably not understanding a word of what he was going on about, but knowing that, when the prattle was done, she had herself a customer.

The young lady I finally zeroed in on, or perhaps she zeroed in on me, I don't recall exactly, was an extremely regal looking woman in a Mayan sort of way. Like the others, she didn't speak English very well. My Spanish was a scant remainder of the high school variety: *"Carumba semiolvedo mi cuarderno!"* or "Darn, I forgot my notebook!" did not afford us the luxury of chatting about the work of Frieda Kahlo or Latin American politics. We did manage to establish a basic rapport, though I did find it somewhat awkward to pop that all important question requesting a possible move up the stairs. Suggesting a price for such a sojourn posed another problem. I was not about to bargain as Donny was because I felt that to be just a bit humiliating for her as well as myself. Somehow she must have magically been able to see through all the foolish rationalizations going through my head at the moment and, placing her delicate had in mine, motioned toward the stairs. I quickly nodded in agreement. Reaching the stairs, she held out her hand, smiled, lightly rubbing her thumb and forefinger together and purred, "Money, honey."

"Now?" I questioned incredulously, "we haven't done anything yet."

Cocking her head, she added sweetly, "No money, no fuckee. Twenty dollar, por favor."

Well, no arguing with that I thought, and dutifully held out a twenty. She smiled again, made the Sign of the Cross, took my money, and disappeared back through the courtyard.

Waiting for her I noticed a steady stream of gentlemen of all ages, and ladies of all shapes and sizes, going up and down the stairs. The only difference, the women coming down the stairs still looked fabulous, but the men were slightly more bedraggled, though to a man or teenager, relaxed and grinning like Cheshire Cats. While waiting, I speculated as to why the ladies crossed themselves after the money was handed over. Perhaps it was a way to ask forgiveness for their sins, which I doubt. If they were all that concerned with sinning they would have vacated the premises along with the nuns. Maybe it provided protection against the evil eye, or pernicious diseases; after all, what is a good saint for? A quick word with Our Lady of Penicillin as a safeguard against the dark angel Gonna Rita and any of her nasty Harpies.

I was jolted out of my bizarre reverie by a playful slap on the chest by my lady for the night, accompanied with a short fellow in tow. Actually "short" is an understatement. He was a dwarf, built like a brick shithouse, muscles bulging out of his ears. Not a person to tango with in a dark alley, or even a well-lit one for that matter. He carried a brass ring with a few dozen keys clanging like jingle bells, an aerosol can of some sort, and two white towels slung over his shoulder, almost dragging on the floor. Climbing a few stairs reaching our level in height, he motioned for us to follow. Taking my hand, the dream girl smiled sweetly, and up the stairs we went.

I was ushered to a room at the far end of the terrace. It had a black iron door like all the others. As if he were an X-rated

Munchkin opening the gates to the Emerald City, he doodled around with the keys, searching for the one that worked. My date for the evening, a Dorothy, who, for the time being, had no desire to ever return to Kansas, was actually looking over the rail, checking out the new prospects arriving without the aid of a tornado. Twisting a key, he finally unlocked the door, pushing it open with a full body block. Yielding against his awesome might, the door opened with a chilling screech, like a steel rake against a concrete sidewalk in autumn. We entered dutifully behind the little guy who began waving the towels around, either to dash away a few imaginary spider webs or get the heavy humid air circulating, or perhaps for both reasons, I didn't ask.

The room was stark and practically empty, except for a grey stripped mattress missing its sheet, a rickety nightstand with a tiny lamp complete with a pleated red plastic lampshade covering a dull light bulb flickering from the vibrations caused by our entrance, eventually going dark. A few empty clothes hooks hung crookedly on the wall. The only other light was provided by a thick silver beam of moonlight cascading through the screenless opening in the thick adobe wall, illuminating an empty beer bottle abandoned on the two-foot-thick sill, casting pale amber shadows on the grey mattress ticking below.

The husky little guy smacked the bed with the towels a few times before throwing them to the foot of the mattress. Vigorously shaking the aerosol can, he attempted to spray the mattress with whatever it contained, perhaps a disinfectant of some sort. Unfortunately, the spritzer was not in the best working order, so it just gurgled a bit, depositing a wet spot on the bed the size of a quarter. Looking at me, he smiled and shrugged his shoulders, said something in Spanish to my rent-a-date, and they both laughed. So much for hygiene, I thought. Leaving the room, he made a lascivious but friendly gesture with his tiny fist, pinched my knee, and then kicked and yanked the door closed behind him.

Once the big iron door rasped shut, the "we aim to please" attitude, already on the wane, disappeared completely. It was business as usual, and I suppose this was understandable as we both knew what we were in that room for. There was no need to offer the usual courting pretense of offering to buy a melon daiquiri or discussing current events. She was not interested in saving whales or impeaching anyone. Considering the moment, neither was I. In a brothel one does not have to worry about keeping up stimulating conversation. The important thing has a tendency to rise all by itself. Primitively brainless, instinct never needs a mind to know when it's time.

I suppose many of the folks visiting the establishment were steady customers and, knowing where their usual room would be, hired one of the roving Mariachi groups to play below its windows at a specified time. With off-key renditions of "Ole Torero," "Maleguena," and "Cu-Cu-Ru-Chu Paloma" wafting through the breezes, blanketed only in moonlight, on a sheetless mattress, somewhere in the state of Quintana Roo on the Yucatan Peninsula, I became one with the ages, and communed with the Universe. Quite a lofty accomplishment for only twenty bucks, no?

Sometime later I was awakened by a mixed bag of sounds seeping in from various places. Through the wall on my right, I heard the sounds of girls laughing and water sloshing about. From the left came a gruff male voice complaining loudly about his time not being up, goddamnit, as he was just warming up! Outside a heavily accented but rousing rendition of "God Save The Queen" was being wailed, presented by a group of Mariachis.

Rolling out of the scratchy bed to the cold stone floor below, I limped to the window, carefully climbed into the dusty opening, and looked out. I saw Carlos below, peering up toward the windows, trying to figure out who was where. A difficult feat, as the windows were a story or two above the jungle below, some still protected with iron bars or grillwork, a throwback to the convent days, I suppose. Noticing me sitting in the window sill and gazing out the window, he wrangled a group of Mariachis to the area directly below, so happy to see a familiar face. Doffing his straw sombrero, he bowed deeply and announced proudly, "This I dedicate to you Señor!"

The band began a brassy version of "The Star Spangled Banner" and Carlos attempted to sing along, though he didn't remember many of the words so he simply hummed through the forgotten stanzas.

Thanking him with a nod and a wave from my perch in the window, I then gingerly climbed down out of the sill into the dimly lit snuggery. Funny, first entering the room it looked rather dingy in a romantic sort of way, but viewing it now retrospectively, it was still just as dingy as before. The special performance of "The Star Spangles Banner" changed suddenly to "Cuando Caliente El Sol" after a few choice Spanish expletives were growled from one of the windows, followed by the sound of a beer bottle crashing through the thick jungle below. So much for the dedication.

The guy in the room to my left was still grousing and complaining, his words muffled somewhat by the thick adobe wall, but the laughing and splashing was still trickling in from the right. I decided to investigate the sweet sounds coming from the right and not the barking coming from the left. I suddenly realized that my lady was not in the room and instantly feared my wallet wasn't either. Panic stricken, I searched for my trousers, not remembering in the slightest where I had left them. I had visions of being stranded in this place forever, not having cab fare back to the ship or a pair of pants to wear for the journey.

I had nothing to worry about, for hanging neatly on the wall were my pants, shirt, shoes and socks, each on a separate hook. My wallet was still in my back pocket, unmolested. Even a flattened Trojan I purchased in a gas station in Acapulco months ago in anticipation for an evening like this was comfortably plastered to the side of the billfold. I carefully peeled it off and was going to flick it out the window but placed it on the nightstand instead as a gift to the next adventurer visiting the room.

Stepping out of the room clothed only in moonlight, I walked on the terrace searching for the source of all the laughter and splashing. Not an exhibitionist by the slightest inclination, I surprised myself, not at all concerned about taking a late night stroll unattired as I was. If anyone on the patio below noticed, they certainly didn't say anything or threw a beer bottle my way, so I suppose no one was offended. No one laughed, pointed or suggested hormones.

The room next to mine appeared to be the source of the laughing and splashing. Peering in shyly, I was treated to a sight that any kid who ever fantasized about a peeking into a busy girls' locker room, might have dreamed about. The room was as dimly lit as all the others, simply in silver shadow from moonbeams streaming in from a number of window openings. Prancing about in delicious silver silhouette were young naked women. Like blasé water nymphs from a piece of Baroque porcelain, some combed a sister's long black hair, some sat under a gently flowing faucet, a few pinched and played a short lived game of tag, while many filled large basins with water flowing from spigots lining the wall, then dumped them over their heads, shivering attractively in the silver blue whiteness of the moonlight.

As with all good things, this feast for the eyes and senses didn't last forever. After entering the room I was quickly discovered.

"Mira, hermanas! El Senor Calor!" one called from the wetness. I was flattered to later learn it meant, "Look sisters, it's Mr. Hot One!"

In a feeble attempt to defend their honor, basins of water were immediately thrown my way. Laughing playfully while slipping and sliding all over the place, each ran toward me with a bowl brimming with crisp water and heaved it in my direction. Making no attempt to defend myself, I folded my arms, leaned against the Spanish tiled walls and permitted them to do their worst. Only one loosed her tin basin at me as well as its load of water. So embarrassed at the bowl hit, she rushed over and began showering kisses over the area the basin hit. Unfortunately, it was my elbow.

Gliding out of the splashing darkness, I recognized my consort of the evening looking even more attractive and alluring than before. Her long black hair, wet and supple, hung languorously about her shoulders and breasts as though she were a Polynesian princess from a Gauguin painting. Coquettishly slapping my behind, she led me from the room like a precocious child, as I "*adiosed*" and "*buenas nochased*" all the ladies good night. Heading back to our room, I could still hear the girls laughing and chattering in Spanish, no doubt commenting on the crazy gringo mistakenly wandering into the ladies shower room. But I had one on them: it was no mistake. Bless each luscious moment, no mistake at all.

After being attentively dried and dressed by my lovely, she gave me a quick peck on the cheek and politely chirped, "Adios Senor Calor. I go now," and she walked toward the door.

"Hey wait a minute!" I called, "*Uno momento por favor!* Ahh. What's your name? *Como se llama Usted?*"

"*Usted es no importa Señor.*" She answered jadedly, "*Me llama Maria.*"

"Maria." I repeated, letting the name flow like music, "*Le Madre De Dios*" I added with a smile.

She recoiled just slightly, furrowed her brow with a slight smile and shook her head as if to say, never in a million years, buddy boy, and she was gone.

Gathering my wits about me, I rose from the bed and made my way for the open door and terrace, slamming into a half-dressed Donny chasing after the girl he had obviously spent some time with.

"What the hell do you mean my time's up? I didn't even come yet!" he wailed.

"You want to go again Big Boy, and don't be soft as a rag this time? 'Es okay, twenty dollar!" and she swung around like Carmen after delivering an aria, and headed straight for the stairs.

"How the hell do you like that?" bemoaned a somewhat shattered Donny to no one in particular, "I didn't even..."

"Yeah I heard." I said, surprising him.

"Huh? Oh hey, how you doin'?" he said, recognizing me, then continuing, "and you know, I wasn't even thinking about baseball or anything. I mean, like I was really trying!"

"That's life in the big city, Big Boy." I made every effort to muffle a laugh.

"Very funny, man." pouted Donny, quickly adding, "you know she even had the nerve to ask for five bucks extra 'cause I turned her over."

"You don't say."

"Really, no shit." Donny assured me, "aw but what the hell, it was probably because of all the booze. It happens sometimes, you know?"

"Yep," I commiserated sagely, "It must have been the booze." Genuinely trying not to, I began laughing once again.

"Damn broads," concluded Donny, throwing an arm over my shoulder, finally beginning to laugh himself, as we made our way to the stairs. Halfway down, Donny's lady stood waiting alluringly. The laughter vanished and he began whimpering once again.

"Es no problem Big Boy, you want to go again? Twenty dollar!" Eyelashes fluttering like a butterfly on uncut cocaine.

"Twenty bucks again? You gotta be kidding. What a rip-off! Now listen, how about ten dollars and we'll just begin where we left off, okay?"

"Twenty dollar." she insisted flatly.

"Look, how about some bitchin' rap tapes?"

"Come on bozo," I said, dragging him toward the door, noticing the hefty transvestite who ran the concession usually selling ashtrays and T-shirts with "El Convento" and palm trees printed on them. She was watching what was happening on the stairs and had begun tapping a rather lethal looking shark bat on the counter.

Once safely outside, we were greeted by Carlos and a fresh bottle of mescal with an assortment of chubby pink worms dancing around toward the bottom of the bottle. He escorted us to his car with our very own Ricky sprawled out over the hood. Smiling broadly, even though he was in a drunken stupor, he wore a wet stained El Convento T-shirt stretched over his uniform shirt. He looked like a victim of an extremely rare Equatorial affliction, covered as he was from the top of his blond forehead to the tip of his white bucks, with thick red splotches that were no doubt placed there by numerous pairs of adoring lips, hoping to be the one to pop a "Cherry Boy" into manhood.

Sobering up a few weeks later, we asked if things had worked out for him at "El Convento." He was evasive, mumbling something sounding like "Gimme' a break guys" and quickly changed the subject. An interesting note is that, while answering his voice didn't crack, he didn't stammer, and blushing suddenly seemed a condition of days gone by.

A few moments later Nigel bounced out of the place, slamming the door behind him. Briskly brushing his hands together, he congratulated himself on a job well done. Stuffing his last Balkan Sobranie into his long tortoise shell holder, he lit it, took a puff, and said, "Well lads, how was it?"

"Terrible!" groused Donny, kicking a clod of dirt.

"Not bad." I answered, almost simultaneously.

Bemused, Nigel went on, "Well, that about covers the gamut then, doesn't it? Did he have a jolly time?" he asked, motioning with his chin toward Ricky, still stretched out on the hood, chortling and smiling in his stupor, "or shouldn't I ask."

"Don't think you have to ask," I said, "what about you?"

"Yes, well I must say I had a cheeky one."

"You too?" moaned Donny, fingering the gold penis hanging from his neck.

"Yes," Nigel went on, "she insisted I married her in '95. Even claimed to have a ruddy daughter. Named her Hibiscus, of all things!"

"Is it true?" I asked curiously.

Nigel thought for a moment and said, twirling his moustache, "Can't remember, actually." He then took a long deep breath of the jasmine scented air and added, "can't say I care very much, either. Hello, is that another bottle of mescal, then?"

"Si señor." said Carlos brimming with pride.

"Well then, Carlos, my good man, bloody well hand it over. By the way, did I ever tell you about the island wench who. . .?" Tossing his arm around Carlos' shoulder, they walked off into the parking lot.

The two photographers were next to come rolling out, laughing and gamboling like weasels, having a difficult time keeping one foot in front of the other. They made it to the car, threw open the back door and, after a few unsuccessful tries, managed to crawl into the back seat. They continued snorting, chortling, and carrying on as if they were privy to the punch line of a very ribald joke only the two of them had ever heard.

Donny watched as they settled down in the back seat and didn't utter a word, burying his head in his hands even deeper, grumbling something about "twenty dollars for twenty minutes, she had a hell-of-nerve."

I later learned the photographers had paid for a special treat and became involved in a unique procedure known as a "Spinning Robin." I was never able to get the exact details out of them, but it seemed to involve two girls and a hammock made out of a surplus fishnet, wound up tightly, attached to a hook high on the ceiling. One of the ladies was positioned strategically inside the net, the other served to aid in the spinning and aiming. It was then allowed to slowly spin down, landing pleasurably atop anyone who was patiently waiting and properly positioned below. Pinpoint accuracy was of the utmost importance.

Periodically the iron door rumbled open and a few souls departed, some happy, some not so happy, and most too drunk to care. Tim was nowhere to be seen.

"Well," declared Nigel, surprising me from behind, "Do you think our Tim will be able to walk out on his own, or will we need to go in and fetch him?"

"We just might." I said, thinking Tim, shy as he is, could probably take care of himself as up in the National Parks I bet he hand fed jelly beans to Grizzly bears occasionally.

"That's it, goddammit!" Donny exploded, "We're going to miss the ship because of the little twerp. For all we know, he's locked himself in a bathroom! I'm going to get him."

"Oh now, now, now. Be a good sport laddie," said Nigel, "We'll make the ship in plenty of time. Not everyone's first time is over in a few minutes, now is it?"

"What the hell is that supposed to mean!" Donny demanded, puffing up like a fighting cock.

Before Nigel was able to reply with a devastating repost, the big iron doors opened slowly. Out walked Tim with an expression sadder than if someone had just told him Smokey the Bear was actually the Secretary of the Interior playing dress up.

"It's about time! Where the hell have you been!" boomed Donny.

"I think she was mad at me." he confessed like a kid in grade school admitting he didn't lift the seat in the restroom.

"Why?"

"After doing it about three times, I think she wanted to do it again, but I thought you guys would be waiting for me and I didn't want to miss the ship."

"Three times!" Donny brayed, "three goddamn times? I can't believe it. You mean to tell me, we were waiting for you out here while you were in there! Three times! Aaaaarrgghhhh!" he screamed, running off into the night.

"Golly, what's the matter with him?" asked Tim innocently.

"Nothing. Don't worry about it," I said, "Hey Carlos, we will be able to find him, won't we?"

"Oh si señor. There is only one road in and one road out. We find him. But for now, I think it better he run off some of his passion, yes?"

"Bloody right. Sure didn't get rid of anything in there, did he? Better for all of us." affirmed Nigel, "Well then, let's get old Ricky boy into the car and be off then," casually slapping Tim on the back, almost sending him flying.

"You know something else guys?" warbled Tim, recovering his step, while Nigel and I were peeling Ricky off the hood of the car. "She was really a nice girl."

"Really do you think you're in love?" I asked just a bit sarcastically.

"No, but she kept her boots on during the whole thing."

"What?" I asked.

"Into leather, was she?" asked Nigel pleasantly, as we tossed Ricky into the back seat of the car, on top of the snoring photographers.

"No, I don't think so. The boots laced up to her knees and she said she had to leave them on in case there was a fire."

"Yes, well you can't blame the woman for thinking ahead, now can you?" said Nigel, lumbering into the front seat.

"No I suppose you can't," said Tim, squeezing into the overcrowded back seat,, "But do you think she kept her blouse on for the same reason?"

Nigel looked at me and cleared his throat. I lowered my head to the dash and closed my eyes. I needed a rest.

"Carlos, old boy, where are you? Shall we go then?" yelled Nigel, slapping the side of the car to raise some attention. Carlos ran to the car, hopped in, and we took off. A few miles down the road we found Donny sitting on a large rock on one side of the pavement, dejectedly tossing pebbles into a mud puddle. I gave him my seat upfront next to Nigel, fearing what he might do to Tim if forced to sit next to him.

Paying off Carlos, adding a hefty tip, we boarded the ship with five minutes to spare, a millennia of extra time as far as we were concerned. Sobering up on some tar-like coffee before we hit the wharf, Ricky and the photographers were able to board on their own steam, more or less. As a precaution we thought it might garner too much attention if we attempted to trot up the main gangway, so we entered through the crew entrance instead.

Three days later, after we had dined on fettucine carbonara, sipping our espressos, the ship's Doctor plopped a bottle of pills on the table in front of Donny. "Here's the Tetracycline, compari. Four times a day for ten days, no booze, no "milka," and you'll be "tip-toppa" in no time, eh?"

"What's that for?" asked Lotus, dining with us this evening, making a conscious effort not to smear her make-up while she ate.

"Oh nothing." said Donny casually, "I haven't been feeling well lately."

"Oh really?" she continued, "Because you know, an ex of mine, who shall remain nameless, had to take that stuff for six months after catching a dose of the clap in Bangkok," she mentioned in a casual way, while picking a dot of bacon lodged in her front teeth with a long burgundy colored nail on her pinkie finger.

"It's not for that! I assure you. I've had a bit of a bladder infection, as well as a runny nose these past few days. Seemed to have picked up the sniffles during the layover in Yucatan."

"Stops the drip, drip, dripping, doesn't it." suggested our never-again-naïve Ricky, trying hard not to smirk while stirring his coffee.

Donny didn't answer. He glared at Ricky for a moment and then shoved the bottle of pills into his pocket, waiting for the dining room lights to dim in anticipation of the arrival of a flaming baked Alaska.

I excused myself from the table and headed for one of the upper decks. Reaching the stern, I paused while thick white foam crashed up from the screws, creating a stream of white waves behind the ship, glinting in the moonlight while thousands of stars accented the evening's darkness.

Leaning over the rail I wondered if there was a Patron Saint for Prostitution and Poetic Justice. If not, there should be.

CAST THY BREAD UPON THE WATER

Ecclesiastes XI, 1

SHE is sitting at the bar, somewhat dejectedly. SHE wears a sparkling white cotton polo shirt with a chic polo player logo on the left breast, the type alluding to class distinction, while maintaining an air of sporty indifference. The leather laces on her moccasin style deck shoes, very popular with the preppy set from Hilton Head to Bar Harbor, are tied in rigidly tight bows. Her skirt is khaki and of modest length, zipper and slit in the back. SHE is reading from a well-thumbed volume of a Holy Bible, King James Version, containing dictionary and Concordance, the pages marked with Quick Reference tabs.

SHE looks up and sees him enter. HE wears a pink polo shirt with the same equestrian logo, khaki slacks with cuffs and oxblood penny loafers, without socks. HE carries a leather bound Bible zippered shut, dime store diary style. The leather is embossed with his initials in worn gold, as well as being decorated with simple line drawings of fish and birds, with the phrases "Hallelujah" and "Praise The Lord" stamped in Western style lettering on the front. The spine and the cover are stained to a dark patina, as he carries the volume wherever he goes.

Their eyes meet.

SHE

Blushes and returns to her Bible.

HE

Saunters over and stands next to her. HE clears his throat and rubs his nose with his Bible, being sure she can see the front cover with all its decorations and aphorisms.

                    SHE

Looks up quickly, smiles, shifts about in her seat nervously and quickly returns her gaze to her Bible.

                    HE

   Excuse me miss, I really don't mean to interrupt
   your Bible study, but are you by any chance, Born
   Again?

                    SHE

   (blushing)
   For three years now. I gave my life to the Lord
   during the finalmoments of the Wendel Fergis
   Hilton Head Crusade and Revival.

                    HE

   Praise the Lord! "Many are called, but few are
   chosen." Matthew, twenty-two, fourteen. It was a
   glorious crusade, don't you think?

                    SHE

   You were there?

                    HE

   For all three days!

                    SHE

   No, really?

                    HE

   Sure enough! But, go on with your study, I really
   didn't mean to interrupt.

                    SHE

   Well, "Much learning doth make thee mad."
   Acts, twenty-six, twenty-four. Care to sit down?

                    HE

   Well now, thought you would never ask.

HE sits. They both giggle.

                    HE
        (continuing)

You know, when I first thought about taking a
cruise, I just laughed and laughed. Because, you
know, you hear all those stories about the ungodly activities that just go on day and night. But
to tell you the Gospel Truth, I haven't seen any
evidence of the Devil's work anywhere, let alone
experience it, thank the Lord.

                            SHE

Isn't that funny, neither have I. Praise His Name.
Other than that.

SHE motions toward a statue of a fat naked gent astride a tortoise, a repro from the Boboli Palace Gardens in Florence.

                            SHE
(continuing)
And that's just silly, isn't it?

                            HE

Huh? Oh that. Wow. Yeah, that's silly all right.
These "Eye-talians" are really something, aren't
they?

                            SHE
(giggling nervously)
Aren't they though.

There is a slight awkward pause.

                            HE

Care for a drink?

                            SHE

I beg your pardon, sir?

                            HE

A fruit punch. Or something stronger, a Coke
maybe?

SHE
Oh mercy, (she giggles) for a moment there I thought you were suggesting alcohol.

HE
Never touch the stuff. That is, not since I joined the ranks. Lord knows I went through a time of sowing my wild oats.

SHE
All men should I suppose, shows them the Glory of the Right Way. It's to be expected really. I believe it's John, Chapter Three, Verse Nineteen. Or is it Chapter Nineteen, Verse Three? Let me check.

SHE quickly turns to an indexed page of her Bible.

SHE
(continuing)
Yes, it's three-nineteen, "Men loved darkness rather than the Light, because their deeds were Evil."

SHE looks at him, HE at her, and together they say,

HE & SHE
Hallelujah!

There is a slight pause. The air is electric. They turn away from each other.

HE
Waiter, can we have two fruit punches please? Easy on the ice. Thanks much.

He turns to her.

                         HE
(continued)
So what made you decide to take a cruise?
                         SHE
Well, you know, I heard all those stories, too. And I thought if it really was as bad as all that, it would be a super place to practice some personal evangelism. That was my major at Bob Jones, you know.
                         HE
Glory be to God! Mine too! But I went to Oral Roberts!
                         SHE
Really and truly?
                         HE
Well, more or less.
                         SHE
Well then, as you must know, the fields haven't been all that ripe, Now, have they? Mercy me, if I didn't know better, I would think this Bible scares people away.
                         HE
Well, they fear the Word, they really do. But you keep "fighting the Good fight of Faith" Timothy, six twelve, and you never know what might pop up.
                         SHE
Praise His Body and His Name!!

The fruit punches arrive.

                         HE
"Take thine ease, eat, drink, and be merry." Luke, twelve nineteen.

They clink glasses. They sip.

                        SHE
"Let us eat and drink, for tomorrow we die." First Corinthians, fifteen, thirty-two.

They clink glasses. They smile. They sip.

                        SHE
(refreshed)
Well now, what line of work are you in?
                        HE
Oh, I'm just the owner and general manager of Amazing Grace Exterminating Service and Pest Control.
                        SHE
A business in the name of the Lamb. How glorious!
                        HE
Oh, and that's not all. Our motto is, "Bashing bugs is my bread and butter, but the Lord is my Life!"
                        SHE
Hallelujah, no one can accuse you of serving the "creature more than the Creator," Romans, one, twenty-five.

They both laugh. They both sip. HE makes a slurping sound.

                        HE
Oh my, excuse me!
                        SHE
(giggling coyly)
You sure do like your fruit punch, don't you?
                        HE
(looking into her eyes)
Man does not live by bread alone.
                     HE & SHE
Matthew, Chapter Four, Verse Four.

They both sigh.

SHE
(changing the subject)
Ummm, tell me more about your business.

HE
Well, there's nothing much to tell really. I mean, let's face it, the exterminating business doesn't really have that great of a reputation. So I realized one night, after a really deep session of personal prayer and reflection that I was commissioned in His Name to go out in the world and spread His Word.

SHE
Maranatha!

HE
So right there on the spot I dedicated my life and business to the Lord.

SHE
A truly glorious decision.

HE
I think so. And business has never been better. Let's face it, Jesus sells.

SHE
What?

HE
I mean the Lord sells. I mean look it, I admit it, I'm absolutely not non-profit. You know First Timothy, six, ten, says money is "the root of all evil" not evil its own self. Let's face it, the Lord expects us to make house payments, doesn't he?

SHE
Of course. You own your own house?

HE
Yep, two actually, one in town and a cabin in the mountains. And I have to make car payments, too.

SHE
Certainly. What kind of car do you drive?
HE
A small Humvee. And every now and then the Lord expects you to buy some fancy jewelry like everyone else.
SHE
He sure does. Welfare's communism and it just don't work.
HE
That's for sure. And you see, in this way, it's God's business. I treat my customers with the Lord's principles, I mean, hey, I don't think I'm exploiting the Lord either, in fact, we're helping to get the Love of His Word out among the non-believers. You see, I even had glow-in-the-dark bumper stickers printed up for all my trucks...
SHE
Really? How many trucks do you have?
HE
Twenty-five, but we're growing. I mean, how can we miss when we've got, HONK IF YOU HATE BUGS, BUT LOVE THE LORD, and the outline of a fish, glowing in the dark all over town.
SHE
Glory be to God, in his Name!

There is a pause. HE is exultant. SHE is beaming.

SHE
And to think, when I first saw you walk through those doors I thought to myself, Matthew, Chapter Seven, Verse Fifteen, "Beware of false prophets who come to you in sheep's clothing, but inwardly they are ravening wolves."

SHE giggles.

> HE
> You mean, you actually thought I was a wolf? Me?
> SHE
> Well, there's only one way to find out. I mean, "Ask and it shall be given to you, seek and ye shall find, knock and it shall be opened to you." Matthew, Seven seven.

HE looks into her eyes. SHE into his. HE taps her Bible lightly with his and says,

> HE
> Would you like to get together later this evening to study Scripture?
> SHE
> I'd be delighted. But where?
> HE
> Well, how about my cabin?
> SHE
> Sounds good. Shall we go then?
> HE
> (Taken by surprise)
> Right now? It's not even lunch time yet.
> SHE
> (Placing her Bible on top of his)
> Why wait? "Hope deferred maketh the heart sick." Proverbs, Thirteen twelve.
> HE
> (Taking both Bibles and her hand in his)
> I guess you're right. "To everything there is a season, and a time for every purpose under Heaven. Ecclesiastes, One three, or is it Three one.

SHE

Whither thou goest, I shall go, and where thou lodgest, I will lodge."Ruth, One sixteen, or is it Sixteen one.

HE

(Tenderly placing his Bible on her lips)
Who cares?

HE & SHE

Let's go.

They leave. Hand in hand, Bible to Bible, and heart to heart.

THE FUNERAL AT SEA

Many times during the course of a season it was necessary to prepare for a funeral at sea. In some instances bereaved passengers would arrive with their loved one's ashes in a proper urn and utilize the services of our resident cleric, Father Nunzio. They would hold a brief ceremony, during either sunrise or sunset, on the stern of the ship and spill the ashes into the sea. Afterward they would promptly head for the dining room for whatever meal was scheduled at the time. Some bereaved passengers, having large families or groups of friends booking passage as well, would arrange for a "destination" funeral, and then, afterwards, would attend a low key reception set up in one of the show rooms, piano player optional.

Occasionally, members of the crew or staff would pass away during the course of a cruise, due to a myriad of problems. Many of the sailors, knowing their families couldn't afford the shipment of their bodies back to Portugal or Sicily, would opt for a burial at sea. To facilitate this request, the ship sailed with the necessary equipment and supplies to fulfill their final wishes. Unfortunately, the ship didn't have a morgue of any sort. Even though the refrigerators and freezers on the ship were three decks high, the Head Chef adamantly insisted that a dead body wrapped in a blanket would never share space with his sides of aging prime beef or ice sculptures of leaping dolphins. Rarely were exceptions made. Bottom line, if the body couldn't be off loaded at the nearest port for shipment home, a funeral at sea was the only alternative.

During one cruise, Gomez, the male member of our charming, resident Flamenco Song and Dance Team of "Gomez and Pilar," suddenly passed away due to massive heart failure. At the time we were sailing midway between Saint Thomas and Caracas during a twenty-eight day cruise.

Gomez and Pilar were loved by everyone as permanent members of the entertainment staff. When not performing, they gave complimentary dance lessons, both Ballroom and Flamenco, to any passengers who might be interested. On "International Nights" Gomez and Pilar not only stomped up a Flamenco storm in the showroom, with actual sparks flashing off their heels, thanks to metal taps on their shoes and a few strategically, though secretly, placed metal plates on the showroom stage. Pilar was also featured as a singer of popular Mexican favorites and plaintive Flamenco chansons, with Gomez flailing away with his sharply pointed fingernails on his classical Spanish guitar.

Pilar, based in East Los Angeles, couldn't fathom spending two months at sea with the body of her beloved wrapped in a blanket on a freezer slab somewhere on board. To make things even more difficult, the two of them survived, as many entertainers on a ships do, from cruise to cruise, meaning paycheck to paycheck. Therefore, coming up with the amount of cash necessary to accompany her husband's body on a flight from Caracas to Los Angeles was simply out of the question, and she proudly refused to hear any mention of donations or collections from the staff and crew. She opted for a funeral at sea instead. As she was a revered member of the shipboard family, the Captaino graciously acquiesced.

A short time later, Father Nunzio approached me after morning exercises and asked if I knew where his large white special occasion bible was stored, as he couldn't find it in the church storage locker. This particular closet was home to stacks of hymnals, boxes of yarmulkes, incense, candle sticks and boxes and boxes of fresh communion wafers, packed and wrapped in cellophane like Oreos from the Vatican. In all honesty I was using the large altar bible as a prop for one of the Neil Simon comedies running in the ship's theatre. Asked why he needed it, he replied as only a blasé cleric could, "They're throwing the guy who died last night overboard, and I need to find a couple of prayers."

His demeanor grew way more somber when he found out "the guy" was actually our favorite Gomez.

Until then, Father Nunzio has been clad in a pair of red speedos, Ray-Ban Aviator sunglasses, Gucci sandals and a t-shirt reading appropriately enough "Saint Thomas" on the front, but "Shop at Al Cohen's Discount Liquors" on the back. Oh well.

As this was the first death I had encountered on board, discounting many of the Cruise Director's stand-up routines, I decided to attend. The actual funeral was held on a quiet crew deck around eleven in the evening. This was done to avoid any inquisitive passengers from stopping by with their smart phones with built-in flash, and it gave everyone attending the service a chance to stop by the Midnight Buffet at its conclusion. More importantly, the late hour afforded the crew and pursers the necessary time to prepare and rehearse the obligatory procedures. The body, sewn into a white canvas bag, was placed respectfully on a platform and draped with an Italian flag. The platform was spring released so that, at the proper moment, a lever was pulled, the platform rose majestically, and the body slipped out from under the Italian tri-color and into the evening sea.

Not having been used for funerals all that often, the spring lever on our platform was not in the best working order and was somewhat rusted from lack of use and, of course, the all-pervading salty ocean air. The Head Purser who was supervising the set-up improvised a bit and used his shoelace to tie down the spring lever as securely as possible. The bagged body was gently placed in the platform with the flag draped over it. The guys then had a few minutes to stand around, chat about the latest soccer scores, or smoke a cigarette while waiting for the Capitano and the funeral party to arrive.

A curious Portuguese bellboy sauntered into the area wearing his formal night uniform, a humiliating organ grinder's monkey outfit complete with rows of polished brass buttons on the chest and a pert little pillbox hat with a chinstrap. Ignored by the Italians as most of the Portuguese stewards and bellboys usually were, he surveyed the situation. Noticing the shoelace hanging down from under the shroud, and knowing instinctually that was not right, being true to his job of keeping things tidy, he attempted to remove the shoelace with a stealthy tug.

Nothing happened. He tried again. Still nothing. Challenged now, he summoned up all his strength and gave the stubborn shoelace a last and final pull. The shoelace tore off the lever, the spring released with a rusty twang, the platform slowly began to rise, and Gomez, snuggly wrapped in a pristine canvas bag, slid into the sea with a dull splash.

Pandemonium erupted as the hysterical wrath of a dozen Italian officers rained down on the hapless Portuguese bellboy. Smacked on the back of the head, kicked in the rear, and gestured at with hundreds of unique gestures damning his, his family, and all his progeny, legal or otherwise, to a burning neverending hell, his problems were just beginning.

Down the long passageway Capitano, Father Nunzio, and a bereaved Pilar shrouded in a proper black lace veil, appeared, and slowly began making their way to the vestibule where the final rites were to take place. The Head Purser, envisioning being demoted to working the ferry between Brindisi and Piraeus, swiftly decided on an emergency course of action. Tripping in his own shoe minus the shoelace, he grabbed the bellboy by his ear, dragging him out from under the platform where he was trying to hide. With a sharp slap to the head he sent him down to the magazine to procure another body bag, and once that was done, ordered him to meet him in the vegetable pantry. He then urged all the others to stall the approaching funeral party in the narrow hallway until he returned. He ran off, fuming, cursing and tripping.

Meeting in the kitchen, the Purser supervised the bellboy in stuffing the new body bag with one hundred and fifty pounds of fresh Idaho potatoes. Placing the stuffed body bag on the bellboy's back, they trudged back to the forward hatch, the Purser continually threatening the lad and all his bastard sons with castration if he as much as got a speck of dirt on the crisp white canvas body bag.

Arriving not a moment too soon, they hurriedly placed the bag bulging with a week's supply of fresh potatoes on the platform and readjusted the patriotic Italian flag serving as the shroud. Just as the last fold of the flag was tucked in as neatly as possible under the sack of spuds, the funeral party, unable to be stalled any longer with kisses on both cheeks and words of sincere solace and utmost condolence, arrived at the open bulkhead hatch.

Father Nunzio was in rare form. The officers saluted and, on the cue "...we commend his body to the sea," the Purser released the lever he had been holding personally throughout the entire service. The platform rose with a melancholy creak and the white canvas sack of Idahos slipped into the sea with a muffled splash. The flag was folded and presented to the bereaved Pilar, who was reverently escorted by the Capitano and Father Nunzio back to her cabin for a late night anisette. The bellboy was docked for the potatoes, no hookers or DVDs for him in San Juan this trip, and the Head Purser violently shook his hand attempting to bring it back to life, still cursing the bellboy, with an incessant stream of choice Italian invective. Assured in his mind the poor kid was going directly to hell as soon as he got off the ship, the Purser accompanied his cohorts, officers, and members of the entertainment staff who attended to the Officers' Lounge. Once there they shared a bottle of Absinthe reserved for special occasions. An attending steward solemnly passed out the individual little pitchers of water to drip on the sugar cube, or two, placed on the slotted spoon balanced across the rims of their unique Absinthe flutes. When everyone's originally green Absinthe was thoroughly dripped, sweetened, and turning a milky white, they toasted to the memory of Gomez, knocked back the special concoction, and quickly ordered another round.

THE PARTY NIGHT, OR, HO, HO, HO, HA, HA, HA, ARBIET MACHT FREI!

During the course of a voyage we always scheduled a Party Night into our lists of evening entertainments. Now, this should not be confused with other nighttime festivities cruise ships have made famous. The Costume Night is when, to the hair-pulling chagrin of every cabin steward, passengers delight in wrapping themselves in everything from toilet paper to bed sheets, presenting themselves as the Sheet Family, Bull and Horse. Or, Talent Night, when passengers turn show business, and show business turns, well, it just turns.

What else can be said about a spoon band playing "Maleguena" or a seventy-five- year old grandmother from Minneapolis reciting Joyce Kilmer's "Trees" having decorated herself with palm fronds commandeered from the potted plants in the lounge?

In fact, when the Cruise Director announced the coming event over the public address system in the morning, he obviously didn't understand the double entendre of his glorious compliment: "Ladies and gents, I guarantee you will never see any of these acts anywhere else in the world, ever again!"

That is, if you were lucky. Regardless, the Party Night, in all its hectic lunacy, was clearly distinct from all these other nights. So special, in fact that, before the evening commenced, the Cruise Director hosted a chalk talk with the staff, reviewing and assigning our positions and functions as though he were an NFL coach hours before the Super Bowl. My favorite admonition was, "Do not invite cripples to participate in the Grand March!"

Insensitivity notwithstanding, we regularly ignored his arrogant order, inviting anyone who felt the feeling to bump and grind in three-quarter time while the band played highlights from the "Colonel Bogey March," "Gaieties Parisienne," and "The Stars and Stripes Forever."

One evening a man rushed up to me, flushed and out of breath, clutching his chest and pleading for a glass of water. Immediately taking him to the bar, I asked if he was feeling okay, and he gasped, "Oh sure. I feel fine. Just a little tight in the chest. I want to take one of my nitro-glycerin tablets so I don't miss the Grand March." Now, is that dedication to a good time or what?

Luckily, we never lost anyone during a Grand March. Once in a while an overzealous soul tripped over his own cane or someone lost a contact lens. One memorable night, a man's pinky ring snagged a ladies wig, it went flying, and her stash of iridescent condoms went ricocheting all over the ballroom. These were minor problems and we endured.

The actual evening consisted of a series of contests and simple games involving passengers as volunteers and hundreds of balloons, pairs of long johns, spoons, tin cans, top hats, ping pong balls, bottles of beer, drawings for bottles of champagne, dance contests, relay races, sing-alongs, and drawings for more bottles of champagne, with everything culminating in a conga line or Grand March, traipsing all over the ship, ending up back in the ballroom.

You might wonder how a group of well-meaning professional revelers could coerce a ballroom full of jaded folks, still digesting an eight course meal, into the swing of things. It wasn't easy. We usually began by organizing a community sing of the "Schnitzelbank Song," telling our passengers it was an authentic German beer *schlager* sung in beer gardens throughout the Continent. Not really true, as most Germans I've met have never heard of the tune. As the majority of our guests had never been out of their home state, let alone frequented a German beer hall, no one was going to argue. Making everyone in the Main Showroom intertwine arms, we encouraged them to sway back and forth and sing —

"Ist das night ein Schnitzelbank?"

"Ja das ist ein Schnitzelbank."
"Ist das nicht ein Kurtz und Lang?"
"Ja das ist ein Kurtz und Lang."
"Kurtz und Lang, Schnitzelbank..."
"Oh, die shoene Schnitzelbank..."
"Oh, die shoene Schnitzelbank..."

— gathering speed and momentum with each verse, of which there were many, until everyone was blithering nonsense, and having a wonderful time.

Because of our lusty Teutonic opening, we enlisted the help of Ursula, Chief Purser Gino's intermittent traveling companioness. They were close personal friends at least twice a week, and for the remainder of the cruise Ursula waltzed about the ship socializing as best she could, quite bemused from peppermint schnapps and Liebfraumilch, brought on board just for her.

She did come in handy one cruise when a group of German tourists grew petulant because we had them sit with a group of hearing-impaired passengers during bingo. Donny scrawled the numbers on the back of bar menus, Ricky held them up, and I called the numbers. With the highest of dudgeon, the German tourists felt because they didn't speak English fluently, was no reason to treat them like "sick" people. Ursula translated for them after that, and they were happy as hasenpfeffer for the remainder of their trip.

The staff affectionately referred to Ursula as "Eva" because of her thick accent and what seemed like her inability to bend her knees when she walked. We wrote this all off as part of her charm. Occasionally, her congenital air of racial superiority surfaced in veiled nasty comments about African-Americans, Portuguese, English, Russians, and the dreaded "New Yorkers," which we all realized was her code word for Jewish passengers, many of whom, according to her, were her best friends, along with Italians, of whom one in particular she slept with. Extremely sensitive about her forefathers' fascist, perhaps, perish the thought, Nazi past, she retorted to the subtlest of innuendo with a huffy, "Vell, my parents veren't Nazis, you know. Dey vere Swiss."

Certainly, and Mr. Eichmann was a travel agent. But who were we to judge?

There was always talk among the more vociferous Communists among the crew, most of whom were of the ilk who, when asked if they were Italian, replied, "No, we're from Palermo," that they were planning to throw her to the sharks one convenient evening. Thankfully, at the last minute, they always felt a tinge of compassion for the sharks and decided against it.

This one Party Night, the time arrived for the Grand March, so we all assumed our positions throughout the ballroom. Ursula stood center stage, resembling an over-the-hill supernumerary from a Wagnerian opera who, years ago, lost her way in a forest of bratwurst and beer. She gleefully grabbed the hand of a diminutive elderly gent in the front row and, acting as a link, joined hands with the man sitting directly across the aisle. Basking in all her Aryan glory, she led the singing and swaying, while the band clamorously pumped out the tune to, "Ist das nicht ein Schnitzelbank..."

Unbeknownst to Ursula, the small man whose hand she joyously held and swayed with had 769885-D hideously tattooed to his forearm in fading purple ink.

Afterwards, she could not understand why so many people in her section did not get in the swing of things, and merely stared.

No one told her why. Nothing would have changed, history or attitude. Besides, it was just another night on a cruise ship and everyone just wanted to have a good time.

THE ARRIVAL OF BABO NATALE, OR, ISN'T IT AMAZING AROUND CHRISTMAS TIME EVERYONE LOOKS LIKE AN ANGEL

None of the staff looked forward to the Christmas cruise. Being far from home and loved ones was reason enough, but for all of us employed on the ship the holidays held a dubious significance. Granted, we complained now and then about our passengers running the gamut in age between silver haired and golden oldie, but it was always easier dealing with mature adults than with children. Admittedly, at times it was rather difficult to tell the difference. The Christmas cruise held the distinction of having the ship invaded with the pitter patter of at least one hundred little feet under the age of twelve and two to three hundred usually sneakered feet under the gangly yet rambunctious age of sixteen. During a "normal" voyage we expected ten children or fewer under the age of twenty-one, so having four hundred or more screamers descend on our home was certainly out of the ordinary—pestilential, in fact.

The Home Office considered the ship sold out with a passenger manifest of about two thousand or so. With a crew of one thousand, this guaranteed a comfortable passenger-to-crew ratio of roughly two-to-one. Thus, meticulous attention, service and a relaxing leisurely atmosphere were assured. Come Christmas time, all bets were off. With families traveling together, along with children utilizing the pull down bunks in each cabin, the passenger manifest could swell to over three thousand or more, though the dimensions of the ship remained insufficiently the same.

Because of the crowded conditions, we had to go out of our way to accommodate the sudden influx of children while, at the same time, providing the same excellent service our older passengers expected. Five to ten additional children's counselors were hired to compliment the five we had on board at all times. Crates of expensive toys, video games, and toiletries for the teenagers had to be gift wrapped by the staff, usually as punishment for having arrived late to a planned activity or sleeping through a muster drill. We crossed our fingers and privately warned our little imps they would get arrested if they pulled a fire alarm. Worse yet, if they intentionally threw ping-pong balls over the side, we would throw them in to retrieve them. There was little we could do about the teenagers, with sophisticated educations, who decided it was great fun going skinny dipping in the pools after hours. We just prayed they remembered to bring their towels.

Another special treat arranged primarily for the children, although we all enjoyed participating in it, was a Christmas party, or *Feste Di Natale* in Italian. The shipwide festivities climaxed with the arrival of Babo Natale or, as he is known in English, Santa Claus. One of the First Purser's most important responsibilities was staging the arrival of the jolly old fat man on Christmas Day. He hoped, year after year, it would lead the way to an eventual promotion to Chief Purser. As a younger man it was rumored our First Purser had aspirations of being a *directore* of the opera in Milano. He never achieved that goal either, but he did play a Babylonian torchbearer in *Nabucco* some years ago, so his operatic experience was close enough to direct the Christmas Feste on the ship.

This noteworthy Christmas we were anchored outside the breakwater of Puerto Vallarta, Mexico. Instead of docking at the local pier, the Capitano decided to anchor a discreet distance from the town as plumbers were flown in from California to make emergency repairs to the sewage and disposal system. An intricate, delicate system on any ship, the system on the "Luna Sea" was constantly malfunctioning and breaking down. Intermittent clouds and rain had accompanied us all the way from Los Angeles, and many of the passengers were getting cranky with the staff and officers for their inability to procure sunny weather. I overheard a woman complaining to a deckhand coiling a length of rope, who probably didn't understand a word of what she was grousing about, "Well, I'm not blaming you, of course, but what the hell are those lazy bums doing about all this lousy weather?" She pointed off to a group of skinny Speedo-clad gents laying out on the Officers Sun Deck. The fact that it was an overcast day didn't matter to them; time off was time off, so they had to take advantage of it.

In addition to all this, by the time Babo was scheduled to arrive, about one in the afternoon, most of the passengers had already been ashore and were curdling because most of the shops were closed just because it was Christmas Day. We were in very Catholic Mexico and it's an essential facet of the Mexican national character to take time off for celebration and the betterment of one's life and wellbeing above all else. Unlike their North American visitors who, when hard at work may be given a ten minute break in the afternoon and think it's a gift, any self-respecting Mexican will take the entire afternoon off, calling it a *siesta*, and consider it a right ordained by God, or at least common sense. They usually return to work in the late afternoon keeping their shops open into the early evening, but certainly not on Christmas Day. The idea of violating their cultural right simply because a shipload of gringos was wandering about town looking for sombreros and piñatas was absurd, if not downright blasphemous.

Try as we might to explain the nuances of Mexican culture to our passengers, they simply weren't having it. The popular understanding seemed to be that the boarded-up shops were an example of blatant Anti-Americanism, and I'm sure, after the cruise, many Congressmen were notified about it.

Meanwhile, on shore, our First Purser was busy preparing and directing our Christmas Feste. Earlier in the day he had easily managed to persuade our Cruise Director to play the role of Babo Natale. He enjoyed this as much as he looked forward to wrapping his crotch in a small deck towel like a diaper, donning a pink baby bonnet, and then chasing a Social Director who was carrying a boathook, dressed in flowing white robes as a white-bearded

Father Time throughout the ship five minutes before twelve every New Year's Eve.

The First Purser also drafted Lotus, the curvaceous ship's secretary, to play an angel, accompanying Santa on his journey in a decorated dinghy, toward the ship. The problem was that he was at a loss to find another young lady to play a second angel, balancing out the tableau. The Cruise Director came to the rescue. Seems we had a showgirl traveling with us who, for lack of a better name, we'll call Bambi. Because she was not getting union scale for her work, she decided, previous to boarding, she might as well have a good time. She facilitated this wish by attempting to have sex with as many different men as she could during the course of the season. She had been doing quite well up to this point, as many of the staff and crew would gladly agree, although she had not as yet had the pleasure of the Cruise Director's company. The Cruise Director considered it part of his life's work to seek the company of as many women as he could during the course of a cruise. He felt spending any part of a cruise alone to be a sin against all that was holy. Coincidentally, he had not had the pleasure of Bambi's company.

The Cruise Director insisted the First Purser use Bambi as the other angel, figuring it was a dandy way to meet her, as well as solving the Feste's casting dilemma. The Purser, well aware of the buxom young lady's less-than-sterling reputation, was aghast at the mere mention of such a sacrilege. The Cruise Director insisted, threatening to throw the entire Babo Natale costume over the side if he didn't get his way. The Purser, crossing himself and then biting the knuckle of his index finger, reluctantly agreed.

On Christmas morning, I was awakened before dawn by a terror-riven scream emanating from Lotus' cabin. Rushing to her aid, I found her sitting cross-legged on her bed in a heap, smoking a cigarette, wrapped in a fluffy pink chenille bathrobe, no make-up, her hair in a jumble revealing black roots, looking like the star of a government produced film on drug abuse or wife beating. Standing on her nightstand was a pregnancy test, showing the two dreaded red lines. She was with child. Absent-mindedly acknowledging my entrance, I soon realized she wasn't all that upset about being blessed, but was in a complete tizzy trying to figure out who the father was. Leafing through her calendar book like a woman possessed, she was desperately trying to recognize whose time was about right to pin a fatherhood rap on. Principal among the candidates, and there were a few, was none other than Marty, our stalwart Cruise Director, bless his philandering little heart.

Marty had already skipped ashore, Babo Natale outfit stuffed in a duffle bag, and he and Bambi were making a beeline for El Set, a popular beach bar just south of Puerto Vallarta's Gringo Gulch, an exclusive enclave of American ex-pats, hence its name.

El Set was the perfect spot for a few eye-opening cocktails. This popular beach side watering hole was open every day of the year and was supposedly Richard Burton's favorite spot while on location with Elizabeth Taylor during the shooting of *Night of the Iguana* some years back. Touted as one of the film's sets, the place was replete with a thatched roof and assorted movie business paraphernalia. Although few see the famous actor when they enter the wildly decorated establishment, many will swear he was sitting right next to them reciting Welsh poetry by the time they are ready to leave. Must be the potency of the locally distilled mescal, or swallowing too many of the supposedly hallucinogenic worms that float around in every bottle.

Back at the dock, the Purser spent most of the morning supervising the decoration of one of the lifeboats as Babo's nautical sleigh. Using an assortment of tropical flora as well as apples and poinsettia blossoms pilfered from the ship, he also utilized crepe paper streamers taken from our costume night decoration stash, lots of crumpled tin foil, and even a few coconuts netted out of the harbor flotsam. When he was done, he kissed his fingers, congratulating himself on the masterpiece he had created.

He commandeered the showroom band, Il Parmigiana, the name having nothing to do with the popular main course of veal and cheese. It simply meant "The Boys from Parma." The boys were assigned to provide the music. The combo consisted of a snare drum and cymbal, sax, trumpet, trombone, and a guitar.

The Purser insisted they wear the outfits the dining room waiters wore for the "Evening In Paris" night: red and blue stripped boat necked jumpers, black cummerbunds and tuxedo pants, and a red beret, worn at jaunty angles befitting each individual musician's taste and degree of drug absorption. You see, not all that excited about an early morning gig, and being that El Set was ordered off limits to them by the Purser, the musicians stood milling around on the dock puffing on crooked little cigarettes while trying to identify parts of the female anatomy being formed by the darkening clouds, much to the Purser's chagrin and disgust.

The First Purser continued to run around barking orders through a megaphone like Verdi himself preparing for the Grand March during the premiere performance of *Aida*. He was completely oblivious to the threatening clouds and high seas beginning to churn up just beyond the breakwater.

Lotus stormed ashore, ignoring the preparations, as enraged as a Valkyrie returning to Valhalla without a dead Viking. She grabbed a cab and headed directly for El Set determined to confront our Cruise Director with her calendar book and proof beyond question that he was indeed the source of the two red lines in her pregnancy test. She carried the incontrovertible proof in her purse, tightly wrapped in a lace hanky.

Heedless of the coming storm, Marty and Bambi were now licking salt off one another's chins, before knocking back shots of tequila and chomping down on slices of lime.

Stomping into the bar, our prudent secretary realized almost immediately that making our Cruise Director fess up to being a papa was as probable as the Pope endorsing party-colored prophylactics. By now both Marty and Bambi were in advanced stages of boisterous drunken dementia. They were delighting in throwing lime slices at each other as well as spitting mouthfuls of tequila at the restaurant's scarlet Macaw, who was screaming, "Fire!" with each drenching spritz. This situation jolted the otherwise logical secretary into rethinking her position, or at least her approach. She decided to be a lady about the entire matter. No vain displays of hysterics, no violence; style and grace all the way. Calmly approaching their table like a Nun selling raffle tickets, she blew it at the last moment. Smacking the Cruise Director upside the head with her diary, she screamed, "I'm pregnant, you son-of-a-bitch, and it's time to play Santa Claus!"

Exiting with a flourish, she took a waiting cab back to the dock, satisfied she had done everything possible to gain his attention, considering the condition he was in. She concluded getting pregnant was one of those calculated risks a woman has to take occasionally, like going on a blind date or acquiring bikini tan lines. Taking responsibility and paying for her abortion, well, that's another issue altogether. Not wanting to lose precious impression points with Miss Bambi, she felt assured Marty would volunteer to come up with some cash.

When Bambi and her beau finally arrived at the dock, the Purser was beside himself, fearing the pair had been arrested for running around naked on the beach, or worse. Our Ship's Secretary, in her angel dress, wings, and tin foil halo, was smoking a cigarette and sulking at the end of the pier. She refused to take one step toward the lifeboat until the Cruise Director and "What's-Her-Name" were in position ready to go. The band, who had already been in place for some time now, were all getting queasy from the waves knocking the decorated lifeboat against the dock like a bathtub toy. Beyond the breakwater, it looked as though a typhoon were raging. With each set of swells that made it into the harbor, the boat rose a few feet, scraping loudly against the barnacle-encrusted dock, and then plummeted back down the next moment, crashing into the water with an eyeball jarring slap, and then the entire process began once again. The members of the band, holding on for dear life, were all a sickly shade of green, while the decorations were all dripping with foamy seawater.

The Cruise Director, laughing and falling over Bambi as she valiantly attempted to dress him in the Santa suit, tumbled and crawled his way back toward the dock. A light drizzle had begun to fall, so the grass stains on the Cruise Director's knees didn't look so bad, as the entire costume was turning a very dark shade of red, as velvet has a tendency to do when soaking through.

Primping, pushing, and cursing the two of them toward the boat, the Purser had to time shoving them onto the moving boat at the perfect moment. If he didn't, he ran the risk of tossing them into the roiling harbor. The boat was still rhythmically crashing into the side of the dock, picking up momentum as the waves grew bolder. Once they were safely on board, Lotus begrudgingly attempted to step on board, courageously batting off the all-too-friendly hands of the band members rushing to assist her. She assumed her position beside Babo Natale and the "other" angel, her halo askew. The First Purser had to order the band members to assist him on board but, once secure, he assumed a position at the head of the craft, like Julius Caesar crossing the Tiber. After checking that all was shipshape, the angels, one copping an attitude, the drunken Babo falling off his throne, the stoned musicians and a few sailors attempting to keep everything from capsizing, the Purser gave the command to shove off.

All of us who remained on the ship had no idea any of this was going on as we had a few problems own to deal with. We displayed the gifts on the aft section of the Promenade Deck, wrapped and beribboned under a huge spreading palm tree we brought on board expressly for the occasion. The trunk and all the branches were wrapped with white twinkling lights that waved and creaked in the gathering winds. The visual impact was muddled somewhat when we were forced to cover the gifts with the large table sized plexiglass bubbles we used to keep flies off the petit-fours during afternoon tea. Today, they kept the drizzle off the toys and games.

With the waves picking up, and a lightly falling rain, the majority of the passengers had attempted to squeeze under a small canvas awning with wildly jiggling chi-chi balls. The overhang was there to protect the poolside bar and its usually thirsty patrons from what is ordinarily a bright tropical sun. We were quickly reminded just why we had to anchor outside the breakwater when the engineers finally repaired the ailing plumbing system.

Seconds after I announced over the public address system that a strange vessel had been sighted circling the ship with a very jolly fat man in a red and green suit (he was an Italian Santa after all) assisted by two lovely angels, the pipes were flushed out with a trembling grumble. This freed a nasty blockage with fumes to match, and everything exploded unceremoniously from the stern, thundering like a flatulent indiscretion by a hundred-thousand-ton duck. If the ship had been moving, most of the heady fragrance would have dissipated in the wake left behind us. Unfortunately, we were at anchor, being buffeted by a storm coming ashore and not away from us. This caused the entire stern of the ship—the twinkling tinsel, streaming palm tree, presents, passengers, everything—to be enveloped in a noxious cloud of invisible fumes that could have been used in lieu of tear gas by any police department worldwide.

Meanwhile, the band played "Jingle Bells" and "She'll Be Coming Around the Mountain When She Comes," the only traditional American tunes they knew. Our two lovely angels, one drunk and getting seasick, and the other one suffering from morning sickness and who knows what else, were doing all they could to keep the pleasantly bemused Babo Natale seated in an upright position between them. They tried to ignore the fact he was having great fun bailing water out of the overflowing bilge just inches below their feet, keeping in character all the while, shouting, "Ho! Ho! Ho!" and waving his sopping wet cap to the passengers lining the decks. Occasionally he would inadvertently smack one of the doting angels in the face with the wet cap, but everyone just thought it was part of the fun.

The Purser was shouting orders to the deckhands to lower the appropriate cables immediately, as he wasn't exactly sure just how much longer the violently thrashing life boat was going to stay afloat. He was loathe to order emergency conditions as the orange life jackets would have completely ruined the colorful holiday *mise en scene* he had so painstakingly created.

Through all this chaos, the passengers were having a wonderful time, merrily snapping photos and precariously balancing their selfie-sticks with their backs turned from the swaying rail in order to frame the perfect shot. There were comments that ran the gamut from, "isn't it wonderful that an Italian ship went all out for an American holiday," "weren't those angels the prettiest little things you ever did see," and, "who could ask for a jollier Santa?"

Miraculously, the lifeboat was hoisted aboard without incident. Santa, the angels, and the band, seriously drenched to the skin, made their way to the stern and commenced handing out the gifts. The noxious cloud having long since blown toward Vallarta, there was some lingering fragrance wafting about, but nothing one couldn't deal with as long as you didn't breathe through your nose. Alas, Lotus breathed through her nose and ran from the stern, holding her mouth and clutching her stomach, a trail of white chicken feathers from her tattered wings following behind. The Cruise Director and Bambi, both three sheets to the wind, were having the time of their lives distributing gifts to one and all as though they were the stars of a Branson. Missouri Christmas special. I hope none of the guests was any the wiser.

Later that evening, while the ship was sailing comfortably to Mazatlan, the storm long having passed, Bambi pranced down to the Cruise Director's cabin. She was clad in a tiny string bikini she had purchased in Cabo and carried a magnum of Dom Perignon with two frosted flutes sticking out of an ice bucket. Knocking on the cabin door, she purred, "Oh Santa honey, your little helper is here with a surprise."

The door swung open, she twinkled in, and the two of them were not seen or heard from again until late the following day.

Lotus, on the other hand, ever the realist, was seen entering the casino near closing time. Calendar book in hand, she waited patiently at a small table as the dashing baccarat dealer snapped out the last hand of the evening. Though born and raised in Chicago, he called out the game in a beguiling European accent of some sort, making all the ladies drool. He noticed our Ship's Secretary sitting alone, coyly smiling at him and fanning herself with her calendar book. He winked and smiled back at her. She didn't return the flirty gesture because, understandably, patience, even for an angel can run thin, especially during the holiday cruise.

CONCERNING THE REMOVAL OF LUGGAGE

The evening before docking at a major debarkation port all luggage is gathered by the stewards no later than six o'clock the evening before and stacked on the portside of the promenade deck. A sight eliciting a sense of awe from any luggage salesman, the pile was five to six hundred feet long, running the entire length of the ship from the bow to the stern. Piled ten feet out from the bulkhead and just as high, the bags were all bedecked with colorful tags that wiggled wildly in the evening breezes. The tags delineated the order in which they would be taken off the ship. Red went first, blue next, and so on. This was done for two reasons. First, all the folks having early flight connections at the local airports or those who handed an understanding officer a crisp twenty were afforded the luxury of leaving the ship before all the others.

The second reason was a bit more interesting. In all the major American ports, including San Juan, Puerto Rico, all the luggage was removed from the ship even before even an ailing crewman or impatient passenger was allowed to set foot in the terminal. The bags were placed in orderly rows on the dock, and then, out of the early dawn mists, a cadre of Customs agents and their specially trained golden retrievers, German shepherds, and a beagle named "Bucky" appeared. Each dog sniffed at each bag with the specific instructions to find their specialties, exotic herbs, and chemicals from the tropics—ideally marijuana, cocaine, or heroin. Open packages of meats, cheeses, or any agricultural products, in addition to improperly tanned taxidermy, were considered contraband as well. Occasionally, a homemade Mariachi band, consisting of bull frogs obviously stuffed by an amateur, or baby

Caymans, alligators, or an occasional armadillo, eviscerated and cured in the sun and then crammed with cotton balls, were nasty illegal contraband all.

Once a dog signaled with a quiet yelp, then sat down beside the offending bag. It was tagged by an agent and the dog was rewarded with a tasty little treat. The passengers with the tagged bags were herded into another line and the bag was politely torn apart by a salivating Customs agent eager for a bust. The hapless passenger standing behind a thick red line about three feet from the inspection table could only look on in dismay, silently praying the Customs officer didn't notice the night club ashtrays or ships towels that accidently popped into their luggage while packing. After all, how was a passenger going to wrap a damp bathing suit, or store a pair of earrings, or some delicate bridgework?

More often than not, they simply found a half-eaten sausage or a huge leg, complete with black hoof, of Iberico ham, with just a few thin slices missing. Factory-sealed foods were perfectly legal but, once opened, or even slightly sampled on the ship, the tasty snacks became infectious contraband capable of destroying American farming nationwide. To prevent that, the goodies were placed on a table and no doubt became a casual buffet picnic for the agents once the docks were cleared.

One might think an inspection procedure based on an over-zealous Beagle trying to please might be a bit much, considering the strongest drug most passengers used regularly, other than a few prescriptions, was Preparation H or Maalox. Try telling that to the agent who once busted a Lilliputian grandma from Tacoma with a shopping bag from Josephina's Fine Knitting, Caracas with just shy of a million dollars' worth of prime uncut cocaine. I bet you he would giggle.

One sleepless evening I decided to take a stroll along the Promenade Deck, a bad idea to begin with as it had a tendency to attract the heartier insomniacs thanks to its sheltered passageway. Regardless, there I was, leaning over the rail, some ten hours and two hundred nautical miles away from Miami, but very much at sea. I was serenely accompanied by the evening sky, the drone of the engines, and the whoosh of the huge iron swan cutting through the black sea causing a crispy foam to bubble up from under the bow, disappearing mysteriously into the muscular swells. The sea, with moonlight glinting and shimmering off the obsidian blackness, resembled a huge cauldron of undulating smooth black silver. There we were, this white mechanized behemoth cutting easily through it all.

My relaxing reverie was abruptly interrupted by a forceful drilling on my shoulder. Startled, I turned and saw a passenger one would never expect to see on a partially abandoned deck on an almost eerie night like this. She was a mature woman, probably traveling alone, clad in a loud print dress, Cardigan sweater buttoned up to her neck, tennis shoes printed with flowers, and a faux Gucci scarf drawn tightly around her head, tied with a tight bow under her chin.

"Yes Mrs. McDougal, what can I do for you?" After long cruises I seemed to have developed an uncanny ability to remember most of the passenger's names, primarily those who always had something to say about anything and everything occurring on the ship. I forgot their names equally as fast once they left the ship, amazing even myself.

"How come they haven't taken the bags off the ship yet?"

"I beg your pardon?" thinking I had misunderstood her question.

"I said," she repeated growing a bit huffy, "how come they haven't taken the bags off the ship yet? You said we had to be packed by six!"

"Well, let me explain," I began, trying to figure out a way to gently explain this visibly upset soul, the world of illicit drugs, dogs, and overzealous Customs agents looking for commendations.

"Look, I don't want to hear about tags or anything else!" she cut in.

"Well, ma'am, I'll tell you what, just where do expect us to put the luggage? We're still about two hundred miles at sea, you know?"

"That's no excuse!" she scolded, slashing her finger at me as though it were a sabre, "if we had to be packed so early before arrival, all the bags should all be off the ship by now."

"Right! You are absolutely correct!" I finally surrendered to this soul with whom the simplest logic had about as much chance as removing a speck of dirt from your eye with boxing gloves. "If it will make you any happier, why don't you just point out your bags to me and I'd be happy to throw them overboard."

"Forget it! Just forget it! It's too late now. But I'll tell you one thing, this is the last time I will ever sail on your ship!"

"Thank-you." I said, quickly making my way to one of the upper decks, where I should have been in the first place. Amidships, I heard her calling. "Excuse me, sonny boy! I found my bags here. Pull it out for me. I need my toothbrush and suppositories!"

"Look for a steward!" I called back politely, rounding a corner and bounding up a ladder marked Crew Only.

Passengers forgetting essential items in their packed bags occurred often. Once the bags were stacked on the deck though, nothing short of a Papal Decree could convince a steward to dive into a ten foot high stack of overstuffed suitcases.

One morning a stately gentleman and his wife discovered the evening before that they had inadvertently packed all their traveling clothes. By the time they came running to the Purser's office, we were docked and the bags had been brought ashore. By the time we had Customs clearance, their bags had been thoroughly sniffed, loaded on trucks, and were headed for the airport. By the time we rushed the man and his wife to the airport, the ever efficient shore staff had already registered the couple and their bags nestled comfortably in the cargo hold of a 747. The man and his wife flew all the way back to Boston in Brooks Brothers pajamas and a nightgown from Bonwits.

THE END, OR: IT'S GREAT WHEN YOUR SHIP COMES IN, IT'S EVEN BETTER WHEN YOU ARE ON IT

On the last night of my final cruise I threw one of my official ship's ties overboard. I considered dumping the entire uniform but felt a bit concerned for the schools of sharks swimming alongside the ship anticipating the sacks of garbage thrown overboard daily. In spite of what I felt about the uniform, and regardless of what sharks feel about garbage, I was sure they would choke on that much polyester. I could not let that happen with a clear conscious.

When I go fishing, even to this very day, I fear sooner or later I will catch a cabazon, or other such grotesque denizen of the deep with a ship's tie around his gills, tied with an impeccable Windsor knot. I will remove the tie and the ugly fish will metamorphose into an even uglier frog. Oh well, on a journey to becoming a Prince, one should expect to spend some time as a frog. If you are among the lucky, you may eventually be given shore leave by the kiss of a Princess.

If you don't believe me, either book passage on any one of the hundreds of cruise ships currently plying the world's oceans, or better still, hire on as a member of the cruise staff in any capacity available, and you will surely find out for yourself.

The Author, as John Hancock, in a National Tour of "1776", USA, (1975)

Cameraman, "Every Second Counts" Manama, Bahrain, United Arab Emirates, 2010

The Author, conferring with Director, on set of "The New Newlywed Game" Hollywood, c 1991

The Author, with Roger Rabbit and Minnie Mouse, NAPTE Convention, Houston, c 1990

The Author, with Ringo Starr, "All Star Tour", Los Angeles, c 1999

The Author, with Santa, TSS Luna Sea, Puerto Vallarta, Mexico, c 1983

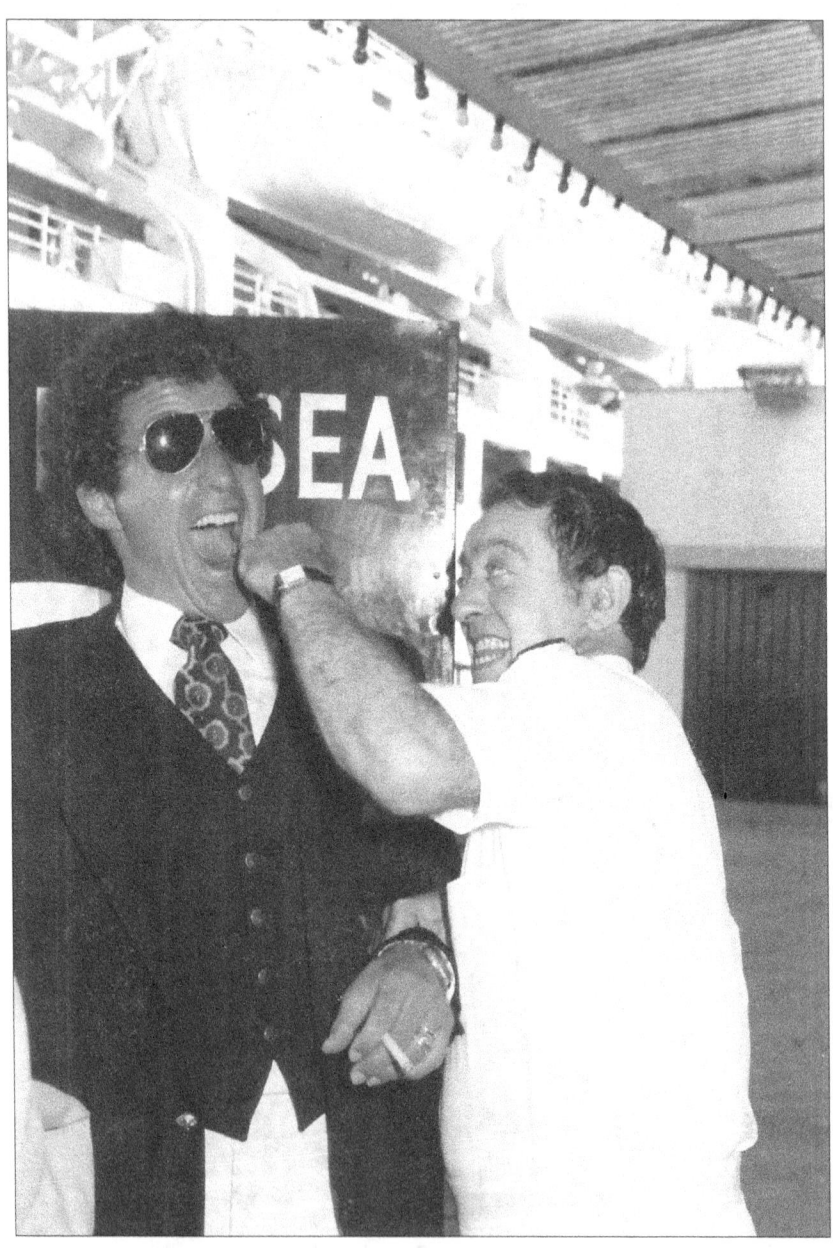

The Author, discussing policy with Capitano, TSS Luna Sea, c 1983

The Author, producing Pet Day, The Dating Game, Hollywood, c 1991

Publicity Shot - "Let's Make A Deal" Walt Disney World, Orlando, MGM Studios, Dick Clark, Ron Greenberg, Bob Hilton, Model, Monty Hall, The Author, c 1988

The Author, with models and Host, "Wheel of Fortune Live!" MGM Grand, Las Vegas, 2000

The Author, Asking questions, "The Dating Game" Pilot, Hollywood, c 1985

Monty Hall, Burt Lancaster, on the set of "Let's Make A Deal" Walt Disney World, Orlando, Florida, MGM Studios, 1988

Hollywood Squares, Mexico City production, c 1995

Lobby Card, Les Cavaliers Du Diable (Vendetta), c 1975

The Author, First Resume Shot, New York, 1974

John Marley, The Author, Lee Van Cleef, on the set of Vendetta, Eilat, Israel, 1975

The Author as Father Time, New Years Eve, TSS Luna Sea, c 1983

A Sales Executive, The Author, Bob Eubanks, Paul Rodriguez, A Producer, on the set of The New Newlywed Game, *Hollywood, c 1991*

Classical Vietnamese Orchestra, playing "Raindrops Keep Falling On My Head" and assorted pop tunes for formal dinner in honor of The Author, having taught a seminar on television production, Ho Chi Minh City, Saigon International Film School, 2015

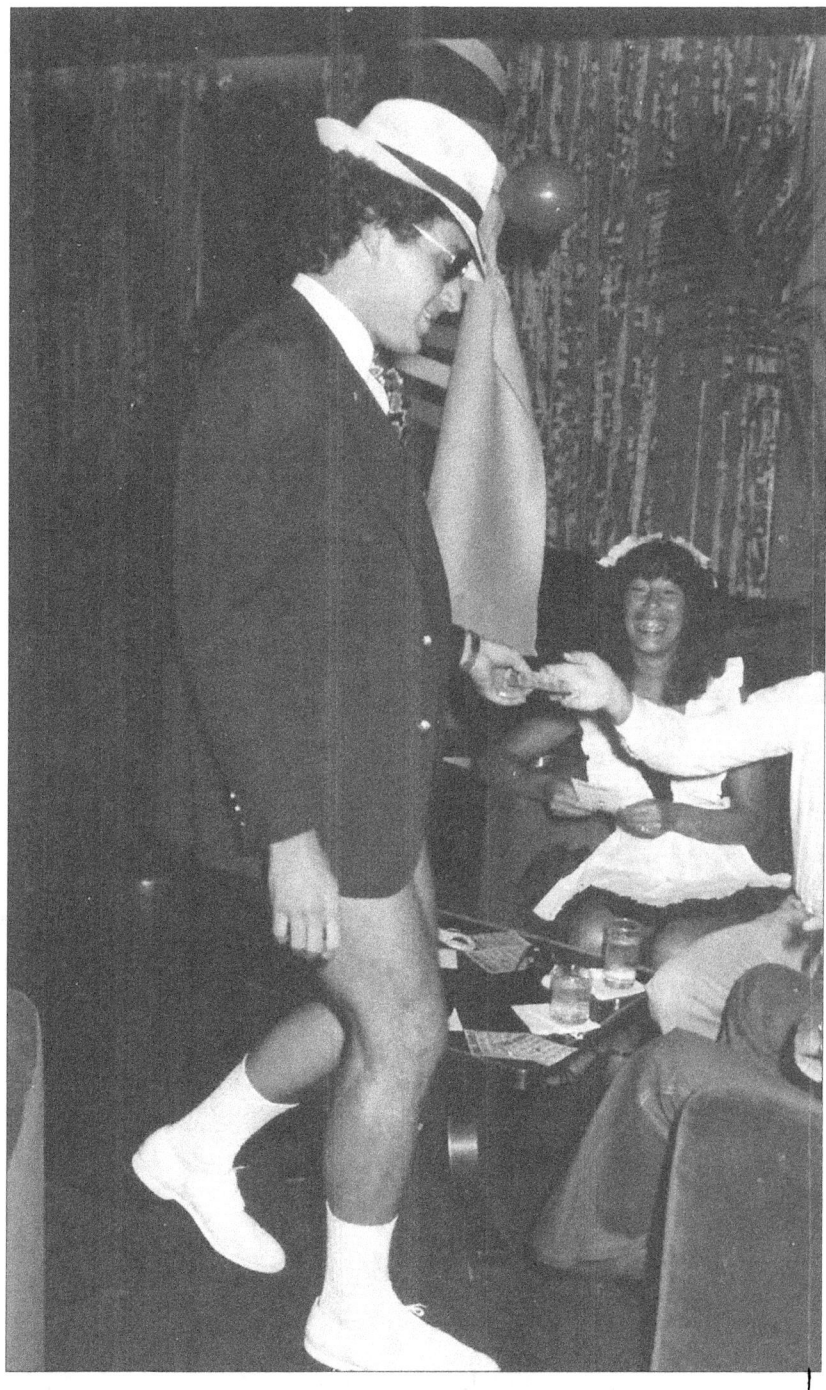

The Author, Costume Night, TSS Luna Sea, c 1983

The Author, wearing pirates hat, at the Writers Table, The All New Newlywed Game *Bob Eubanks Hosting, 1987, Hollywood*

The Author with Ringo Starr, Daughter Peregrine and wife Geraldine, c 1999

The Author, as Toad Of Toad Hall, Mount Holyoke Summer Theatre, 1973

The Author, on guard duty, Golan Heights, Kibbutz Gonen, Upper Galilee, Israel, 1975

"Kid Vengeance" (renamed for American release of Vendetta), theatre marquis in Hollywood, 1977

Catalog Listing, featuring The Author, for The Saigon International Film School, 2015

Shrine to TV Station personnel killed by Russians while defending the station during Russian expulsion, Vilnius, Lithuania, 1990

The Author, leading "Warm-ups" on set of "Let's Make A Deal", MGM Studios, Walt Disney World, 1988

The Author, leading "Warm-ups', on tour with "Wheel of Fortune Live!" 1999

The Author, explaining show rules, "Wheel of Fortune Live!" 1999

The Author, as First Officer of Entertainment, welcoming passengers on board, TSS Luna Sea, Caracas, Venezuela, c 1983

Part II: Still at Sea . . . But Attempting to Plant My Feet in Hollywood

OH, BRAVE NEW WORLD, THAT HATH SUCH CREATURES IN

After a few seasons on the ship I returned to Los Angeles. I had a few dollars in my bank account, so I figured now was as good a time as any to book a flight to somewhere exotic and see what there was to be seen there. A travel agent in Los Angeles suggested the cheapest flight at the time would be a round trip to Reykjavík, Iceland on Icelandic Air. I could then hop a "puddle jumper" to either Cairo, Tel Aviv, or Beirut. Flights to either city cost about the same, and it would get me to the farthest reaches of backpack civilization at the time. After staying a few days or so, I could book another flight to Istanbul and work my way back to Reykjavik via Europe and then back to Los Angeles. Sounded like a plan. I booked a flight to Tel Aviv and then a two-week "student" a.k.a. "no-frills" bus tour of the country.

Boarding the air-cooled (no air conditioning), reconditioned school bus at Israel's Ben Gurion Airport, I threw my backpack on the roof rack and we were off. The tour hit all the major sights: Jerusalem, the Dead Sea, Masada, Haifa, Eilat, and the Red Sea to the south and up north to the Golan Heights. The bus stopped for lunch at a kibbutz named Gonen or Defender at the base of the Golan Heights early one afternoon. I heard a group of people speaking English at one of the tables in the dining hall and went over and introduced myself. They asked where I was from and what I did for a living. I told them I was an actor and an activities director. They listened and then said, "We want to start an acting class here on Gonen. Do you want to teach it?"

"Sure" I replied.

"Great." they said, and went back to enjoying their lunch.

A few moments passed and I said, "You know, I am on the bus tour."

"So get off the bus tour," came a quick reply, and they continued eating.

A bit confused, I went out to the bus, which was already loaded and getting ready to speed off to the source of the Jordan River, called "Banias." I told the tour guide what just happened.

"Wonderful!" he yelled and scampered up the side ladder to the roof rack, found my backpack, and threw it down to me. He then climbed into the driver's seat and yelled, "Lehitriot!" (See you later!) The bus drove off, leaving me standing there in a cloud of dust.

One of the kibbutzniks showed me to a cabin in the Volunteers area, issued some well-worn kibbutz work clothes, blue shorts, T-shirts, and a pair of leather sandals, and I was all set to start picking apples the following morning at 5 a.m. The Volunteers consisted of a friendly group of European and Asian young people from Holland, England, France, Germany, and Thailand. Either they were interested in learning farming techniques or they were "city kids" like me looking for a bit of adventure and three hearty meals a day. The summer work day ran from 5 a.m. to 12 noon. Scrambled egg sandwiches on fresh rye bread and bottles of orange juice were brought out to the orchards for a breakfast break, and then we were brought back to the dining hall at 12 noon for a huge hot meal. Everyone slept the afternoon heat away in their cabins, awoke, and showered around 5 p.m., and a light dinner was served in the dining hall at 7 p.m. Movies were shown a few times a week in the evening, or there was folk dancing with live music. Occasionally professional musicians and pop singers would perform and then spend the night. As we were a border kibbutz, safety and security were still a bit of an issue as soon as the sun went down. We also had a contingent of young soldiers stationed on the kibbutz as part of their service, a year on a kibbutz, a year less of active duty, with the hope they would stay and become active members. They were called "Garinim" or "Seeds." Few ever stayed. I held my acting classes a few nights a week for anyone who was interested and had quite a few regular attendees. There were also art, conversational English, karate, singing, and recorder flute classes available.

One afternoon during lunch a friend pointed out an advert in the *Jerusalem Post*, an English language newspaper delivered daily. A movie company run by Menachem Golan of Crown Pictures in Tel Aviv was looking for an actor who could speak English with an authentic Southern accent and ride a horse. The Southern accent was no problem for me, though I had never been on a horse in my life. I figured in the movies illiterate cowboys knew how to ride, so how hard could it be? I'd just fake it. The next morning, with a few fresh scrambled egg sandwiches and a recently harvested apple in a paper sack, I was hitching the four-hour ride into Tel Aviv in one of the three Peugeot pick-up trucks owned by the kibbutz. The small gray pickup trucks, called "tenders," made daily runs all over the country delivering or picking up people or supplies as needed.

We arrived at the production office in downtown Tel Aviv around noon. I met with the producers, the director, an American from Los Angeles named Joe Manduke, and a few of the Italian creatives. The movie, released as *Vendetta* in the United States (later retitled *Kid Vengeance*), and *Les Cavaliers Du Diable* in Europe, was an American/Italian co-production shooting in the Israeli Negev Desert—a "Spaghetti/Matzo" western for lack of a better description.

The executives were all quite shocked at how well I spoke English for an Israeli. I told them I was born in Miami Beach and had been in Israel for about a month. After they stopped laughing, they told me I got the job and the first table read would be in the morning at the exclusive beachfront Dan Hotel. I asked if I would be staying there as well, and they said no, but they did book a room for me at a very nice two star with breakfast, very conveniently located in the neighborhood. A number of the cast and crew were already staying there as well, so I would be in good company. They assured me the pickled herring in cream sauce on the breakfast buffet was to die for.

Bright and early the next morning, after a sumptuous Israeli breakfast, we made our way to the Dan Hotel, the smell of the sea air still lingering in the morning humidity. We were shown to a large ocean view meeting room with a huge oval table in the center. A script and a few sharpened pencils were placed in front of each chair around the table. No one was sitting at the big table as yet, but were gathered around a giant steaming espresso machine, sampling fresh assorted croissants and pastries, while sipping lattes and cappuccinos.

The director breezed in and invited us all to sit. He welcomed us, encouraged us to enjoy the coffee and pastry, and said we needed to wait a few more minutes for the last few Italian producers to arrive. No one really cared as long as there was fresh brewed espresso and warm croissants available. The stars were already there. Football great Jim Brown was holding court off to one corner. John Marley, (who played the producer who woke to the horse's head in his bed in *The Godfather)* was introducing his much younger wife and their infant baby girl to everyone. Easily recognized from hundreds of character parts in movies such as *The Outlaw Josey Wales, Jeremiah Johnson* and *Will Penny,* though few know his name, character actor Matt Clark was also in attendance, cast as the comic relief in this otherwise serious cowboy epic. Even a cherubic twelve year old Leif Garret, referred to as "the bambino" by the Italian crew, was there with his mother as chaperone; the embarrassing mug shots of his scab marked face and the drug arrests would come years later.

I figured Lee Van Cleef had not arrived as yet either. I leaned over to the guy sitting to my left and said quietly, "Where the hell is Van Cleef?"

"He's sitting next to you." came the reply.

I looked to my right, and the seat was empty, and then it hit me.

"Ooops, open mouth, insert foot," I said rather sheepishly to the big guy sitting on my left. He was wearing a bandana covering his head to his forehead, a big gold ring in his ear, scraggly hair down to his shoulders, a full beard and moustache, a squash blossom turquoise necklace and assorted Navajo jewelry. I thought he was the costume designer. He still had the narrow eyes that were peering at me, and his classic aquiline nose, so there was no doubt about it. I was sitting next to film legend Lee Van Cleef.

"Mr. Van Cleef, I'm so sorry. I was expecting the *High Noon* Lee Van Cleef, you know the black hat, black leather vest and all that."

"That was almost twenty five years ago kid, 1952."

"Really? That was the year I was born." I said ingenuously.

"Okay, now you are pissing me off."

"Mr. Van Cleef, I didn't mean. . ."

"And furthermore, you better start calling me Lee, or else I'm going to get really angry."

After that bizarre first encounter, it was "Lee" for the remainder of the shoot.

The table read went very well. After lunch, we were all flown to Eilat, Israel's international port and resort on the Red Sea just north of the Sinai Peninsula and the all-important Suez Canal. We were checked into a beautiful luxury hotel. The area is crammed full of high-rise luxury hotels representing a number of international chains. A simple three-foot chain link fence running the length of the border over the beach and into the sea separates Israel's Eilat from Jordan's Aqaba. Aqaba was a mirror image of the port and high-rise hotels in Eilat, in addition to being Jordan's only port city. During all the wars in the area neither city was ever attacked by the other. The governments of both sides realized that the steady income from tourist dollars was way more beneficial than having to deal with something as destructive and impractical as a war.

The outdoor western action was shot in the surrounding deserts, complete with covered wagons, horses and campfires. The area was known as the Pillars of Solomon and was supposedly the site of King Solomon's ancient copper mines. When the sound man shouted "Jets!" all action stopped and two fully armed jet fighters zoomed overhead multiple times during the day, headed for the Lebanese or Syrian borders where they would bank sharply to the left and return to the south via the Mediterranean. Another pause would be caused by Bedouins and their camels occasionally passing through the shot even though they were miles away. They didn't do it intentionally; it was their home after all. Regardless, the shot had to be re-racked and done again—without camels.

During one of these pauses, Lee and I remained on our horses waiting for the jets or camels to pass out of sound range, or sight. I noticed he opened a little locket he wore around his neck. He took a pinch of the powder out of the locket and sniffed it up his nose, and then sneezed a few times. He noticed I was watching and he offered me a pinch saying, "It's mint snuff I picked up in Cairo, want a hit?"

I tried a tiny bit and it did have a minty aftertaste, but I ended up sneezing well into the final shot of the afternoon, as my teeth and gums grew mysteriously numb. I also stayed awake for a day and a half. I suppose it was some sort of an Arabic tobacco product, but, then again, I couldn't be sure.

Mrs. Van Cleef accompanied Lee while we were on location and supplied him with small cold bottles of Perrier during the down times. One afternoon she tossed one to me and we started chatting. It seems she was really into jewelry making and asked if I wouldn't mind accompanying her on a search for Eilat Stone during the lunch break. She knew it was out there but didn't want to wander around the desert alone. Resembling turquoise, Eilat Stone is a blue green semi-precious gemstone littering the area in chunks, or veins running through stones of various sizes. After a few days we had found bags of the stuff. Inside their tent she had set up a small lapidary station and showed me how to extract the Eilat Stone from the specimens we found. I suppose Lee was going to be replacing some of his Navajo jewelry with Eilat Stone.

After we finished shooting in the Negev, we had a few nights off in Tel Aviv. One evening most of the cast, Lee and his wife, Jim Brown, John Marley, Matt Clark, and I were relaxing in the lobby. As I was an American who spoke Hebrew, they considered me to be almost Israeli. They had me fielding questions they all had about some of the peculiarities of Israeli culture. Everything closing on Friday night, reopening on Saturday night, along with why the Ultra Orthodox with their curls, round hats, and long coats didn't recognize the State of Israel and wouldn't speak Hebrew.

Even stranger, they thought that in almost every restaurant they visited, pork was never on the menu, but when the waiter heard them speaking English, he would lean over and whisper, *"Yesh stek levan,"* meaning, "We have white steak." The Israeli name for pork. I tried to explain regardless of kosher laws, Israel prides itself on being a pluralistic society, but pigs, for both Jews and Muslims, were considered taboo. So much so, pigs are not allowed to touch the ground in the Holy Land. Unfazed, a kibbutz in the north decided to raise pigs on a sturday wooden platform, as they are an extremely efficient protein. A four hundred pound cow needs four hundred acres for grazing; a pig of the same size needed only a few square feet. Unfortunately, a missile blew up the sty during one of the wars, and the pigs scattered into the Golan Heights. The Golan is now home to hundreds of wild boar, a favorite of sport hunters in the area.

While explaining all of this to the others, an older Yemeni man and his three wives, wearing their colorful native robes, walked into the lobby of the five star Dan Hotel. He found a suitable spot, pulled over a hassock to lean on, and sat down on the floor. He then barked orders to his wives and they quickly returned with a hookah and plates of nibbles which they placed on the floor near him. They then sat on the floor as well, leaning on cushions taken from the designer sofas gracing the lobby.

The hotel manager, losing his mind, was running around apologizing to everyone else in the lobby. Polygamy, though extremely illegal in Israel, cannot be enforced on elderly Jewish immigrants arriving from Arab countries after they had been married for many years. So the man and his wives had to be made welcome while lounging on the floor.

In an effort to make my cohorts welcome, I ordered a round of arak (Arabic ouzo) and a small pitcher of water for everyone. When the drinks were ready, I wished everyone "L'Chiam," we downed the anise flavored white liquid, and I quickly ordered another round.

The next morning we were taken to a small town west of Tel Aviv called Petah Tikva. The film company, with the help of a few

Italian designers, constructed an extremely authentic looking western town. The "town" had a livery stable, a saloon, a sheriff's office and jail, everything a western town should have, except it was located in an abandoned ancient olive grove in Central Israel. Serge Leone used the town in a few of his movies, as did a number of other well known "Spaghetti Western" directors. It was nearby, cheaper than renting Italian sets of the same quality, and in close proximity to a number of desert locations, providing one could disregard the camels and cruising jet fighters.

The morning we arrived on the set, the crew had already been there since dawn preparing for our climactic ride into the town. The property was actually Bedouin land, so when a film company wasn't shooting, it became a slightly secret curiosity and would become littered with sheep droppings, a crumpled cigarette packet, or an empty Maccabee beer can or two. All this had been swept away before our arrival.

When action was called, the "gang" began its slow ominous horseback ride into town, the camera shooting the entrance at the far end of the sandy street. Suddenly, out of nowhere, a lone sheep scampers into the center of the street, and stops and looks at us. The director screams for us to keep going, and the sheep runs down the wadi, or what we would call an arroyo, running parallel with the town. Then another sheep appears, then another and another. The director is losing his mind, we keep riding into the shot. Finally a flock of at least a few hundred sheep descend on the street, slowly walking through the town toward the wadi, baying, bleating, jumping on each other and doing whatever sheep do while being led to a new pasture with no regard to a visiting film crew. Directly behind them a Bedouin appears wrapped in his characteristic black robes, carrying at least an eight foot crook. He walks to the center of the street, looks at us on the horses, gives a quizzical glance over to the camera crew feverishly covering the camera equipment to protect it from the rising dust, and a director throwing his script on the ground and screaming like a lunatic. The Bedouin shrugs his shoulders, then shepherds the remaining sheep into the wadi with his crook.

Lee looks at me and says, "Can you fucking believe this?"

"Of course I can. Remember the guy and his wives sitting on the floor in the hotel last night? Shit happens here every day, but no one told the sheep." The entire gang started laughing.

The Assistant Director yells, "Lunch!"

The Director adds, "Does anyone know where I can score a few Xanax!"

We keep laughing and head for the Commissary Tent.

A few years later I was cast as a Detective Hernandez in a short-lived mid-season replacement series that shot on the Paramount lot called *Dog and Cat*. The show starred veteran actor Lou Antonio, and the beautiful Kim Bassinger in her first television role after rising to fame as a Cosmo model. First day on the set, the Chief of Police walks in and he's played by Matt Clark, the same guy playing the comic relief in *Vendetta*. I walked over to him during a break and said I was the guy in the Israeli movie with the Southern accent and Confederate army uniform. He recognized me immediately, even without my beard and long hair. During down times for the remainder of the series we would reminisce about *Vendetta*, the sheep, the camels, and being buzzed by the Israeli air force. I lived a few blocks from Paramount, but he insisted on giving me a lift home after every time we were on the set together. Talk about a small world, and a very nice man.

THE RETURN OF THE PRODIGAL

Returning to Los Angeles after my time in Europe and Israel, I knocked around town for a while, hustling jokes to comics in the parking lot of the Comedy Store or hanging out at Tiny Naylor's, a fifties Googie-styled coffee shop on Sunset that never closed, or Jerry's Deli, open 24 hours, in the Valley. I would always notice depressed guys sitting at the counter with a cold cup of coffee and a half eaten bagel as their price of admission. Sitting there, they would sigh while pondering, and then jot things down on a yellow legal pad, nowadays replaced with an iPad. They were supposedly working on their new killer sitcom, or smash hit screenplay, or soon-to-be bestselling novel, very few of which ever saw the light of day.

As a union "actor," the thought of going into the production end was considered a complete sell-out, short of taking a job as a full time teacher, or heeding my parents' constant urging and enrolling in law school. Yet, as I started to fall behind on my rent and Swanson Hungry Man frozen dinners became a way of life, I realized perhaps a production job might not be a bad idea. I called a friend who was working as a daytime producer at NBC and asked her if she knew of anything going on anywhere. I warned her I had no production experience but had been hired to work as a "three days or less actor" on a number of series, *Barnaby Jones, Incredible Hulk, Rockford Files* and so on. By the way, I added as an afterthought, I just finished working a stint as an Assistant Cruise Director on an international cruise line.

"Really?" she said getting interested, "I just heard that a game show company in town, The Hill-Eubanks Group, just signed up to do a pilot for CBS, a new version of Art Linklater's *House Party*. They are looking for someone with a handle on ladies parlor games, and silly stunts like that. Why don't you give them a call?

They're great guys, repped by William Morris, it might be perfect for you."

I didn't need more convincing than that. I thanked her, hung up, and called their office immediately. I was called in for an interview with Michael Hill, the Hill of The Hill-Eubanks Group. Game show host Bob Eubanks was the "Eubanks" in the company name, but he wasn't very active with the development end of the company, so he didn't participate in staff interviews and the like. I told Mr. Hill I had been an actor for the last few years, but just got off a cruise ship as the Assistant Cruise Director or First Officer of Entertainment. I had absolutely no production experience which, I suppose, in retrospect, wasn't the smartest thing to fess up to during an interview for a production position. He asked if I had any experience with "ladies parlor games" as he put it, and I told him I had a notebook of over two hundred stunts and games we used on the ship on a regular basis.

I was hired on the spot and offered two hundred dollars a week, a paltry sum even then, to become a researcher on the current *House Party* pilot they were working on. Mr. Hill was a bit embarrassed by his offer, but claimed most of the staff had already been hired and the staff budget was depleted, and promised there would be a decent salary for the next pilot, if I survived this one. I thought "survive" was an odd choice of words, but as it was my first gig in production I wasn't going to make a fuss about being called a researcher or being paid peanuts. I was just happy as a clam to get the job after my first and only interview for a production gig. Being concerned about survival would come later.

Even though I was responsible for creating games and stunts, writing host patter, writing game instructions, writing ins and outs for commercials, and writing the show, the "researcher" title remained for the duration of the project. Turns out I was promoted to "writer" for the next project, as promised, and for all the shows following. I was eventually told I had to join the Writers Guild. Not a bad thing, as it guaranteed a specified salary, health benefits, and an eventual pension. My first year as a writer I earned more money than ten years as an actor, so that was the end of my acting career. To this day I'll never know if that meant I was a better writer than I was an actor, but when it came time to buy a house, send my daughter to private school, and even vacation with my wife at the Ritz in Paris, I was happy to have made the leap into production and never looked back.

As a game show company, the writers would come up with ideas and stunts in the morning and then, after lunch invite celebs, represented by the same agency that represented us, the William Morris Agency, to come up and try out the patter and games we had created earlier. The carrot was a possible position as a host on a game show if it sold. David Letterman, Jay Leno, Arsenio Hall, David Brenner, Ruth Buzzy (*Laugh In*), James Hampton (*F Troop*), Howie Morris (*Your Show of Shows*), Arte Johnson (*Laugh In*), even improv artist Andy Kaufman all showed up on a regular basis. One of the improv artists Andy introduced us to was a woman named Geraldine. She was so good at character improv, and so hysterically funny, we eventually realized we didn't need to hire half a dozen comedians for a run through, just her. We would give her any number of situations, as needed: "You're a butcher's wife" or "You drive a diaper delivery truck" or "You're Cher's make-up artist." She would then riff off hysterically from there until we told her to stop so we could catch our breath. I eventually married her, and we have been laughing together for over thirty five years, but this is a story for another time.

Game shows were developed in a very specified manner. After creating a decent idea, it would be taken to a network to be "Office Pitched." The Office Pitch consisted of just a few executives, a story board, perhaps, and some colorful cue cards. If they liked the pitch they would give us a fee, usually about ten thousand dollars, to produce a non-camera run-through in a rental event hall or in a large meeting room at a neighboring hotel. Beverly Garland's Howard Johnson's Motor Inn in Studio City was a very popular run-through venue. If the non-camera run-through was a hit, a decent budget, perhaps $150,000 or so, was awarded and a pilot was scheduled to be shot in one of the network's studios. Three or more cameras, lighting, bells and whistles, everything necessary to create and edit a complete game show were budgeted. Real people/actors were even hired to play the contestants, and prizes were displayed and awarded (but never left the studio). The taped and edited show would be delivered in the can for affiliate opinions and possible purchase. Most important was the eagerly sought-after gold ring, a scheduled network or syndicated airdate.

After taping a pilot, Mike Hill would always treat all of us to a nice dinner at any number of fine restaurants in town— Scandia, Musso & Frank, Spago, to name a few. One evening at Scandia, one of the most revered restaurants in Los Angeles at the time, we all enjoyed a few bottles of frozen Aquavit, poured from a bottle frozen in a block of ice, pounds of gravlax, prime rib carved at the table, and an ample desert of flaming Cherries Jubilee. Mike received the check and went over it, as any good Executive Producer would. He stopped, tapped a glass with a fork to get our otherwise boisterous attention, and asked, "Who ordered the two silver serving platters? You owe the table eighty bucks."

We all looked around, surprised and somewhat bewildered. That is, everyone except one of the senior producers named Arty, who decided he couldn't live without two of the serving platters brought to the table covered with thick slices of gravlax. When empty, he surreptitiously slipped the trays one at a time off the table and into the purse of one of our secretaries, unbeknownst to anyone at the time except him, the secretary, and a very observant waiter. After slumping down in his chair as far as he could go without slipping under the table, we knew he was the culprit. We refused to leave until he paid up or returned the trays. The secretary, having a previous engagement planned, pulled the trays out of her purse and threw them on the table, clanging and crashing directly in front of Arty. A rousing inebriated cheer arose from our table. He paid by adding eighty bucks to the tip, and returned the trays. We all cheered again.

One morning we were informed that Pat McCormack, the head writer for *The Johnny Carson Show* as well as a respected and revered comic around town, wanted to come up and pitch a game show idea he had been developing for quite some time. There was no way we could or even wanted to refuse, so we scheduled an afternoon pitch meeting. We set up our Game Room for the meeting, a round table and a mini-bar with assorted soft drinks and snacks. Pat arrived, big, robust, back slapping and full of laughter. Before sitting down, he asked if he could use the restroom and we showed him where it was, just down the hall. He returned moments later, sat down, handed out his game show proposal and, before beginning his pitch, he let loose with a booming sneeze. A jagged little white ball came flying out of his nose, and bounced on the table. Before anyone could move, let alone say anything, he pressed his sausage sized thumb down on the little white morsel, and inhaled it back into a nostril, with a brief snort.

"Sorry about that fellas," he smiled, "Now where were we?" He then proceeded to pitch his show, explaining all the entertaining nuances as well as twists and turns. Mike didn't buy the show that afternoon, but he invited Pat to come back and pitch us again anytime he wanted to, next time encouraging him to bring enough of the magical white powder to share. We would even send out to Art's Deli for lunch, our treat. Everyone laughed, Pat thanked us for our time and was on his way.

Occasionally a producer would come along as part of the package for a game show we were asked to develop. There was no problem with that as long as he was not one of the "OG's" or original gangstas, as it was sometimes difficult for the "new guy" to fit in. Case in point was this fellow brought in to supervise the development of a show he sold to our company. We would work in the morning and come up with material, which we would run by him when he arrived around eleven. On the drive in he would burn a few joints amid the bumper-to-bumper Hollywood Freeway traffic and simply fall down in uncontrolled laughter when he read our stuff. We loved that. Later in the afternoon when he began to come off his morning high, he would do a few lines of cocaine. Storming in to the Writers Room, after re-reading the same material he had just read a few hours before, he would threaten to kill the writer who created it as well as his entire family. This went on for a few weeks, with pithy criticisms like, "These god damn laughs are killing us! What the fuck is wrong with you guys?"

One day just before an afternoon meeting, one of the older writers, who still wore bell bottom jeans even though they had been out of style for a number of years, said in exasperation, "Look, we'll show him the stuff. When he starts to scream, just point to your left."

Knowing this would drive him absolutely crazy, we couldn't wait for him to come back after lunch. He never did. Seems he was stopped for a routine traffic stop and the policemen found all sorts of illegal goodies in his car. Lots of it. His car was impounded and so was he. Last we heard he was growing tomatoes while incarcerated in a minimum security prison in central California. We never went to visit.

One morning at Hill-Eubanks we were called together and told we were being asked to perform a "mercy fuck" for the William Morris Agency. We were involuntarily getting a new member to our team. Seems our company, represented by the Morris Office, and our agent, asked Mike and Bob to do a huge favor for the agency and hire an artistic young man looking for a job in show business. His name was Tommy Lasorda, Jr.

Obviously an offer one couldn't easily refuse, Tommy Jr. arrived in loose fitting pastel yoga pants, a gossamer shirt and a few painted finger nails. Mike decided Tommy would be the resident "Designer," not that he'd ever designed anything, let alone a television game show set. But he was happy with the job title and came in every day with sketches and drawings he created that really had nothing to do with the project we were working on. We actually relied on the design services of more professional folks when the need for a set arose.

One afternoon, Tommy Jr. and I were sent to an art supply shop in Studio City to get some material for an in-office run-through we were planning. Tommy presented his credit card at the register and the name on the card was, of course, Tommy Lasorda, Jr. The clerk looked at the card and then looked at us, and said with a curious smirk, "Which one of you is Tommy Lasorda, Jr.?" Tommy identified himself demurely. "Really?" said the clerk in shock.

"Just run the card pal, okay?" I said, jumping in, not liking where I feared the conversation was going. Which he did quickly and handed the card back, staring at us in amazement, as we trundled out of the store with long rolls of paper, cases of markers, and assorted cardboard tubes and art supplies.

On the way back to his car, Tommy Jr. said, "Jesus, Mary and Joseph I hate it when that shit happens."

To which I quickly replied, "You know what? Fuck him if he can't take a joke."

We looked at each other and broke down in goofy laughter as we loaded up his small two-seater sports car with the art supplies we had just purchased.

A year or so later, Tommy Jr. passed away amidst an early wave of the AIDS epidemic. During his funeral, Tommy Lasorda, this model of macho masculinity as the manager of the world champion Los Angeles Dodgers, eulogized his son by saying, "Thirty three years ago if God came to me and said, 'I can give you a boy, but you can only have him for thirty-three years. What do you want to do?' I would have looked God straight in the eye and said, "Give me the boy!"

I realized one does not become Hall of Fame member Tommy Lasorda, a leader of men, without being someone very, very special: even in sorrow, the quintessential "Team Manger" who appreciated all his teammates, regardless of inclination.

One morning Michael Hill came into the Writers Room and announced he was doing a new pilot with the very popular nationally known disc jockey Rick Dees as the host. The only problem was Dees was demanding a fifteen thousand dollar payment for the two hour taping and was refusing to rehearse as well. Mike wanted to know if we would be willing to go a few weeks without pay so he could pull this off. He thanked us without waiting for an answer, and was gone.

That afternoon I bought a bottle of brandy in a gift box, attached a note thanking Mr. Hill for all he had done for me, but asking me to work for an indeterminate number of weeks so he could pay a prima donna fifteen thousand dollars for two hours of work was beyond the pale. I tendered my resignation.

I was told he threw the bottle of brandy in the trash, and I never heard from him again.

The Hill-Eubanks Group closed shop and ceased developing game shows a short time later.

CHUCK BARRIS

Within a few weeks of my leaving The Hill-Eubanks Group, Bob Eubanks was hired by Chuck Barris to host a new version of the classic *Newlywed Game* to be called *The All New Newlywed Game*. Thankfully, Bob brought me along starting as an Applause Puller and Entry Level Writer. An Applause Puller is the cheerful soul who stands in front of an audience and, at the proper moment, waves his hands frantically in tempo with the flashing APPLAUSE sign. It is his job to let everyone know when, and to what intensity, they should cheer and applaud. I did that for a season and was soon promoted to a full-fledged writer, without having to pull applause, which I appreciated greatly. Seems Chuck had a nephew he promised a job to, so Applause Puller was it. That was fine with me.

I was a writer on *Newly* before computers. One had to sit in front of an IBM Selectric, a beautiful state of the art typewriter at that time, insert an index card, color coded to your name, and wait until the muse hit you to create a funny question guaranteed to get anyone answering it in trouble with his or her spouse. We were responsible for thirty-five to forty killer questions per day, mandated to put either of the newlyweds "in the soup," as we liked to say. First Round were the guys, so we engineered the questions to yield answers that would get the wives angry or embarrassed or both. Once an angelic wife was made angry or embarrassed, there was no telling what she would say to get back at her husband during the second round. Angry wives slamming husbands with cue cards, pouting, screaming, and occasionally punching the poor guy was comedy gold, and we lived for those reactions. Why? They were funny.

We would interview a few hundred couples to choose four for each show. We used codes on the audition forms, so if any of the couples saw their forms on our table as they were leaving the audition they wouldn't know what we had written down about them. TL was "The Look" we were looking for, NTL was "Not the Look." B & F stood for "Back & Forth," meaning they would argue about nothing. DAOS stood for, "Dull As Owl Shit" (we did have to entertain ourselves after all). HK stood for "Hate Kill" meaning this couple hated each other so much, if we didn't book them on the following tape day, they would probably kill each other. Venomous couples arguing with total abandon about whose mother looked most like a frog was *Newlywed Game* comedy at its finest.

After being picked up for our second of five seasons, I was promoted to Producer. The studio threw a cocktail party to celebrate the second season pickup and Chuck Barris actually attended, Believe it or not, he was a rather shy guy and didn't attend too many parties or get-togethers. I was introduced to him as the new Producer of the show, and he smiled and shook my hand. Not knowing what to say to this television legend, I mentioned I was good friends with Steve Friedman, the fellow who produced the show the last time it was on the air a few years ago.

"You know Stevie?" asked Chuck rather flatly.

"Yes, for a number of years, we worked together at King World."

Before I could finish the sentence, Chuck grabbed the front of my shirt, pulled me down to his level and said, "No fucking monkeys." and he smiled menacingly.

No monkeys, I thought, thinking monkeys was some sort of code like NTL, or TL

"Not to worry Mr. Barris, no fucking monkeys will ever set foot on my stage," not knowing what the hell he was talking about. He smiled, turned away, and began chatting with some others waiting their turn to mingle with the god of television game shows.

A few weeks later, Steve Friedman and I arranged to meet for lunch at Jerry's Deli in Studio City. He came in, sat down, and the first words out of his mouth were, "So what's it like working with Chucky Baby?"

"Fine." I said. "He's never around, I've only met him once at the Second Season Cocktail Party. He said something really strange though."

"Really? What"

"When I told him I knew you, he got really serious and growled, "No fucking monkeys."

Steve started laughing, and said, "Oh man, I can't believe he's still pissed about that!"

"Pissed about what?" I asked, my interest aroused. It seems when Steve was producing the show, they received a trip to Lion Country Safari to give away as a Dream Date. Steve thought it would be drop dead funny to substitute chimps instead of eligible bachelors, though the boys would be standing behind the seated chimps. Using a tight shot on the chimps and rubbing their lips with honey just prior to a question being asked, they would move their lips as if they were actually talking, and the boys standing behind them would answer. Great idea! Brilliant! Emmy Award winning stuff!

On tape day, our chosen Bachelorette asked a question. The monkeys moved their lips, and the young man standing behind the chimp answered the question. The audience went crazy.

Our Bachelorette asks the remainder of her questions to the Bachelors of her choice, the chimps answer, and audience members are falling out of their seats with laughter.

She chooses one of the Bachelors, Host Jim Lange suggests we meet the others. He starts with Bachelor #1 and reads a list of accomplishments that would make a Rhodes scholar jealous.

"Let's meet him!" says Jim.

Out walks one of the chimps wearing a beret. The Bachelorette almost faints. The audience is gasping for breath while laughing.

"Okay, no further playing around; here is Bachelor # 2!" and the second chimp saunters out wearing a cowboy hat, vest, and chaps. The Bachelorette is beginning to swoon.

"Okay, all kidding aside now! Let's say hello to the guy you really picked, Bachelor #3, come on out!"

The third chimp ambles out wearing a space suit and carrying a helmet. The Bachelorette starts screaming and crying and falls to her knees.

Host Jim Lange is also on the verge of tears as he calls out the real boys standing just beyond the asterisk-studded wall to come out and save the day. The Bachelorette is inconsolable, will have nothing to do with any of them, and runs screaming from the set. The chimps are laughing, hooting, and doing flip-flops as Jim bids everyone a fond farewell. He reminds the boys, who are a bit confused, to throw the farewell *Dating Game* kiss as rehearsed earlier, and the credits roll.

I looked at Steve in amazement and laughingly said, "So Chuck didn't think that was funny?"

"Well he never aired the show, we gave the all the kids trips to where ever they wanted to go and a year's supply of Kinney Shoes, and everyone was happy."

"Except Chuck." I added.

"I suppose," said Steve, "but he never mentioned anything to me. So 'no fucking monkeys!' Really?"

"Really." I said in finality.

"That's just a shame, because you know, monkeys are always good for a laugh!"

I ended up producing the show for a total of five seasons and never used any monkeys, though on one of my shows, I managed to squeeze in an elephant.

During one of the seasons, now hosted by Jeff MacGregor, who had aspirations of being a talk show host, it was decided to extend the show to an hour. Jeff was a good looking young guy, touted as the son of one of the stars of the popular TV series *M*A*S*H*. We were never able to find out who and, as Jeff wasn't on speaking terms with his father, he had no intention of telling us who it was either.

The first half hour of the newly tooled program would be the usual raucous show everyone knew and loved, and the second half would feature an interview of the couple recently returned from their "Dream Date" somewhere in the world.

Prior to their appearance we would interview the couple in order to produce their segment. During an interview of a couple we sent to Bangkok, Thailand, the fellow mentioned the highlight of his trip was learning how to ride an elephant. The girl disagreed and claimed he couldn't do any such thing. Within moments of their leaving my office, I was on the phone ordering an elephant to appear on their segment. In Hollywood you can rent anything. An elephant, "studio trained" (meaning he wouldn't stampede if startled by loud noises or bright lights) was actually easy to find.

On tape day, the elephant arrived all cleaned and fresh, with freshly polished black toenails. We parked the elephant outside the studio with a handler, a few bales of hay, and a bushel of carrots. The elephant was beside himself in joy and happiness, or so I was told. Everyone was excited about the show except the studio manager. It seems our stage was built as the "tank" set for Columbia Pictures back in the thirties, meaning it was actually a giant four-foot-deep swimming pool in which it was rumored all the *Tugboat Annie* films, *Captains Courageous*, and even a version of *Moby Dick* were shot. The pool hadn't been used for years as they built a stage over it to enable additional studio space for shooting cowboy shows which had become very popular in the forties and fifties. Studio management recently received word from the Humane Society that in order to support an elephant, or something as heavy as an elephant, in any sound stage, the actual floor had to be supported with foundation supports no more than three feet apart. If more than three feet apart, there was no way the stage would be up to code, and the entire tape day would have to be cancelled, except for paying the three thousand dollar fee for the elephant rental. Seems the elephant had a "pay or play" deal, guaranteeing he had a payday regardless of what emergency may befall the show. The studio rep demanded someone had to go under the stage with a tape measure and a flashlight to confirm the dimensions of the foundation supports. As it was so close to taping, I had no time to spare arguing with studio management. I borrowed an electrician's overalls, a five celled flashlight, and under the stage floor I crawled. It was dark naturally, musty and thick with spider webs, with little showers of dust showering down from footsteps on the stage floor above. I even heard squeaking and the pitter patter of little feet scurrying who knows where, but hopefully far away from me. The foundations were less than two feet apart, yippee, problem solved. I bid an extremely hasty retreat out of this hell hole. Sneezing uncontrollably from the dust I inhaled, I told everyone the supports were two feet apart, and I received a round of applause by those standing in the vicinity. It seems the stage was actually rebuilt to support horses, extremely important during the cowboy show era, but in our age of litigiousness, studio management had to be reassured it would support an elephant.

The show went on as scheduled. The couple arguing as planned, the boy bragging he learned to ride an elephant while on the date in Bangkok. The girl adamantly disagreed. Voila, out came the elephant to everyone's surprise! The boy hopped aboard, straddling the huge animal's neck just behind his floppy ears, and the audience roared its approval.

I didn't stop sneezing for a week, but at least we delivered a great show.

A number of celebrities also made appearances on *The Dating Game* long before they became famous. Back in those days, actors liked to go to auditions with a reel of appearances to show to the casting directors and an appearance on *The Dating Game* was perfect. Among the celebrities making appearances were Arnold Schwarzenegger, John Ritter, Farah Fawcett, Sally Field, pre-moustache Tom Selleck, Richard Dawson, Cuba Gooding Jr, and Paul Ruebens, who came to the audition as himself but showed up on tape day as Pee Wee Herman. Finally, no one could easily forget Rhonda Shear, currently of Home Shopping fame, showing up in a flaming hot, form fitting pink latex body suit. Those were the days.

Chuck was a rather easygoing boss to deal with, except if you insulted him. He did have a full drum set in his office which he played with reckless abandon every so often, and whenever the felt the urge, would dress up in a trench coat with a hat pulled down to his ears, telling us he was going on a mission for the CIA. He would invariably return with grocery bags filled with sandwiches and quarts of Cole slaw and potato salad, so we knew the "mission" must have gone well, or at least had been in the vicinity of Nate & Al's Deli.

One weekend a senior producer decided to throw a costume party at his home and invited Chuck to come by. Chuck rarely attended parties, but this particular evening he decided to attend. He arrived without a costume. The host of the party refused to let him in and actually turned him away. We were all shocked at how amazingly stupid the host of the party was, but after Chuck had left, he continued with the merry making as if nothing had happened. The following Monday morning when we arrived at the office, the glass-enclosed office belonging to this producer/host of the party was completely cleaned out and empty, as if no had ever been there. The producer didn't show up either, and no one dared mention his name, or the costume party, ever again.

AL AND FLO JOYNER

During one of the contestant auditions for *The New Newlywed Game* a cute young couple showed up and modestly mentioned on their audition forms that they recently qualified to represent the United States in track and field in Korea. No mention of the Olympics. After the audition I called them to the table and inquired if they were going to Korea for just another track and field competition, or something else? With wide eyed innocence they replied, "No it's for the Olympics, we forgot to mention that." They both smiled apologetically. I fell off my chair. It was Al and Flo Joyner who, in addition to just getting married, were receiving all sorts of press as track champions. I booked them to tape a show immediately. When I briefed Bob Eubanks before their show, I told him to mention they were bound for the Olympics. They both blushed and smiled modestly when he did, almost embarrassed at earning spots on the United States Olympic Team.

During the interim between *The New Newlywed Game* and the Olympics, Chuck Barris sold the company to Burt Sugarman, famous for owning a cement company and producing nine seasons of *The Midnight Special*, a rock and roll variety show which made announcer Wolfman Jack a household name. Burt Sugarman hired Hollywood fixer and bulldog Jeff Wald to run things. Jeff was a rather aggressive sort of guy with a very direct sense of humor. After watching my wife audition for a possible replacement host for *The New Newlywed Game*, Jeff came up to me afterwards and said, "Hey Starin, your wife is fucking hysterical! I didn't even think she could speak English!"

Geraldine's maiden name in Spanish meant paper, nee Papel. A few weeks later Jeff had *The Gong Show* producer, Rac Clark, cast her as a celebrity judge between Jimmy JJ Walker and Norm Crosby.

By the way, Rac Clark was Dick Clark's oldest who son. There is a rule in all Hollywood unions that only one actor or member can have any one particular name. Since Dick Clark was already taken with all the unions, his son decided to call himself by his initials RAC, for Richard A. Clark, instead.

Jeff Wald also had a claim to fame as the ex-husband and manager of Helen Reddy, Rosanne Barr's personal manger, and the list of celebs he worked with and protected was endless. He had a reputation in town and internationally as the go-to guy to get anything done in Hollywood for anyone needing his assistance. In fact, there was a copy of the iconic photo hanging in his office of Elvis Presley meeting Nixon in the Oval Office. What is usually cropped out for publication are Jeff and Colonel Parker in a cowboy hat, standing off to the side, smiling proudly.

One morning, Jeff called my home at 6:30 and my wife told him I was at the gym. He then called the gym, had me paged, and a fellow at the gym led me to the phone, towel wrapped around my waist, still dripping from a few laps short of my daily mile in the pool.

Without skipping a beat Jeff explodes, "The Joyners just won all kinds of gold medals in Korea. Find them and book them for our Kenny Rogers pilot this afternoon. You know them, right? You booked them on *Newly*, remember?"

"Yes, of course I did, but I wouldn't say we were friends, I booked them on the show, that was it. Where in Korea are they?"

"Hell if I know. There's a promoter in Japan named Tats Nakashima, maybe he can help. At least he can set up and send out the video crew. Call him."

"What's his number" I asked.

"How should I know? Call Directory Assistance in Tokyo, and when you get to the office pull a tape of the show they were on, we'll need it for Kenny's pilot." With that he hung up abruptly.

Seems Jeff had a brainstorm at dawn that morning, after way too many cups of his favorite espresso, to get the Joyners as video guests on a talk show pilot he was producing with Kenny Rogers as the host. Getting the Joyners on the pilot would be a fabulous idea and a genuine publicity coup. Once I found them, I was also tasked with setting up a live video feed from wherever they were to our studio in Hollywood during the actual taping of Kenny's pilot. It would be a logistical nightmare in itself, provided I was able to find the Joyners in the first place.

Just how successful was Kenny Rogers at the time? When his wife wanted to go shopping, a helicopter landed on their estate and flew her to a corner of the parking lot of the appointed shopping center. A limo picked her up at the landing spot and took her to the entrance of the mall where a golf cart was waiting to take her wherever she desired to go. When she was ready to leave, the process took place in reverse, golf cart, limo, helicopter. That's how successful Kenny Rogers was.

I arrived at the studio and ran up to my office, my hair still wet from the pool, and began calling hotels in Seoul, Korea. No one knew anything, let alone the where the Joyners were, or who they even were. Growing manic after my fifth or sixth attempt, I was transferred to someone who was with the American Olympic contingent and he told me the Joyners had left for Japan the night before. I asked if he knew where in Japan and he had no idea. I thanked him and, as soon as he began asking who I was with and where I was calling from, I hung up and started calling the best hotels in Tokyo.

There were quite a few to choose from, The Peninsula Tokyo, Mandarin Oriental Tokyo, The Ritz Carlton Tokyo, Hotel Okura Tokyo Bay. The ladies who answered the phones in schooled English were extremely polite and as helpful as they could be, though not being able to assist me at all. Finally one hotel operator, out of the blue said, "Hold on please, sir. I'll ring their room." My heart started to palpitate as the phone rang. Once. Twice, and then a groggy female voice answered, "Hello?"

"Hi" I said quickly, "is this Flo Joyner?"

"Yes" came the tentative reply.

"Good morning Miss Joyner," I said. "I'm sure you don't remember me, but I'm the producer of *The New Newlywed Game* who put you and Al on the show a few months ago, remember?"

"Yes, I remember" came the reply a bit more cogent, and just a bit friendlier.

"Well I'm working for the same company and they are producing a talk show with Kenny Rogers as the host, and they would love to have Kenny interview you and Al live, right from your hotel room."

By this time, Al was chiming in. "When do ya'll want to do this? We are leaving for the States tomorrow."

"Later on today, no problem. The crew will be arriving early in the afternoon to set up. You guys cool with all of this?"

"Sure," they said, laughing a bit.

"You're the best!" I said, "Now don't go anywhere, order anything you want for breakfast from room service and we'll pay for it."

"It's actually almost dinner time."

"Order the best dinner they have, throw in a bottle of champagne..."

"We don't drink."

"No problem. Make it orange juice, or Cokes or anything you want. Now I have to run, I have to get the production crew to your room. You guys are great! Congratulations on the medals by the way, that was fantastic, the entire country is talking about you."

"The medals are sitting right here on our dresser."

"Well don't let them out of your sight. I'll be getting back to you!"

With that, I hung up, thrilled beyond belief, but all that was dashed in a heartbeat when I realized I still hadn't found Tats Nakashima, who I had hoped would set up the video crews, and time was flying by.

I then did what Jeff suggested and called Directory Assistance in Tokyo, figuring I had nothing to lose, and they actually answered. I asked for the number of a Tats Nakashikma, and they actually gave it to me! Hoping against fate that he was only Tats in Tokyo, I dialed the number. It rang a few times and a gruff voiced answered, "Hi"

"Hi" I replied, "Is this Tats Nakashima?"

"Hi" came the reply, even gruffer, sounding like a cranky Yakuza.

"Jeff Wald gave me your name, He said you can do anything for anyone in Japan. This is true, right?"

"Hi, Jeff good man, what you need?"

I told him as succinctly as possible what the situation was. We had the Olympic Gold Medalists, Flo and Al Joyner standing by in their hotel room, we needed to set up a live feed to air on the Kenny Rogers show taping this afternoon in Hollywood. Could he make that happen for us?

"Kenny Rogers, the Gambler?"

"Yep, that's him alright, I can even send you an autograph picture if you like"

"No Picture. No problem. I make happen. Tell Jeff he owes me."

"You bet I will Mr. Nakashima, Domo, Domo Arigato. . ."

"Okay, your Japanese very bad. I call you in three hours."

Three hours to the minute later, he called. The live interview from their hotel room, to our Sunset/Gower Studio in the heart of Hollywood with Kenny Rogers chatting back and forth with the Olympic Gold Medalists, Flo and Al Joyner in Tokyo, went off without a hitch. Everyone was happy. I was unbelievably relieved.

A few days later Jeff called the entire staff into the office Conference Room and told them what I had done. I was a little embarrassed as I figured it was all in a day's work, just a few phone calls actually. Jeff then hands me an envelope, extends his hand for a handshake, and gives me a "job well done" slap on the shoulder. I shook his hand of course, while the entire staff started cheering and applauding, and a photographer, brought in for the occasion, took a few shots in rapid flashing succession. I modestly acknowledged the cheering staff, and then reminded everyone we had a show to produce, so let's all get back to work.

As we were leaving the conference room, a few of my people came up and asked what was in the envelope. I told them it was probably just a thank-you card, and not to worry about it. Once back at my desk, I immediately opened the envelope. There was no thank-you note, no congratulations, nothing. Nothing but a check from Barris Industries made out to me for five hundred dollars!

Jeff once shared a show-biz life lesson with me, telling me he always arrived in his office at least an hour before the official start of the day. It gives you time to get things sorted before all hell breaks loose.

I arrived early the next morning, check in hand and went to Jeff's office. He was in the midst of getting a haircut from his private barber.

"Excuse me Jeff, may I interrupt?"

"Sure" he said, "What's up?"

"Thanks you for this, but it really wasn't necessary." I said, waving the envelope gently.

"Really?" he smiled, "Then give it back wise guy."

"No way that's going to happen; it's already spent. The baby needs a new pair of shoes, if you know what I mean."

"Sure I know, just wait till she starts hocking you for a car," he said and winked to the barber, who smiled back knowingly. The barber removed the white sheet with a shake, and then fussed all over Jeff with a soft long haired brush. "Hey kid you want a haircut?"

"No thanks, that's okay"

"Come on, don't be an asshole. Get a haircut. Give the kid a haircut."

With that command, the barber shuffled me into the portable chair, wrapped a piece of tissue paper tightly around my neck, threw the sheet over me, and I was getting a haircut in Jeff Wald's office. I looked up and realized I was under the faces of Elvis, Nixon, Jeff, and Colonel Parker, all smiling down on me from the Oval Office in the White House.

There was something very gangster about Jeff, but very lovable at the same time. I could never forget the time he affectionately put his arm around the waist of a pregnant agent from William Morris who was visiting the studio to observe a taping of *The New Dating Game* and cooed, loud enough for everyone around to hear, "You know, pregnant women make me hard."

"That's great Jeff, I'm so glad you still have something that gets hard." said the pretty agent without missing a beat, "Now where am I sitting, god damnit, I'm pregnant!"

Obviously she was quite adept at dealing with powerful executive producers in Hollywood. Everyone, including Jeff, started laughing.

After the third season of *The All New Dating Game*, Bob Eubanks decided to leave and was replaced by comedian by Paul Rodriguez. One tape day, Jeff and I had to meet with Paul in his dressing room. Jeff was carrying a child-sized Dodger uniform on a hangar he had pickup at a game for Paul's infant son. That little boy is now a professional skate boarder known worldwide. I knocked on the door and Paul called out, "Just a minute guys."

No telling why he wanted us to wait, Paul always brought an entourage of his friends to the tapings who partied in his dressing room while he was getting ready and snacked on trays filled with an assortment of Arby's roast beef sandwiches. Jeff was getting a little cranky with the wait and yelled, "Come on Rodriguez, you have two Jews waiting for you out here and I can guarantee that's never happened to you before. Open the damn door!"

The door swung open, with Paul standing there in his boxer shorts and munching on a roast beef sandwich. "Come on in guys. Anyone want a sandwich?" A tray of Arby's roast beef sandwiches was sitting on a side table. I began reaching for one, but when I heard Jeff grumble, "No thanks, we got business to talk about." I quickly decided no Arby's for me that afternoon. Paul was partial to Arby's as he had purchased a franchise for his mother and father to run. He once told me he bought them the restaurant after he started making some money as he didn't want them picking vegetables in the Central Valley any more. That could have been just part of Paul's self-deprecating humor, as he also claimed early in his career he sold bags of oranges on the freeway exits to make ends meet, but who knows?

MIKE TYSON

I first met famous boxing promoter Don King in the rest room of the Barris Industries offices in Santa Monica. He came in, washed his hands, and took a urinal right next to mine. I glanced over at him and he announced, "I always wash my hands before I pee!"

"Okay, good idea" I said, and then I realized who he was. "I'm one of the producers here and I'd shake hands but I'm involved"

"I understand, Mr. Producer" he boomed, "God bless America!" and smiled broadly. Which I was to later learn was one of his favorite expressions.

When boxing legend Mike Tyson was in town without Mr. King, Jeff would get a call from the famous promoter asking him to keep an eye on the Champ while he was visiting. Jeff eagerly agreed.

Mike came up to the office for the first time a few days later. He was shy, almost bashful, and I was surprised at how much shorter he was than me, though he was built like a fire hydrant. This was the innocent Mike if you will, with a big friendly smile filled with assorted gold teeth, before serving time on trumped up rape charges, before biting Evander Holyfield's ear off in the ring, before the tattoos on his face, and before quite a bit of cosmetic dental work. Not hip to custom made clothing at the time; he wore a pair of crisp new Levis with folded cuffs. In order to get them over his muscular thighs, he had to get a waist size way larger than his actual athletically trim girth. The pants fit with a two-inch gap around his waist. He wore a simple oversized polo shirt, allowing for his huge biceps and thick chest and neck, but it hung down way below his waist. For shoes, he wore what was to become his signature, unlaced red high-top sneakers, without socks. He carried himself as if he were simply another husky kid from the mean streets of his Brownsville neighborhood in Brooklyn, New York. At the tender age of twenty, he was also the youngest World Heavyweight Boxing Champion of the World.

Jeff called me into his office and introduced us. We shook hands and I expected a bone-crushing grip, but was a bit taken aback when his clasp was unexpectedly light and delicate. Jeff then said he had courtside seats for the Laker game that night and asked if I wanted to come along. Well, no need to ask me twice I thought, of course I would come along.

"Great. Here, you're in charge of these."

Jeff tossed a manila envelope toward me. Inside were a few 8x10 glossy photos of Mike posing with his championship belt. I knew exactly what the photos were for. Bob Eubanks and I were stopped a few years back clocking eighty or more down the San Diego Freeway. Bob was driving and we were late for a taping of *Newlywed* at Sunset/Gower Studios in Hollywood. Bob got out of the speeding ticket when he gave the officers a few custom autographed photos made out to each of them by name, and almost every member of their families. Lesson learned, when traveling with celebrities "in the street" always carry a few 8x10s for custom autographs, just in case.

I carefully stuffed the photos of Mike into my shoulder bag and we were off.

We walked downstairs to the parking garage and climbed into Jeff's huge BMW. I was quite proud of my tiny brand new red Honda Civic at the time, so this behemoth seemed as large as an aircraft carrier. Mike got into the front seat with Jeff and we were off to the arena. Eventually we made our way to a line of cars all headed for the valets at the VIP entrance. It was a long line and, after each time we inched forward, the person behind us would beep his horn at us. This went on for a number of times, and we were all getting a little annoyed. Move a foot, beep. Move two feet more, another beep. Finally, Mike leaped out of the front seat, and began making his way to the car behind us. Jeff yelled to me, "Go get him damnit, and make sure doesn't hit anyone! " A professional prizefighter hitting anyone in the street can lead to jail time.

By the time I got to the car behind us, Mike was leaning against the person's car door with both hands. I heard Mike's high-pitched voice talking to the guy through the rolled down window. Needless to say, the guy was in shock and disbelief. I patted Mike on his shoulder, which was as hard as a rock, by the way, and said, loud enough so the driver of the car could hear me, "It's okay Champ. Don't worry about it, I don't think he'll beep at us anymore. Will you?" and I glared at the guy at the wheel.

"No, no of course not," said the guy, quickly shaking his head from side to side as though he were shivering. "No problem."

"Let's get back to the car, Champ."

Mike continued glaring at the fellow for a moment or two. The longest moments of my life, as I thought at any second Mike was going to lash out and cold cock the guy with a right to his nose splintering it into a thousand pieces. Mike sighed, patted his hands once lightly on the guys car, and then I let him lead the way back to Jeff's Beemer.

Once inside the arena, we were treated like royalty and escorted to our courtside seats. Mike sat between Jeff and me and the game began. Jack Nicholson walked by and gave us a nod, hyperactive Spike Lee bounced by a few times, and each time he passed he shot Mike a clenched fist salute, and I could swear the stars on the court, Magic, Kareem, Kupchak, Rambis, all gave us winks or nods as they ran back and forth during the game. Before halftime, I got up for a head start to the VIP snack bar. I asked Jeff and Mike if they wanted anything to drink, and they declined. Before heading up the aisle, Jeff warned me with a pointed finger, "Make sure you're back here before half time." He meant that we both were needed to run interference for the Champ, if need be, as if he could not take care of himself, but legally that was not an option.

As I stood on line at the snack bar, the guy behind me tapped me on the shoulder and said, "Hey, remember me?"

"No" I said, off handedly, "Should I?"

"I'm the guy who was the car behind you on the VIP line"

Oh, great I thought, the guy who almost got his face rearranged by the best boxer on the planet.

"Really, that's wonderful. Enjoying the game?"

"Oh yeah, its fine. Hey, do you think I could get Mikes autograph? I see where you guys are sitting. Best seats in the house, huh."

The last thing I wanted was this guy to bug Mike courtside. "Hey, I'll tell you what, I'll get you an autograph. Just stay right here. Do not come down to the seats, and I will set you up. Okay?"

"Sure! That would be great!"

"Okay, stay right here and I'll be right back. If you get to the counter before I get back, get me a Perrier." I reached for my wallet.

"No, no, no way my treat!

"Fine" I said and was off to courtside. When I got there, I immediately pulled a photo from bag, and told Jeff and Mike about the situation.

"Make sure the asshole doesn't come near us," Jeff said looking around the arena suspiciously.

"Don't worry, he's fine." At least I hoped he was. Mike signed a copy of his photo, and across the top added "Beep Beep!" and an unhappy face emoji. We stuffed the photo into an envelope, and I ran back to the snack bar.

The guy was waiting there like a well-trained puppy, holding a bottle of Perrier, and I handed him the envelope. He handed me the bottle of water, and then tore open the envelope like a spoiled kid on Christmas morning, and exclaimed, "This is great, who would ever believe this?" Not bothering to answer, I made my way back to the passage to courtside. He ran after me and pleaded, "Hey buddy, do you think you could get me a few more?" Not believing the guy's chutzpah, I looked him squarely in the eye and said just a little ominously, "I think you should quit while you're ahead." He thought about it for a nano-second, and then chirped, "Yeah, I guess you're right."

I smiled and bounded back to Jeff and the Champ. They were just getting out of their seats and beginning to make their way to the VIP Lounge for some refreshments during halftime. An usher accompanied us, running interference, blocking any enterprising autograph pros from ambushing us on the way out.

Toward the end of my five-year tenure at Barris Industries, Chuck called us into his office one morning and announced he was handing off operation of the company to Burt Sugarman and was headed back to the south of France. This was not the first time Chuck surprisingly gave up on producing his shows and moving off to France, as he had done it a few times in the past. Burt Sugarman handed the shows off to Peter Guber and Jon Peters. Though they were a famous movie production team, they had little experience with game shows, and we eventually closed down.

DICK CLARK, OR, LETS ROCK AROUND THE CLOCK

After five years with Chuck Barris I grew quite comfortable with show business, but after he left Hollywood and returned to France, I found myself once again adrift in the great sea of the unemployed. Not bothering to sign with an agent, I thought my job with Chuck would go on forever. That's not the way it works. During a weekend party, with the usual giant brie and assorted beers from Trader Joe's, venerable *Price Is Right* announcer, and long time friend, Charlie O'Donnell told me his agent was looking to extend his operation to include TV producers. He promised to put in a good word for me, which he did.

I called a few days later. The office was expecting me and invited me to come in for a meeting with Richard Lawrence, the head of television for a well-known talent agency in town called Abrams, Rubaloff, and Lawrence. It seems Dick Clark Productions and NBC had just procured the rights to a retooling of *Let's Make A Deal* with Monty Hall to be produced from Walt Disney World in Orlando, Florida. Richard asked if I would be interested in relocating. I was nodding yes before he finished saying "Orlando."

I was sent to Dick Clark's personal office building. Rumored to be a onetime funeral home, it was now an ivy-covered, red brick edifice directly across the street from NBC Studios in Burbank. I met with Dick's second-in-command, producer Fran La Mania. Things seemed to be going quite well as we chatted about Hill-Eubanks and producing with Chuck Barris. He asked me about the relocation, and I said it wouldn't be a problem, as my wife was a professional stand-up who was well acquainted with being on the road, and my daughter was just three years old. Fran started smiling and laughing and finally was able to say, "You're perfect!"

I smiled modestly. We shook hands and that was it. I called my agent immediately afterward and told him how the meeting went, but, more concerning to me, was what Fran said about me when I left. The lobby was filled with a dozen other producers I knew, obviously interviewing for the same gig. Was he being sarcastic? Did he hate me? What?

"Well, at least he didn't say you suck, so don't worry about it." said Richard, making an agent joke. A few days later Richard called and told me to start packing, I got the job.

Prior to "relocating" to Orlando, I was given an office in Dick Clark's building to begin pre-production. Dick loved rock and roll memorabilia and stray dogs. He had hundreds of items displayed in the conference room. Among them, the white cape Elvis wore in Vegas in a frame on the wall, a pair of gold sequined high heeled boots (the one-time property of Elton John), and an assortment of Ringo's drumsticks in an English beer mug and about two dozen autographed guitars, including a Gibson acoustic signed by Orville Gibson himself. My favorite was a framed early resume of Barbra Streisand which listed her contact phone number as JU 6-6300. That number belonged to an extremely popular answering service in Manhattan which I used as well when pursuing an acting career. It was cheap, about six dollars a month, and catered to all the show business hopefuls in Manhattan. Every afternoon you would call in for messages and the gum-snapping operators would either say "yes" and relate the information, or the dreaded, "All clear, honey cakes!"

I loved thinking Barbra Streisand endured the same nervy operators as I once did.

During the Hard Rock Café era Dick decided to open his own version of a rock and roll restaurant. Instead of sending out his priceless collectables to decorate the walls of the restaurants, he had multiple replicas made of everything in his collection and sent them out instead. Unfortunately Dick's venture into the restaurant business didn't prove to be a rollicking success, but the antiques and priceless rock memorabilia never left the office.

Dick may not have been the best restauranteur but he remained sly as a fox when it came to preserving his rock and roll treasures.

Arriving early in the morning to the Burbank office, I occasionally walked up behind Dick arriving in his white limo. The door would swing open and five or more dogs of various shapes and sizes would tumble out and wrestle with each other for a moment before heading for the front door of the office building. Immediately following a sneakered foot would extend from the limo door, attached to Dick Clark himself. If I reached the heavy curved oak door first I would hold it open for him with morning greetings, or if he reached the door first he would hold it open for me and wish me a good morning as well. The dogs would roam the halls and offices at will. One in particular, a rotund Weimaraner named Daisy, would visit every office and rout around in the trash cans looking for half eaten sandwiches and other yummy goodies. She did this so much that Kari, Dick's wife, had to send out a memo to everyone not to allow Daisy to snack from the trash baskets as the vet said she was getting dangerously overweight.

Dick hated the smell of food of any sort in his hallways and banned smelly lunches or snacks in the building regardless of Daisy's preferences. To make up for that stern rule, he had soft drink soda fountains installed on each floor. In the conference room, he purchased an entire English pub, with an oak bar complete with an authentic brass rail, mirrored back wall and shelving with working soda spigots and English pub pull bars for beer kegs he would order for staff meetings.

Rumor had it he had one of the offices made into a comfortable bedroom. No one knew for sure why, but quite often in the afternoons he would disappear for a few hours. During late afternoon and early evening production meetings, while the rest of us were collapsing, he was always bright eyed and bushy tailed. To that end, Dick also went on vacations for a few weeks every year. He returned looking years younger and quite refreshed. If anyone inquired what spa he went to, we were told not to mention anything about his time away. Enough said.

Four weeks after being awarded the gig, we sublet our house, packed our bags, and Dick Clark had booked all three of us in the First Class cabin of a Pan American 747 headed for Orlando International. During the five hour flight my daughter asked the Flight Attendant for some peanuts. She was presented with a silver bowl of fancy mixed nuts placed on a doily with nary a peanut to be found. She endured the attention like a champ. It was the very first time anyone of us had flown First Class in our entire lives, and it was certainly something one could get used to. Who needs peanuts with your mixed nuts anyway?

The show was produced from a state-of-the-art studio that was part of the Disney-MGM Theme Park. The viewing audience of three hundred and the costumed contestants were chosen from locals as well as theme park guests. As a new twist, in addition to the three curtains, which were a staple of the show, we added a huge video wall setup above the curtains to accent with a live action presentations of motor boats, sailboats, and cars, before revealing them behind a curtain if they fit. If not, we rolled them out on stage. The studio was the largest ever used to produce the show.

We edited the show at the Disney edit facility. The edit bay itself was quite spacious with a dark glass floor to ceiling window making up the left side wall of the studio. It seems we were part of the Studio Tour, and every few minutes lines of guests would be ushered into a stand-up gallery on the opposite side of the one way glass. They were able to view, but not hear, an actual edit session. We couldn't see through the glass or hear the Tour Guide's patter unless the tour guides turned up the lights in the darkened gallery. Concentrating on editing the show, we eventually forgot about the tourists on the opposite side of the glass wall and just went about our business.

One afternoon Dick decided to join us during an edit session. Always high energy, Dick took his position pacing behind the desks facing the dozen or so monitors on the wall in front of us. During the episode we were editing a contestant who made an odd hand gesture and the question arose if the guy was actually flipping off Monty Hall. Somehow the conversation strayed to the variety of ways people around the world used hand gestures to insult one another. Dick was adamant as he demonstrated the two finger English "V" hand gesture, opposed to the one-finger American version.

"In England, this," demonstrating the English two finger method, "means the same as this in the U.S.," and he thrust his middle finger up in the air. He was facing the dark glass wall head on.

"Dick," I mentioned quietly, "You just flipped off fifty guests from Omaha."

Speechless and in visible shock, he covered his face with his hands, fell to his knees and began trying to crawl under the nearest edit console. We were able to hear the laughter through the thick glass as the Tour Guide turned on the lights and we saw the guests laughing and some feigning covering their children's eyes, and some admonishing Dick by waving an index finger. Quickly regaining his composure, he grabbed an editor's pen and wrote, I AM SO SORRY!" on a piece of paper and held it up to the still-laughing crowd behind the window. Their laughter turned to applause and, ever the showman, Dick took a deep bow and then threw a few kisses. When everyone in the edit bay started applauding as well, Dick was jolted into the realization he was paying hundreds per hour for the edit session, and ordered everyone to cut the crap and get back to work. He remembered to wave goodbye to the tourists behind the glass wall, the lights went out, and we continued with our edit session.

ANDREW DICE CLAY AND THE AMERICAN MUSIC AWARDS

During the earlier days of television, Dick grew to believe *The Grammy Awards* were just a bit too stuffy and old fashioned for the burgeoning rock music industry. Powerful enough to be reckoned with, and having more than enough musical talent in his camp, plus rights to the all-important footage of their performances from all his *American Bandstand* days and more, *The American Music Awards* were born.

Everything about the show he created was new, fresh, and included all genres of pop music. It proved to be, and still is, a perennial favorite among all award shows.

Everyone working for the company realized it was never a good idea to upset Dick Clark. We never minced words when he asked for our opinion, but if we were told Dick wanted something done in a certain way, we were sure to get it done exactly that way.

During rehearsals for an episode of *The American Music Awards*, Andrew Dice Clay was scheduled to appear. He promised to do his act "clean" but during the actual taping he delivered the dirtiest, nastiest, and filthiest performance possible. The three-second delay bleep was sounding throughout the entire performance. When it came time for Clay to deliver an award, he did so, and then added in closing, "Fuck you to Dick Clark!"

Why anyone would be so stupid to say something as idiotic on live TV, true to your "character" or not, boggles the mind.

When I arrived at the office early the next morning, Dick was already there. He was in his office, pacing back and forth like a caged lion, in front of a monitor playing and re-playing the show. We were told not go near him for any reason.

No one knows what happened next, but Andrew "Dice" Clay's standup days on network and cable television were basically over.

He was rarely seen again after that date. No more HBO Specials, no network comedies, nothing. In fact, MTV imposed a lifetime ban on Clay when he pulled the same stunt during one of their award shows. It was lifted after twenty-two years.

MONTY HALL AND CLINT EASTWOOD

Working with Monty Hall under the auspices of Dick Clark proved to be quite a memorable experience. Monty and his partner Stefan Hatos, a PT boat Commander during World War II, created *Let's Make A Deal* years ago. Hatos kept all his records and notes in military precision on legal pads turning brown with age. Before we created any new "deals" we had to run them by Stefan and Monty first. They rejected most outright. Fortunately I was able to get copies of a number of old shows and reviewed each one. Next time we pitched the "boys" we would explain that a contemporary deal was exactly the same as the XYZ deal they used first used in 1975. We just used different terminology and props. They were okay with that.

Disney was another entity we had to deal with. Standards and Practices from NBC were insanely concerned with what they labeled "Creeping Disneyana" or Disney trying to plug themselves or the park every chance they had during our show. A case in point was the use of the "Disney Cow." Here's how it worked. One aspect of the show was the use of a "Zonk," or a worthless booby prize, sitting behind one of the curtains.

If a contestant chose a curtain with a "Zonk," they either lost everything they had won up that point or received nothing at all. A new car had been lurking behind a different curtain perhaps, and we were certain to reveal it before moving on. Disney approached us saying they had just acquired a big black and white cow that actually had an outline of Mickey's head on his body. It was affectionately known as "The Mickey Cow." They wanted to know if I wanted to use her as a "Zonk." How could I refuse?

A member of NBC's Standards & Practices Department from New York decided he needed to attend a taping in Orlando that week along with bringing his golf clubs just in case he had some extra time for a few rounds. No problem; we welcomed him with open arms and gave him a front row seat.

The cow was placed surreptitiously behind one of the curtains, as were the other prizes in the remaining curtains. A representative from the Disney Farm stopped by to check things out and was happy with the placement of the Mickey Cow as well as the lighting on the Mickey logo, and left the studio. We began the rehearsal and, when it was time for the "Zonk" to be revealed, the curtain zipped open and there was the Mickey Cow in all her glory! The Standards and Practices executive hyperventilated in panic and ran from his seat to the set claiming the cow was a blatant example of "Creeping Disneyana" and it had to be replaced immediately. That wasn't going to happen, but I did agree to turn her around, as the Mickey logo just appeared on one side of the cow, which had normal black splotches on the other. Problem solved. The Standards and Practices exec began breathing through his nose once again, and we had a great rehearsal, and taped an even better show later that afternoon.

Two days later I receive a bill from the Disney Farm for $800.00 for cow transportation and rental. I immediately called the Farm Office and asked what was going on, and was told if they saw the logo, the cow would have been free, but as we "hid" the logo, we had to pay the standard rental costs and fees as one would for any animal rental. I called our offices in Burbank and told the accountant the story, to which she replied, "You have to talk with Mr. Clark. Hold on I'll transfer you."

Not knowing what to expect, but knowing it wouldn't be good, Dick got on the line, and I explained the situation.

"Fuck Disney, send the damn bill to NBC!" and he hung up.

I sent the bill to NBC and never heard back from them again about "Creeping Disneyana" or "The Mickey Cow."

Dick called me at 9:00 am every Monday morning in Orlando, 6:00 a.m. in Los Angeles, for a full report. He was mainly concerned why the show we taped the week before ran few minutes over. It seems the overtime dug into Dicks' personal profits, or "cake" as they say in the carnival business, and, this for him, was an intolerable situation.

During one taping Burt Lancaster walked out onto our set to chat with Monty. He was shooting a made for TV movie in the studio next door playing Supreme Court Chief Justice Earl Warren. He had a few minutes to spare, so, dressed in his long black robes, Mr. Lancaster walked over for a visit. Monty introduced him appropriately and the audience applauded reverently. Ignoring the noise, Monty and Burt stood there center stage on our set chatting like two school boys. After a few minutes, I approached and asked very politely if we could move things along. Lancaster gave me an extremely nasty look and then ignored me. Moments later, they finished chatting, Monty announced him once again, and he waved to the cheering crowd as he walked back to the neighboring studio.

After the taping I asked Monty what was so important to delay the show for twenty minutes. He told me Burt wanted to invite him and his wife to a barbecue in Palm Springs the following weekend.

Dick called bright and early the following Monday morning and wanted to know why we were twenty minutes over. I told him the story and the fact when I tried to move things along Burt Lancaster gave me a look that was so evil, if looks could kill, I'd be a dead man. Besides that, Monty told me Burt wanted to invite him to a barbecue in Palm Springs next week. I actually heard Dick laughing slightly on the other end, and he said, "Okay. Monty has forty years' experience on us, whatever he wants to do, let him do it."

As a rule, I always delivered my shows with time to spare. Unfortunately there was no bonus for that. Running long just happened once in a great while. After delivering a show thirty minutes over, Dick was hot on the line the next Monday morning.

"What the hell happened?" he asked, as though he had already downed a few too many cups of coffee.

"An alligator was blocking the one lane road to the studio and the Disney cops wouldn't let anyone through."

"So, why didn't you just throw a rock at it or something."

"Dick, I actually suggested that! But the Disney cop told me all wildlife 'on property' were protected, so if I disturbed the monster, I'd be arrested."

"Just remember, if it happens again, I would love a new pair of alligator shoes." He hung up, and I was amazed he'd actually attempted to crack a joke.

Florida has a monsoon season of sorts, and every afternoon during our time at the studio complex, there was a cloudburst. Like magic, little red kiosks selling Disney rain ponchos sprung up all over the park. The dense rain cleared up after an hour or so and the sun came out once again as if it had never rained. The kiosks disappeared as quickly as they had appeared.

During one such storm, accompanied with thunder and lightning, our studio building was struck by an errant bolt. All the lights went out, and a wisp of smoke rose from the console in the Control Room. The Director and technicians backed away carefully and then ran for the exits. In moments, the emergency power kicked in and a dull light filled the control room and the studio halls, as well as the studio itself, so none of the audience panicked. A very long hour later the Disney electricians cleared the studio as safe, and we all went back to work.

Dick called on Monday morning as expected. Before he could utter a word, I said, "Dick, the building was struck by lightning. All the lights blew out, and there was smoke coming out of the Director's panel in the Control Room."

There was a long pause. He finally said, "You're doing a great job kid. Keep up the good work." He never called back again.

Between shows Monty would relax in his dressing room and delighted in telling me stories of his early days a growing up in Winnipeg, Canada. His favorite story was about his father, a butcher, making him haul raw meat on a sled through the snowy streets of Winnipeg for the weekly deliveries. Never forgetting his humble roots, he once asked me what charity I supported. None really, I answered, I was just happy keeping my wife in make-up and my daughter in private school.

"That's unacceptable young man" he said shaking his head. It turns out Monty was Chairman for Life for the Variety Club, the Children's Charity, Hollywood Chapter, dedicated to the support and welfare of children. In addition to sponsoring and supporting The Boys and Girls Clubs of Los Angeles, the hand painted Disney decorations for the entire children's ward of County USC Hospital, as well as new and replacement equipment for "other-abled" children. Children outgrow their expensive motorized wheelchairs and other equipment necessary for comfortable survival, so new ones were supplied by the Variety Club on a yearly basis. Quite a legacy and responsibility for a guy known mainly for giving away washing machines to people dressed like scarecrows.

Within a week of returning to Los Angeles, I found myself on the Board of Directors of the Variety Club. Because of my experience, I became responsible for the video and film needs of the organization. During a fundraiser at the famous Chasen's Restaurant in Beverly Hills, we were honoring Prince Edward, Elizabeth's youngest son, as it seems he was active with a comparable children's charity in the United Kingdom. I had already set up all the cameras and equipment but had to run out for an additional box of tapes. When I reached the door a frail older woman was struggling to get it open. I reached forward and pilled it open for her. Surprised she looked up at me, extended her hand and said, "Good evening young man, I'm Carol Channing."

"Yes Miss Channing, I know who you are," I said and I introduced myself. "Are you here for the Variety function?"

"Yes I am. You know the chili here is to die for."

"I've heard. Let me take you back." Don't ask me why, but I extended my arm and she graciously held on as we walked to the back patio.

"I can make it from here. Be sure to try the chili!" and she joined friends at one of the tables.

The buffet began and there was a huge cauldron of Chasen's famous Steak Chili, among other delicacies, so I'm sure Carol Channing was quite happy. The function was running very well, and legendary comedian Sid Caesar, who was the emcee for the evening, made an announcement, in six or seven of his "pseudo languages" that Prince Edward would be arriving shortly. Immediately after that announcement Bea Arthur, of *Maude* fame, who it was rumored to be slightly hard of hearing, asked her companion, rather loudly, "Edward? Isn't he the gay one."

Her words hung in the air like a tiny explosion of fireworks. I immediately grabbed a camera and announced, "Okay everyone, before the Prince arrives I'm going to come around and take a few candids for our party reel! Start smiling, here I come." For some reason a few people started laughing nervously and some started applauding. Bea had no idea why.

Another big fundraiser for the Club was having a celebrity shoot a short trailer to be shown in movie theatres and then have the ushers pass around collection cans though out the audience. Monty had a friend at Warner Brothers, and this friend suggested we approach Clint Eastwood to shoot one of our filmed donation shorts. Clint was thrilled to donate his time and energy to the project. Known for being a serious actor with an ominous, "Go ahead, make my day" demeanor, the real Clint couldn't have been friendlier. Warner's donated a studio and camera operator, we brought in a director, and I wrote the copy. Clint had his words down pat on arrival, and suggested we let the cue card person enjoy her Saturday, which we did. No arguing with Mr. Eastwood.

As the kids and their families arrived, Clint greeted the parents and kids individually. The parents were in awe, and the kids, most in wheelchairs, not really knowing who Clint Eastwood was, reflected their parents' thrill and wonder. We set up the simple shot, Clint standing center with all the kids positioned around. We were ready to shoot in a few minutes, and Clint was friendly and helpful throughout the set up and camera rehearsal, but the very moment, "Action" was called, he immediately turned into the "Go ahead, make my day" guy.

His eyes narrowed, he spoke in his threatening but calm monotone, and when he suggested we donate whatever we had for the Variety Club, we all reached for our wallets. "Cut" was called and this snapped us all back to reality with some nervous laughter in the studio. Clint instantaneously turned into the same friendly guy he was before "Action" was called. He started asking if everything was okay, was the lighting correct, did he lisp, was he blocking anyone, should we do it again from a different angle? We assured him everything was perfect and we got it in "one take." A compliment all film actors love to hear. We invited him to join in a little punch and cookies reception the ladies of Variety had set up in his honor in the back of the studio and he gladly accepted. Clint laughed and joked with everyone as he signed autographs and posed for cell phone photos, smiling and kneeling down to be near the kids' happy faces.

After the kids had left and we were striking the set, all the ladies of Variety introduced themselves as the President, or the Vice President, or the Treasurer and so on, and shook his hand in thanks. They were amazed he knew them by name, forgetting in the excitement they all wore name tags as one is expected to do at functions such as these. My wife introduced herself and not an officer of Variety, simply stated her name and, in that magical voice of hers that made even the simplest statements sound funny, she said with a smile, "I'm just a nobody."

Clint started laughing, and by her name tag saw that we were related, and said, "By the name on your tag I bet you're somebody to that big guy standing over there." Gesturing toward me. "May I?" he continued, looking my way. I nodded sure, not really knowing what was coming next, but knew my love could handle it. "You're not a nobody." he said smiling, and then bent over and kissed my wife on both cheeks.

All the ladies began laughing, that particular snarky laugh unique to all "Ladies Who Lunch." If visualized it would be seen as teeny tiny little daggers of jealousy jetting through the air toward my wife's heart. We quickly asked Clint if we could accompany him to the parking lot and he agreed. Once we reached his modest Mercedes, I thanked him again for helping us out and he shook my hand and winked at my wife. He then drove out of the studio gate on to Warner Boulevard and blended into the midday glare of Burbank traffic.

WILL GEER, AMERICA'S GRANDPA

While I was attending Emerson College in Boston during the early seventies, Will Geer was appearing in a pre-Broadway tryout of a play about the devil called *Scratch*. One of the professors knew Will and invited him to come over and chat with the drama students about the business. Our student union was directly across the Public Garden from the Colonial Theatre where *Scratch* was playing, so it was an easy walk for Will and he gladly accepted. He spoke with us for a few hours, regaling us with stories of the blacklist, Woody Guthrie, and, of course *The Waltons*. Afterwards, the school threw a little reception, and I went up and introduced myself. He took one look at me, and said,

"Hell you're a big one. You could hunt a bear with a switch."

"Maybe." I replied, and we smiled and that was the end of it, as he had to go back across the Garden to get ready for a matinee.

Years later, I arrive in Los Angeles after my stint on the cruise ship and sojourn in Europe and the Middle East, and I called a woman I went to school with. She was living in the Hollywood Hills with a friend who, it turned out, I worked with in summer stock.

Talk about a small world! I asked them what they were doing one Sunday wondering if they would like to hang out. She told me she was in charge of costumes at Will Geer's, Theatricum Botanicum in Topanga Canyon. I told her I never heard of the place, but I did I meet Will some years before at Emerson, so she invited me to come along with them to the theatre early the next weekend.

We arrived at Theatricum Botanicum at dawn on a misty Sunday morning, the air redolent with live oak and pine. My friend immediately found Will, who was feeding his chickens, and brought me over to properly introduce us. We shook hands, and

I told him I met him during his tryout of *Scratch* in Boston when he came to speak at our student union. I then mentioned he told me I was big enough to hunt a bear with a switch. He smiled and stepped back and gave me the once over.

"Well," he said, "You're still a big one. Wanna be an assassin in *Julius Caesar* this afternoon? We need a guy."

"Sure." I said, "But I don't know the lines."

"Don't worry, there are none, just join in stabbing old Julie when the others do. Get him a toga!" He walked off, a red bandana hanging from the back pocket of his denim overalls, to finish feeding his chickens. Just like that, I was part of the company.

During his prime, back in the earlier days of Hollywood, actor Will Geer bought five acres of land in the famed Topanga Canyon. The canyon actually connected the San Fernando Valley with Malibu via a circuitous two-lane road. Topanga had a trickle of a brook running through the canyon most of the year, turning into a raging river during the rainy season. In addition, the canyon was filled with an assortment of live oaks, aspens, chaparral and even a waterfall or two, also appearing mysteriously during the rainy season. The canyon was famous for being the respite for a collection of artistic types, free spirits, assorted hippies and even a nudist colony. Will moved in and named his homestead Theatricum Botanicum. There was a shack on the property where, supposedly, Woody Guthrie lived while in Los Angeles. Will built a small cabin on the property on stilts as protection against the seasonal floods that occasionally tormented the canyon. Will's wife of many years, actress and activist Herta Ware, lived in the cabin well into her eighties, even after they divorced amicably years before.

As a onetime blacklisted Hollywood socialist, Will was convinced theatre belonged to the people and as such it should be available at no cost to every human being on the planet. To facilitate his philosophy he had a natural amphitheater dug out amid the five acres of hillside property and created a free weekend Shakespearean showcase.

At the entry to the Amphitheatre, he installed huge curved wooden doors, which were supposedly used as the gateway to Rome in the silent *Ben Hur*. He purchased the doors at a back-lot prop sale at MGM a few years earlier. There was no charge for admission, and of course the actors weren't paid either, but they were given the invaluable opportunity to perform and hone their craft. During the shows Will, in overalls and a tattered straw hat, would putter around the rows of stadium style bench seating, tending to and pointing out to anyone listening all sorts of herbs and plants mentioned at one time or another in Shakespeare's plays: "This is rue. This is sage right here. Here is some rosemary. Ophelia mentions all of them in Hamlet."

Will was married for a number of years and fathered a few children. One daughter, Ellen, still runs the theatre for profit these days. Nevertheless, in his dotage, Will developed an infatuation for young teenaged boys. A favorite joke of his was greeting an established married member of the troupe playing Puck in *Midsummer Night's Dream*, with "So how's my favorite fuck? Excuse me, I mean Puck." He would amble off, chortling and giggling.

Many times on a misty Sunday morning, Will would show up in the costume tent with a new young surfer type in tow. He would vaguely introduce the kid and tell the Costumer, who was the friend of mine from college and who actually found a toga for me when requested, to put the kid in an appropriate costume of some sort, as he was going to be part of the show that afternoon. No one would argue, though the Costumer did warn the kid that, if he as much as opened his mouth and uttered one word during the play, she would come out on stage and punch his lights out. Will never disagreed, he just smiled and chuckled, as he shuffled off to begin tending the herbs and flowers sprouting in every nook and cranny of his rustic aromatic amphitheater.

Basically, hanging out at the theatre was just something to do on a Sunday afternoon. After performances, we would gather on the deck of his cabin to enjoy an ample slice of Herta's fresh banana bread or any organic snack of the day brought in by one of the cast members to share with everyone. We would lounge about, perhaps sharing a joint or two, as the evening chill and fog began creeping in. A large stone fire pit blazed and crackled off in a corner, and the sun began going down in pink and orange Maxfield Parrish splendor over the idyllic canyon.

After passing away in 1978, Will was cremated. He had requested his ashes be mixed in with the roots of a young apple tree being planted on the property during his funeral. While the impromptu planting and internment ritual of sorts was taking place, one of the troupe began playing bagpipes from a neighboring hill in tribute and memory to the avuncular legend. The tunes wafted through the live oaks and chaparral like melancholy sighs from an ethereal chorus of angels.

It was Will's dream that, every year going forward, a young actor or artist would be able to pick one of the newly ripened apples, take a big bite, and then remark how tasty Will still was after all the passing years.

UNCLE MOISHE

Before attending college in New England, before tramping around Europe and the Middle East, before the T.S.S. Luna Sea experiences, before any of my life began to unfold as spectacularly as I feel it has been, I was born on Miami Beach and raised in Coral Gables, a comfortable suburb of Miami. Back in the late fifties, my parents occasionally had a visitor from Miami Beach who had a quirky habit of dropping by unannounced on Sunday afternoons at our small house in the "Gables." Uncle Moishe would arrive in a black chauffeured Oldsmobile and he always brought a small strange "hostess" gift for my mother, a bottle of Canadian Rye (always Canadian) for my father, and something for my brother and me. My father and Uncle Moishe would then retire to my parents' bedroom and only the two of them would chat for an hour or two. Afterward they would come into the "Florida Room," an attached pre-air conditioning room unique to Florida. The rooms were built with floor to ceiling Jalousie windows which, when opened, were supposed to allow the trade wind breezes to waft through, making it the coolest room in the otherwise sweltering house. My mother would make lunch, cold tuna or salami sandwiches on white bread with a glass of Cott's Black Cherry Soda, Uncle Moishe's favorite. It was my job to take a sandwich and a glass of cold soda out to Uncle Moishe's driver sitting behind the wheel of the black Oldsmobile reading *The Racing Form*.

One Sunday afternoon of note, my parents were out of the room and my brother and I were building something from the Erector Set Uncle Moishe had brought over. I distinctly remember him saying with a sigh and a Polish accent, "You know something boys, in life, you should never trust nobody. Harvela (my older brother Harvey), I don't trust you, and Brucela (maybe I was seven or eight), I don't trust you, and you know something boys?

Sometimes, just sometimes, I don't even trust myself!" and we all laughed.

My parents had returned by then, and my mother was carrying a plate with a large chunk of chocolate cake wrapped in tin foil she had made for lunch. Anyone else would have gotten waxed paper, but Uncle Moishe, tin foil. My mother asked if he wanted to take some cake back to his apartment, but he demurred politely, patting his stomach and saying his doctor warned him to watch his sugar and his salt, waving his hand in disgust. He then got up, kissed my mom on both cheeks, shook my father's hand, donned his white Panama hat, and slowly ambled out to the driveway. His driver, I remember, was wearing a white loose-fitting four-pocketed "Cubaverra" shirt and you could see a packet of Camel unfiltered cigarettes in the top pocket. He opened the back door of the black Oldsmobile for Uncle Moishe who lumbered into the back seat with a grunt.

For quite some time as a kid, I always thought when people reached a certain age they all started speaking in foreign accents and grunted a lot. You can imagine my amazement when one day I saw a little old grey haired Southern lady in the local Winn-Dixie grocery actually speaking English exquisitely, with just the slightest Southern drawl, and no Central European guttural throat-clearing at all. I was amazed.

As the big Oldsmobile started creaking, tires crunching down the driveway, my eyes met Uncle Moishe's through the back seat window. He shot me a wry smile, and winked while scrunching his nose in a funny way. I smiled and waved goodbye and didn't know how to wink, though I tried, as the massive car rumbled away toward the "Beach."

Years later, after Uncle Moishe had long since passed away and was buried in a cemetery across the street from my old elementary school, my parents thought it "safe" for a short visit and asked me to drive them over. My father, aided by his cane, slowly stepped forward and delicately placed a stone on the marker. The flat red granite stone was dappled with sunlight and dancing shadows like little characters from Disney's *Fantasia*. He then stepped back, sliding his arm around my mother's waist, a bit for affection, but mainly for support, and they quietly stood there for a few moments longer.

The gravestone had a Star of David carved into it as well as the phrase "Always in our Hearts." The name on the stone left me uncomfortably confused, as it simply stated, "Meyer Lansky."

GEORGE ABBOTT - PRODUCER, DIRECTOR, PLAYWRIGHT, SCREEN WRITER, LEGEND

I met less notorious, but nevertheless famous, celebrities while growing up in Florida. In my senior year in high school I took an unpaid job as an apprentice at the Upstage of Coconut Grove, Florida. The theatre was above the local post office, hence its name. Bordering Biscayne Bay, Coconut Grove was the oldest incorporated city in Miami, and was renowned for its artistic sensibilities with galleries, coffee houses, and theatres cramming its narrow streets. Legend had it that Samuel Beckett's *Waiting For Godot* with Bert Lahr premiered in the Coconut Grove Playhouse in 1956 billed as the "laugh riot of the century." Half the audience walked out before the second act.

The hippie culture was rampant at the time (1969) and I reveled in hanging out at the parks and cafes with the long-haired "artsy" types. Identifying as one of the resident hippies during the hot humid days under the palm trees, I had to drive my mother's turquoise Mercury Monterey home to the toney suburb of Coral Gables every evening—certainly not the crib of a starving artist, as I envisioned myself to be, but no one had to know the truth at the time.

Working as an apprentice at the Upstage meant I did everything from sweeping the stage to replacing the rolls of toilet paper in the rest rooms. As I was a very mature looking seventeen, I also understudied any number of roles in the shows produced there, including the works of Harold Pinter, Jean Genet, Jean Claude Von Italie, and many other avant-garde playwrights of the era.

One evening as I was assisting with the ticketing in the box office before my understudy performance in Pinter's *The Homecoming*, an older fellow came up to the window and asked for his three tickets, one for himself, one for his wife, and one for an assistant who was with them. He said his name was "Abbott." R. Laurence Tobin, the owner of the theatre, who handled all the money, smiled and asked. "Oh, is that as in George Abbott?"

"Yes." replied the gentleman modestly.

"*The* George Abbott?" pressed Tobin, his eyes widening to the size of coconuts.

"Yes, I suppose so," replied the man.

"Here, by all means, the tickets are on the house. Please be our guests!" babbled Tobin.

"No way, that is not necessary. Take my money at least as a donation. It's my pleasure. Truly."

Tobin reluctantly took his cash and handed him his tickets. He then slammed the box office window shut with *Back In A Flash* permanently imprinted on the glass and grabbed my shoulders in hysterics.

"Listen carefully," he said. "Go backstage and tell everyone to give the performance of their fucking lives! You understand what I'm saying!"

"Cool," I said, as blasé as a seventeen-year-old wanna-be hippie could be, and I went backstage.

The older actors were all chatting, putting on their make-up, and getting ready for the show in our tiny dressing room while sitting on a communal bench in front of the long mirror illuminated with bare light bulbs all around it. A few crispy yellowing telegrams were hanging here and there, as well as being stuffed into any available crevice in the vicinity. They moved over to make room for me at the very end of the bench.

"Hey guys," I began, "Tobin wanted me to tell you to give the performance of your lives tonight because there is some famous old guy in the house."

"Really? Like who?" came the reply as, occasionally, the theatre was frequented by Jackie Gleason and various local television and radio personalities.

"Some old guy." I replied, "Named George Bishop, or Pope, or some sort of name like that."

"Oh, I bet you mean George Abbott" joked one of the female actors, smiling at her joke and nudging the actor, sitting next to her.

"Yeah!" I said remembering his name, "That's it, the guy's name is George Abbott."

The dressing room of actors looked at me in astonishment, their mouths agape, eyes widening to the point of exploding.

"*The* George Abbot?" came the chorus.

"Hey, that's the same thing Tobin said. Who the hell is this guy?"

The dressing room erupted in bedlam, everyone rising all at once, with me still sitting on the far end, so one end of the bench shot up into the air and I landed on the floor with a make-up sponge filled with Max Factor Tan #2 pancake smearing into my left eye. No one cared; they were all running around the tiny dressing room like hundreds of hermit crabs just released back on the beach from captivity in a shoe box.

The performance went off without a hitch. During the show, and unbeknownst to us, Mr. Abbott sent his assistant out across the street for a chilled magnum of Cordon Rouge Champagne and some plastic flutes. After the audience cleared out, Mr. Abbott and his wife gathered us all in the theatre lobby and proposed a toast to our performances and to our little eighty-seat theatre on top of the post office.

He then came around a shook everyone's hand. When he came to me, I remember him saying, "Good show young man. They tell me you are only seventeen."

"Yes sir," I said, probably blushing a scary shade of crimson, "I'm off to Emerson College in Boston in September."

"Emerson? You are a very talented young man. Be sure to listen carefully to your professors and when it comes doing a show, do anything they ask you to do." He moved on to the others, sharing a handshake and a brief chat with each.

The following year I took a course in Contemporary Broadway Theatre and learned that Mr. Abbott was responsible for either writing, producing, directing or doing all three for a variety of Broadway hits including *Jumbo* (1935), *Boy Meets Girl* (1935), *The Boys from Syracuse* (1938), *Pal Joey* (1940), *High*

Button Shoes (1947), *Where's Charley?* (1948), *Call Me Madam* (1950), *Wonderful Town* (1953), *The Pajama Game* (1954), *Damn Yankees* (1955), and *Fiorello!* (1959). The school decided the big musical my freshman year (1970) was going to be George Abbott's *Fiorello!*, a show about the life and times of flamboyant New York Mayor Fiorello LaGuardia. During set up I was given the job to crawl under the stage and paint all the braces and platforms underneath in a flat coat of black paint, most of which splattered all over me and my corduroy Levis.

I didn't tell anyone that George Abbott once treated me to a flute of Cordon Rouge after a performance, or that he told me "Do whatever they ask you to do." I painted the underside of the set on my back in a stunning shade of flat black with the determination of Michelangelo as though it were the ceiling of the Sistine Chapel. At the end of the year, I was cast as Bernardo in *West Side Story*. A casting coup for a freshman. Thanks for the advice Mr Abbott.

AUNT SARA, UNCLE IRVING, AND ABBIE HOFFMAN

Aunt Sara and Uncle Irving, my elderly Godparents, were dedicated socialists who, even so, owned one of the Art Deco dowagers on Collins Avenue facing the Atlantic on Miami Beach. The hotel was named The Pelican and stands there to this day, a pastel pink and blue *petit four* part of the Historic District. It was air "cooled" in those days by the unobstructed winds and breezes directly off the Atlantic. According to my Dad, before the war, he and Irving used to hang out in the same poolroom in New York's Lower East Side. They remained friends over the years; in fact, Uncle Irving supplied my father with a small second floor apartment that protruded out a bit over Collins Avenue, enabling my father to see up and down the busy two-way street. An extremely important architectural feature as, after World War II, my father ran a little off track betting parlor in the space and needed to see any police cars racing up or down the street toward the hotel. If so, he could touch a continually lit cigarette to his result sheets which were always written on flash paper, tissue paper pre-soaked in kerosene, then dried and worked until pliable. All the evidence would disappear in an instantaneous wisp of smoke.

The Pelican, with its lobby forever smelling of mothballs and cigars, was sold years ago. All the old snowbirds were forever sitting on the porch with their canes and walkers, and some of them actually died while sitting out there. James Michener once wrote that Miami Beach is filled with people who spent their entire lives waiting for the right time to do something they always dreamed about. Now they have the time, but would rather be in bed by 7:30. The elderly retirees have been replaced by trendy young men with pony tails accompanied by sexy girls with four-inch heels and skin-tight leopard print pants, sipping espressos from tiny cups pulled from a huge copper espresso press, crowned with an eagle where the wooden newspaper rack used to be,

Having spent an inordinate amount of time in the tenement slums of New York during the thirties and forties trying to organize the inhabitants, Aunt Sara contracted tuberculosis and lost a lung to the disease. She was sent to a recovery sanitarium in the Berkshires that she referred to as "The San." While incarcerated (her word) she once told me she organized the cafeteria staff and the other residents because of the "horrible, horrible food they served." She was released early.

Sara's home was a sprawling cathedral-ceilinged, faux-adobe structure in an older section of Miami. Screened porches surrounded the entire house; the screens were installed in wooden frames on an inward diagonal from the roof to the outer walls so even during the heaviest afternoon downpours you did not have to close the windows. This allowed the breezes to continue cooling the house. The house was filled with thick rattan furniture with flamingos and palm trees printed on the heavy yellowish fabric. It was not until later I realized all the framed original artwork in her living room was by Frida Kahlo, Rockwell Kent, and Diego Rivera, erstwhile socialists every one, though some might even say Communists. In fact, for my Bar Mitzvah, she gave me a complete volume of all of Shakespeare's works, plays, sonnets and poetry illustrated by, who else, fellow traveler Rockwell Kent, of course.

The Republican convention of 1972, nominating Richard Nixon, was held on Miami Beach. Sara eagerly volunteered to hand out literature at a kiosk for the Students for a Democratic Society (a.k.a. SDS) in Flamingo Park, an oval track and field stadium on South Beach where the protesters were herded for safekeeping. Sara was arrested during a sweep of the "politically motivated young people," as she liked to call them, once the city tired of being nice to the protesters. Her husband couldn't bail her out, as the only car they still owned was a Cadillac from the fifties that couldn't be driven but which they kept parked in their weed-riddled driveway, even though all the tires had gone flat years before. They felt it made the house look "lived in."

My father and I were elected to head down to the Miami Beach Police station to bail her out. That proved to be a somewhat risky situation due to intermittent rioting, a curfew, and clouds of tear gas still wafting around the town in defiance of the evening ocean breezes. My father, an old denizen of the "Beach," knew a back way to the station (no telling how he learned about that), and we arrived in the early evening. When we told the Desk Sergeant who we came to bail out, he said, "Oh, Joan Baez's grandmother, it took you guys long enough."

Seems Sara was leading the arrested protesters in rousing renditions of Pete Seeger and Woody Guthrie songs, much to the annoyance of the cops in the station.

First words from Sara when she saw us were, "I hope you didn't tell these pigs anything!"

We told her to quiet down and quickly headed for the station exit. As we were leaving, the Desk Sargent mumbled, "Have a good evening Sara."

To which she replied, with a clenched fist salute, "Power to the people, Sammy! Hey, how are the kids?"

"Tommy is at University of Miami, and Mary Ann's been accepted at Florida State."

"Bless their hearts, tell them I send my love. Next time they are on the Beach, tell them to stop by the Pelican for a Coke. We just got a new machine."

"Sure Sara, no problem." He turned away to answer the phone.

We smiled sheepishly to grumpy Sergeant Sam (who knew?) and hustled her out of the booking office.

Outside on the landing, there was a tall thin fellow standing there with a huge Jewish/Afro haircut, patched jeans, and wearing dark aviator sunglasses, even though it was well into the humid evening. He was smoking a cigarette while listening to the sound of the waves crashing on the beach a few blocks away, accented by the eerie wail of sirens off into the sticky night. Sara then politely inquired, "Abbie? Abbie Hoffman? Abbila, darling, what are you doing here? Do you need bail? Is there anything we can do for you?"

"We?" I thought to myself.

He then said, much to the amazement of my father and me, "Sara what the hell are *you* doing here."

"Abbie, you of all people should know, the struggle against these fascists pigs will never end! I'll be back in Flamingo Park bright and early tomorrow morning, and I expect to see you there as well!"

Thus gently chastised, Abbie smiled back and looked at me and said in a recognizable New England regionalism, "She's your grandmotha?" (sic)

"Godmother," I corrected.

He laughed and said, "Well I'll tell you one thing, she's a pistol, no doubt about it. Hey, how about you joining us, we'll be around all week?"

"Sorry, but I'm headed back to school in a few days." I said.

"Where?" he replied.

"Boston." I said.

"Boston?" he replied somewhat incredulously," I was born in Worcester." Which he pronounced "Woosta."

"We'll be back there in two weeks. We can use a big guy like you!" He winked at my Dad and shot him a clenched fist salute. My father, not known for his liberal sensitivities, ignored him, of course, and continued hustling Sara toward the parking lot.

"Don't worry Abbie," she called back, "he'll call, I have the number of the SDS Boston office in my appointment book!"

He began laughing and said, "Don't spread it around, sweet-haaart; it's actually my apaaartment numba!"

Speechless, I looked at my godmother as she nodded knowingly and shot him a clenched fist salute. Just then, Abbie was called back into the police station. "I'll look forward to hearing from you, Sara, and you too, my man!" He gave us all a two finger peace sign and began blowing kisses and goofing around with his uniformed escorts.

I returned to Boston in the spring —Abbie and I never managed to get in touch with each other—a few months later I received a packet of seven plays in the mail with my lines highlighted in each from Mount Holyoke College Summer Theatre in South Hadley, Massachusetts. My summer stock gig for that year. The ice had begun groaning and breaking up on the Charles River, the tulips were blooming through the defrosting soil, and I never re-connected with Abbie Hoffman.

Some time later, I read that he had committed suicide.

Shakespeare once wrote, "Out, out brief candle, life is but a walking shadow, a poor player who struts and frets his destined hour upon the stage, and then is heard no more."

As Abbie once said, "Freedom is the right to yell 'theatre' in a crowded fire..."

ESTHER WILLIAMS – THE MILLION DOLLAR MERMAID

During the mid 1990s my wife had a very close friend whom she met years ago when they were both improv comedians working the comedy club circuit in Hollywood. They were troupe mates and audience shills for Robin Williams, Andy Kaufman, and many others. Turns out, a few years later, this woman evolved into the ex-wife of Esther's fourth husband which, in Esther's ultra-hip, avant-garde world, made us all part of her family. That was fine with us. While visiting at her Beverly Hills estate on numerous Sunday afternoons, at no particular time, Esther would decide it was time for lunch or dinner. She had her husband pull her gold Rolls Royce convertible with cream leather interior out of the garage and into the driveway. We would all climb in. She insisted on driving, her head wrapped in a Gucci scarf and oversized dark sunglasses, and off we would go. Careening down the narrow circuitous streets in the Hills, we would eventually make it to the flats. I wouldn't say Esther drove with reckless abandon, but she certainly enjoyed her time in command of her classic automobile. Driving up or down one way streets or short cut alleys, answering honking cars with "I'm a movie star, calm down!" as she would continue on her way.

Arriving at one of the very famous Beverly Hills eateries with a world renowned outdoor patio where there were always swarms of paparazzi milling about the sidewalks and entrances, many of whom Esther just may have told her husband to tip off before our arrival. She refused to use the valet but, instead, parked in the nearest handicapped spot, even though she did not have a proper placard allowing her to do so. To avoid the $500 dollar fine, she would place a little prepared note under the windshield wiper that she took from the glove compartment. Written on delicate personal stationary with a flowery border it read: "Officer, if there is a problem, please come in and see me, table six. Best regards, Esther Williams"

We would all walk down the sidewalk, Esther elegantly acknowledging the paps as well as signing just a few autographs.

No one ever disturbed our lunch, though many times when returning to the car, the note was gone, and Esther would grouse, "Damn, now I have to write another one."

When my daughter turned thirteen we invited Esther to her Bat Mitzvah celebration, both the morning service and the reception afterward. We never expected her to show up at the Synagogue in Brentwood on a Saturday morning, but to our amazement and surprise, there she was, in full makeup and hair, looking like a queen. Prior to the service, it's customary to hand the Rabbi a list of family and friends who will be called to the stage during the reading of the portion of the Law, or the Torah, designated for that day. The Honorees get their names mentioned during the opening prayers and are then instructed to delicately touch the portion of the Torah that is going to be read in their honor with the Rabbi's prayer shawl. It's called an "Aliya" or "Calling Up." Not expecting Esther to attend, we did not include her on our list. Luckily, our Rabbi was nobody's fool and, seeing a Hollywood legend in his congregation that morning, "called her up" as the last honoree. The murmur in the congregations was palpable, but Esther performed like royalty. Not understanding a word of the classical Hebrew being sung, she stood there with noticeable awe and respect. When the ritual was over, our diminutive Rabbi extended his hand for a handshake, as is the custom. Esther, a tall woman with broad athletic shoulders, shook his hand heartily, and then kissed my daughter on both cheeks. She then turned, grabbed the Rabbi's shoulders with both hands, and drew him in for a big kiss on the cheek as well. Not something usually done in religious ceremonies, but it was so sweet and ingenuous everyone in the congregation burst out in laughter and then applause. Esther returned to her seat slowly and majestically, modestly acknowledged the crowd as though she had just received an Academy Award®.

We held the reception for my daughter on the Queen Mary at permanent anchor in Long Beach Harbor. The party was held in huge oblong room on the main deck toward the rear of the ship, the onetime first class lounge and club. It boasted ceiling-high windows running the length of both sides of the room revealing twinkling light views on the opposite shores, both port and starboard. There was a raised bandstand toward the back of the room and a slick Art Deco wooden parquet dance floor spreading out from the bandstand into the room in the shape of a huge bouquet of tulips.

Esther arrived quite early that afternoon and, while apologizing, told me she had made the crossing on the Queen Mary a number of times in the "early days" and wanted to have some time to look around, just for old time's sake. I told her that wouldn't be a problem, in fact, we were given the Royal Suite for the night as part of the package for throwing the reception, supposedly the favorite of the royal families from George V up to and including Queen Elizabeth as a child with her royal parents. The suite consisted of a huge Art Deco sitting area and a separate bedroom, adjacent to servant's quarters. I asked Esther if she wanted to see it and she agreed immediately. Seems when the Royals weren't traveling they made the room available to Hollywood elites. The stars accepted the invitations wholeheartedly, as the studios were paying for it.

Esther sauntered in and grew a little faint. "This is it. This is the stateroom! The furniture has changed but I'll never forget all the built-in shelving. Loved the port holes, I always demanded they open them because the air on the North Atlantic was the best on the planet, bracing and a bit brisk. Why don't you open them?"

"I can't, they're sealed." I said, having already tried when we checked in.

"What a pity." she purred and quickly asked, "Can we see the pool?

Earlier in the day, we had taken a complimentary tour of the ship and the pool had been closed for repairs. Rumors were rampant it was haunted, as well. I told Esther as much and she said, "Oh young man, I was the Million Dollar Mermaid, don't forget. They'll let us in, let's go."

Although the pool was deep inside the bowels of the ship, Esther knew exactly how to find it. Unfortunately, it was early evening, the entryway doors were locked and chained, and there was not a soul around who could open them. Two round windows in the doors were frosted with age, so you could not see through them, but Esther tried peering inside anyway, to no avail.

"Oh well" she said with a sigh, "it was a tiny pool anyway. Let's get back to the party."

While the festivities were gaining momentum, there I was, walking down the Promenade Deck of the Queen Mary toward the Club, arm in arm with Miss Esther Williams. I expected to see Cary Grant, in a white jacket sauntering down the opposite way.

Esther's current husband was a debonair fellow named Eddie, with greying temples and a very suave demeanor. He met us at the door of the reception, "Where were you guys?" he asked with a furrowed brow.

"Checking out the pool, but it was closed," I answered immediately Didn't say anything about the George V Suite for fear of raising any undue suspicions, as, after all, this guy was her fourth husband.

"No problem, come on doll, let's dance." He extended his hand and she delicately placed hers in his, and off they went to elegantly "cut a rug" on the slick parquet tulip dance floor.

She gave my daughter a copy of the coffee table book *The Century* by Peter Jennings and Todd Brewster, as a gift. The following inscription, on a piece of her personal flowered stationary was tucked inside.

February, 2000

Dear Peregrine,

This is a book about our Century. The next one is yours. Go with love, we send ours.

Good Luck and Long Life!

Esther and Eddie

A few years later, in 2013, Esther passed away from natural causes. She was 91. At the time she was still living in her hilltop mansion high above Beverly Hills. Her ashes were scattered in the Pacific, as any revered mermaid's should be.

We were told, on the morning of her passing, like she did every morning before breakfast, she had swum a few laps in her pool.

WHEEL OF FORTUNE LIVE!

Just before the "turn of the century" 1999, I was hired by Sony to create and produce a live stage version of *Wheel of Fortune*. We called the show *Wheel of Fortune Live!* and it consisted of various puzzles from the TV show, live stage stunts, and videotape collections of memorable scenes from a variety of game shows that just happened to be Sony properties. All the contestants were chosen from the audience at random. This caused an occasional problem, as we were unable to pre-screen the contestants as we did with the television show. Because of the random nature of choosing a contestant, we had to deal with an older man in Birmingham, Alabama who didn't know how to read (at least he didn't know the alphabet) and another who, when asking for a vowel, would recite any letter in the alphabet that he could recall. After a number of tries he finally hit on a vowel and the audience gave him a warm, understanding round of applause. Our host, Bob Eubanks, was a master at dealing with any type of contestant, regardless of education, or lack of it, and he was able to work with a myriad variety of audience members from farmers to brain surgeons. Invariably the farmers did better at the games than the brain surgeons, but that's show business.

We traveled all across the United States and Canada from as far south as Palm Beach, Florida, to as far north as Edmonton, Alberta, Canada. We played huge arenas, small theatres, baseball stadiums, open air theatres, county fairs, high school auditoriums and occasionally a hockey rink or two. In one particular hockey rink, rather than replace the ice, the promotors had the ice covered with a thick slab of compressed paper known as homasote. This was standard operating procedure in many of the hockey rinks we played, as the hockey arena was the largest public building in many of these small towns. The city fathers were proud of the concerts, road shows, and even a circus or two that had played there before. Our show was quite flexible and we had the ability to adjust the performance for any running time the promoter desired—two hours, an hour and a half, even one hour if that's what the venue desired. The running time was usually predetermined by contract, according to the needs of the fair, sporting event, or wherever we were scheduled to appear. The fairs didn't want a few hundred people in a confined space for too long and not on the midway spending money.

During one matinee performance in a hockey rink in North Dakota, the promoter came up to me mid performance and asked if we could cut the show in half. This was after we had already begun and were turning letters, solving puzzles, and giving away air conditioners courtesy of the local appliance store. When we asked why he wanted us to cut the show once we had already started, he replied that the old folks, the majority of our audience, who were sitting on the homasote covered ice, were beginning to get chills and were rather uncomfortable. I grabbed Eubanks during a video portion of the show and I told him what was happening. As soon as he was able to stop laughing, consummate pro that he was, he went back out on stage and ended the show within minutes, with no one, cast and crew included, being any the wiser as to why.

The *Wheel of Fortune Live!* show traveled with one bus outfitted for touring. We also had a semi-trailer truck with the sets, video, sound, and lighting equipment. Our tour bus was custom-fitted and owned by the driver. It came equipped with a living room area and a kitchen, a restroom, bunks for up to twelve, and a private cabin in the rear. The rear cabin, or Star Cabin, was equipped with a King sized bed, sofa, writing desk, and a small fridge. In addition, it had a large flat screen television as well as an entertainment console with stereo headphones, radio, television, DVD player, and Video Disc player. There was a picture window across the back wall of the cabin and it came with a hatch in the ceiling that could open and close for fresh air or replace smoky air that had had a tendency to accumulate in the very comfortable space when Bob was not in residence.

Bob and I usually met the tour bus at the airport nearest the venues where we were going to play that weekend, Thursday through Monday. We would fly in together and then travel on the bus the entire weekend, then usually flew back to Los Angeles on Monday or Tuesday. One afternoon while zipping through a never-ending Idaho filled with cow pastures so remote that wild, prong horn antelopes mingled with the grazing Guernseys, I was having a down moment while staring out at the rapidly passing landscape. Bob joined me and asked if anything was up. I told him my wife just emailed me some papers claiming the tiny house we just purchased in Studio City for $120,000 had been purchased by the seller a few years before for $60,000. I felt we had been taken. Bob laughed and said something I'll never forget: "If you stay in show business long enough, some years your house will earn more money than you will."

Bob went on to tell me he bought a hundred acre ranch in the barren Santa Ynez Valley in 1965 for less than $100,000. His closest neighbors were ostrich and emu farmers. He built a modest hacienda, riding rings, and a barn, as he wanted a place zoned for horses. When not hosting game shows, he was an avid rider and dressed the part with cowboy hats, boots, and large rodeo buckles holding up his Lee Jeans. Thinking he was an avid camper and outdoorsman, I once started questioning him about what types of tents and camping equipment he was partial to, and he started laughing and said, "Are you kidding me? I've never slept in a tent. Camping for me is the ground floor of the Holiday Inn!"

The ostrich and emu farms are now long gone, and the area now crammed with Native American casinos, hotels, shopping centers and suburban homes. When I asked Bob how much his acreage is worth these days, he would smile coyly and tell me to mind my own business.

Every spring, Bob volunteers to emcee and serve as auctioneer for a western art show on his property to fund the local Chamber of Commerce. The year we attended, he took time off from his varied duties, saddled two horses, and took my daughter riding around one of his equestrian rings. On the drive back to Studio

City, my pre-teen daughter was very impressed with the fact that her dull, boring parents actually knew a cowboy. Sitting in the back cabin with Bob, after our return, the pastures passing by in a blur, we would occasionally find empty bottles or containers of Airwick or some such room deodorizer. No telling why.

Bob Eubanks is a straight arrow and, even though he promoted and produced the Beatles' first appearance at the Hollywood Bowl, as well as shows with the Rolling Stones and more, he claims he has never smoked a cigarette or even tasted a beer, let alone anything stronger. During a long flight, I was going over our contract rider for the venue where we were headed. A rider is the list of personal needs an act asks for its engagement. This includes the types of food served for various meals, the snacks in the dressing rooms, the refreshments available for the crew and, in some cases, even the number of fresh towels and type of soap for the stadium showers. All this was supplied cheerfully, as it is an integral part of the touring business.

Bob told me about the rider he once received for a rock group he was promoting early in his career. This one band added on their rider that it will "snow" in all the dressing rooms on the day of the show. Bob had no idea as to what they were talking about, as he had booked the show into two venues where it never ever snowed, as they were both in sunny Southern California, the Long Beach Auditorium and the Hollywood Palladium. He thought they were just trying to be funny so he ignored it. On the day of the show, the Road Manager came screaming out of the dressing rooms complaining that the needs on the rider had not been met and there will be hell to pay. It seems there wasn't any "snow" in the dressing rooms as requested. Bob tried to diplomatically remind the Road Manager it never snowed in Southern California. That's when he quickly learned the "snow" they were requesting was actually cocaine. Bob never told me how he solved the problem.

Traveling with Mr. Eubanks was a hoot. Usually, when he was recognized at the airline ticket counter, we were immediately upgraded to Business and occasionally First Class at no extra charge. Timing was of utmost importance here. If it seemed Bob wasn't recognized and we were not going to score a free upgrade, he would ask the agent how much an upgrade would cost, and then look at me, as if I carried the checkbook, and I would shake my head and say, just loud enough for the agent to hear, "No Mr. Eubanks, it's just not in the budget, but let me call Sony, and see what's going on." I'd pretend to dial a number on my phone and then say, "Hi sweetheart, this is Bruce. We're at LAX, I have Bob Eubanks with me, we are on our way to do the show. There aren't Business Class tickets here for us, what's going on?'

Realizing, finally, that he or she was dealing with a celebrity, the agent would interrupt and say, "Mr. Eubanks, not problem; this happens all the time. Here are your upgraded tickets. Have a good flight, and thanks for flying with Delta today!"

We took the tickets, thanked the agent profusely, and hurried to the gate before the agent could change his or her mind.

During one flight in business, Bob ordered an orange juice and I ordered something a little stronger. After a few moments Bob grew a little impatient and said he was going forward to see what was taking so long. He was gone for about thirty minutes and finally returned with his orange juice. Sliding into his seat, he turned to me and said, "You're not going to believe this, but I was just sitting in the cockpit with the pilot and co-pilot."

"Sure you were," I said, "and my name is Orville Wright." Even though this was years before 9/11 and onboard airline security was practically non-existent. I was still very skeptical.

"Seriously." he said, "The flight Attendant recognized me and asked if I wanted to sit upfront and I said sure. She knocked on the door, it opened, and in I want. It was great. I told them about you and they are waiting for you, go tell them who you are."

An old joke in Hollywood—"tell them who you are" or "tell them who you were" and you might get a seat or better service—was a sarcastic line we suggested to friends all the time. Eubanks was a famous practical joker, so I was sure he was trying to set me up. Moments later a smiling Flight Attendant came to our seats, Bob pointed at me and she motioned for me to follow her. I did, and in moments I was sitting in the cockpit with the pilot and co-pilot. The pilot was sitting back in his seat with his foot propped up on the console. The co-pilot was reading a *Popular Mechanics* magazine and gobbling from a box of Good & Plenty. We chatted briefly about this and that, and the pilot asked if I was ever in a cockpit before.

"Are you kidding? Of course not!" and they both started laughing.

Something crackled through the radio which I didn't understand and the pilot returned to a proper position. I noticed that the section of the console where he was resting his foot was rubbed bare to the metal, so he wasn't the first pilot to rest his foot there. The co-pilot offered me a snort from his box of Good & Plenty, I refused politely, and he began relating some sort of official jargon into his radio. I figured it was time for me to leave. I thanked them, they nodded and waved back, and I returned to my seat.

I don't think flight crews are offering random passengers a shake of Good & Plenty, let alone entrance to the flight deck, anymore.

We played a variety of entertainment venues including baseball stadiums, Native American casinos, small theatres, large theatres, open arenas, amphitheaters and, oddly enough, race tracks with sulkies and horses racing by in the afternoons. During a race, we had to hold perfectly still while installing the set so as not to spook the horses as they ran by. In the evening the promotors would set up chairs on the sandy race track itself and we did the show on a covered stage right next to the rail in the infield.

During the annual county fair at a famous racetrack in Lexington, Kentucky it had been raining all day and I suggested we cancel the show. The promoter said that would be impossible as they had never cancelled a show during their thirty-five year history. I agreed that was a wonderful record, but if we called a contestant up on our stage and they slipped and broke something we would be liable. The promotor assured me that wouldn't happen, but if I could produce a waiver guaranteeing if someone hurt themselves due to the weather, we wouldn't be blamed, he would gladly sign it.

I was on the phone in minutes with the Sony lawyers in Los Angeles and within two hours received a waiver, in triplicate, for the promotor to sign, relieving the show and Sony from any responsibility in the event eager contestants tripped and hurt themselves running up to, or on, our possibly rain soaked stage. When the time came for the performance the eager audience, some protecting themselves with a rainbow of umbrellas, were ushered to their seats on the dampening track, the rain by then having subsided to an intermittent drizzle.

During the show, I noticed that Bob and some of the contestants on stage were being pelted with little balls of race track clay. Bob calmly walked over to me during a video break, steaming mad, and said some jerk was throwing crap at him and the contestants. I immediately called the promoter to the production table and told him what was happening. I threatened to end the show if it continued.

"Don't worry," he said calmly, "It's "Dingleberry Dan." He does it at all the damn time, even though he's been banned from all the shows. We'll find him and throw him out. I'm really sorry, boys."

Bob and I were not convinced. Moments later three husky lads with SECURITY printed on their black T-shirts descended on the audience and grabbed a skinny teenager. They dragged him from the audience kicking and attempting to scream, but a large hand pressed over his mouth prevented him from causing too much of a ruckus. No telling where they took him, but then again, his welfare wasn't our problem.

The rain had stopped. The show continued without a hitch. No one slipped, no one fell, and Bob told the audience if they were called up to please leave their umbrellas at their seats.

After the show, as we did at all the venues, we prepared for a meet & greet in a dry area backstage. Enterprising Bob charged ten dollars, cash only, for a signed photograph, twenty dollars if they wanted a photo with him and them posing by the Wheel. We had brought along a system that could develop the photos within a few minutes, so before we had even completed striking the set, the photos were ready, delivered in a souvenir envelope, and the happy audience members and contestants were on their way.

A few weeks later we were playing a convention center outside of Chicago that had various arenas and meeting spaces of differing sizes. We played a small hall able to handle our expected audience of a few thousand or so. The largest venue, with an audience capacity of over seven thousand, also served as a basketball arena when concerts were not scheduled in the hall. During our performance, we heard explosions going off nearby and we all grew quite concerned. I went out to investigate and it turns out this particular weekend the fantasy rock group KISS was playing there. They were on a summer tour that year. Many bands and performers travel all spring and summer playing one night stands or weekends at arenas, fairs and stadiums, and our small *Wheel of Fortune Live!* show was in that mix. Many times we shared an arena or fairground stage either before or after a one night or weekend stand by an assortment of shows including *Brooks & Dunn, George Clinton and Funkadelic, Santana, Cheryl Crow, Travis Tritt, Tim McGraw* and many more.

One evening we were performing next door to KISS, whose act was complete with fire breathing, shooting rockets, levitating drum sets, and more pyrotechnics than a Fourth of July celebration. Setting up and running this complex show was a large team of roadies and technicians who were all home based in Nashville. That is where all the rehearsal halls are located in a part of town filled with hundreds of non-descript Quonset huts that were actually rehearsal stages available for rent. The entire area looked more like a Hollywood studio backlot that stretched on for miles than a neighborhood in Nashville. Regardless of show, the roadies were all pals and looked forward to visiting each other when two shows met at a venue. Some carried scrapbooks with innocent looking sunflowers or wheat fields decorating the covers, while the inner pages were crammed with Polaroids of their sexual conquests with whom they affectionately referred to as "arena rats" or the groupies who hung around the venues and truck stops. The faces of the men and women in the lewd photos had their faces burned away with a lit cigarette, so only an empty circle remained where the face once was. They would spend hours hooting and laughing trying to identify each other by tattoos, physical attributes, and more sexual positions than listed in the Kama Sutra.

Disregarding photographic recognition, all our people knew the KISS crew and they knew our guys. We did a late afternoon show. Afterward, our Road Manager and crew invited me to come along with them to say "hey" to the KISS boys and check out the installation and performance of their show, as well as any scrapbooks that might have been traveling with them.

The first thing that impressed me was the army of tour busses and semi-trailer trucks traveling with the show parked in precise order behind the building. In contrast with our show traveled with one tour bus and one semi-trailer truck, KISS moved with quite a few more. There were five custom designed tour busses, one for each member of the band and their families, and one extra that was used as a mobile office. There were an additional five busses for the crew with accommodations for twelve as described earlier. This caravan was accompanied with ten semi-trailer trucks for their sets and equipment.

The KISS stage boasted floor to ceiling speakers on either side of the stage, which I thought was unbelievably impressive. Turns out those monstrous speakers were simply non-operational stage props, the actual sound amplified from large standard amps on stage. Even with my fantasy shattered, I was still amazed. The stage was equipped with a huge crane with a cherry picker basket attached to the front end. During the show a member of the band, with a special guitar, would jump in the basket and it would stretch out over the screaming crowd. Between hot solos, accompanied with jets of fire spewing out from the actual guitar, the aerial guitar player would shower handfuls of guitar picks on the appreciative crowd below. Many members of the crowd would leap vertically in the air to catch a souvenir pick, like dolphins leaping for a fresh kipper.

Backstage, in full view of any of anyone passing by, was what they called the Air Sofa. It was a long worn, Goodwill store style sofa with an oriental rug spread out in front. It had four oxygen tanks replete with tubing and breathing masks placed intermittently behind it. After a break in a rousing riff, a few of the band would rush back, collapse on the sofa and start breathing heavily through the masks. The makeup and hair people were also hovering around to supply any touchups that might be needed.

My Road Manager and I were standing in the wings. The sound was deafening, but we still had a clear view of the action going on backstage as well as the ongoing performance on stage. I turned to my right and towering above me in full KISS drag, The Demon himself, with cape, shoulder spikes and high heels, was Gene Simmons. He was checking out the performance as were we, after a refreshing hit of pure oxygen, waiting for his re-entry cue.

Our eyes met, and I shouted "Nu manishma habibi?" which was Hebrew/Arabic slang for "Hey buddy, how are you doing?"

I knew Gene was born and raised in Haifa, Israel as Chiam Witz, the son of Holocaust survivors, so I gave the Hebrew a shot, not being sure what to say to a seven foot tall rock star, getting ready to dash on stage. He reeled back just for a bit, and then shouted back somewhat incredulously, "Atah Israeli?" (Are you Israeli?)

"Lo ani lomed Everet bi kibbutz bi Galil Eliyon?" I replied quickly. (No, I learned Hebrew while living on a on a kibbutz in the Upper Gallilee.)

"Galil Elyon?" he replied, "Ata yodea Joshua Rabinowitz?" (Upper Galilee? You know Joshua Rabinowitz?)

"Slach li, adoni, aval lo" (Sorry sir, but I don't.)

At that moment, a Stage Manager came running over yelling, "Gene, it's time!!"

While carefully beginning a slow belabored strut to the stage, Gene looked back at me and with a big smile, said in English, "My father was "Sir." I'm Gene. Lehitriot habibi!!!" (See you later buddy!)

"Lehitriot, chaveer, Mazel Tov!" (See you later friend, Good Luck!) I yelled back.

He waved his hand and shouted back, "With these fucking shoes, I'll need all the luck I can get!"

He slowly hobbled out on stage, balancing on the six-inch platform boots, stuck out his insanely long tongue, and the audience roared to a decibel level that almost caused my ears to bleed. KISS broke into a rousing rendition of "Rock and Roll All Nite."

Later that night, relaxing with the crew and a cold one in the living room area of our bus, a Willie Nelson disc playing quietly in the background, our Road Manager made a big announcement that I was a close personal friend of Gene Simmons. I denied the accusation, mentioning that Gene just wanted to know if I knew an old friend of his. That seemed to settle everyone's curiosity.

EDMONTON, ALBERTA, CANADA

We headed up to Canada after the KISS date and spent two days driving through nothing but wheat fields from one end of the horizon to the other. Occasionally a red barn or silo broke up the monotony, but not often. In an attempt to maintain our sanity, we stopped at an archeological site known as Head Smashed In Buffalo Leap. It seems stone age Canadians would drive thousands of buffalo over cliffs, falling to their deaths on the jagged rocks below. This provided the entire tribe with an abundance of hides, horns, bones, and certainly meat and assorted edible goodies to last an entire winter. In the deepest recesses of my mind, I just hoped the modern day Canadians of Edmonton, Alberta, didn't have the same fate waiting for us. I had absolutely no reason to think this was even the remotest of possibilities, but after two days of driving though wheat fields as far as the eye could see, one's mind has a tendency to wander. By the end of the third day of passing through even more horizon-to-horizon wheat fields, Edmonton appeared in the distance shimmering as though it were the Emerald City of Oz. We were relieved that we had finally reached our destination until we pulled into the parking lot of this venue, the largest shopping structure in the Western Hemisphere, the West Edmonton Mall.

We were scheduled to play at the Mall Amphitheatre, and when we asked where it was, the lonely security guard at the entrance to the parking lot told us it was in the center of the Mall, just keep driving for about a mile or two, and then follow the signs to the load in area. It was impossible to miss. He wished us good luck, gave us a snappy salute, and directed us forward.

Eventually arriving at the load-in dock, we thought it might be a good idea to check out the venue before unloading. We climbed down out of the bus and innocently entered the Mall as a group. We were immediately dwarfed by what had to be the largest interior space on the entire planet—so large, we were told, the building occasionally generated its own interior weather. Directly in front of us dolphins were leaping out of a lagoon to the delight of hundreds of people gathered in an amphitheater surrounding the water feature. Beyond the leaping dolphin show was a water park with colorful tube slides intertwining with each other above the crowds, emptying into the largest indoor wave pool and sandy beach in not simply Canada or the Western Hemisphere, but in the entire world! So large in fact, surfing lessons were offered at specified times throughout the day, as well as catamaran rides on the raging surf for the more adventurous. If this weren't enough to amaze and entertain, there was a submarine ride that snaked through the mall, no telling what was on view in the murky depths.

If people were in the mood for a dryer experience, there was a roller coaster speeding by above our heads as well as snaking throughout the mall, dipping in and out of the building accompanied by the roar of the wheels and lots of screaming. There was also an amusement park with a Ferris wheel and assorted rides for the younger set. Not forgetting it was a shopping mall after all, there were also over eight hundred shops, popular emporiums, and restaurants available for one's shopping and dining pleasure. If this proved to be more than one could take in in one day, there was also a hotel on the property in which a tired soul could relax and rejuvenate.

The Fantasy Land Hotel within the mall itself boasted three hundred fifty guest rooms and one hundred twenty themed rooms. The themes included The Igloo Room, The African Room, The Polynesian Room, and our favorite, The Newlywed Room, featuring a rotating heart-shaped bed and a pink claw-footed bathtub with Jacuzzi.

We were told to set up on a round stage in an amphitheater usually reserved for the dolphin and assorted sea creature show, featuring a walrus, several seals, and a waddle of penguins. The performance pool for the sea animals was directly in front of the stage, their living quarter pools backstage. This meant human participants would have to run down the aisles of the amphitheater and cross a rickety bridge to greet a welcoming Bob Eubanks on our set. The lucky, though usually out of breath, contestants would then have their shot at spinning the Wheel, choosing a letter, or buying a vowel and eventually solving the puzzle.

Obviously this all works well on paper, but the promotor failed to warn us that nothing stopped the roller coaster from roaring overhead intermittently throughout the show. Neither were we told the stage was covered with a thick, dense-celled rubber pad to protect the sea creatures during their appearances. It looked dry enough but remained sopping wet like a huge sponge throughout the day, giving up a squish and a puddle with every step. The stage hands from the venue assured us the little souvenirs occasionally left by the herd of dancing penguins would be cleaned up, and they were, but little greasy green splotches remained as a not-so-pleasant smelling reminder of their having pranced by a short time before.

Bob, ever the trouper, reminded me of that old show biz axiom, "You gotta make hay when the sun shines!" and had no problem doing the show, but only after making me promise to buy him a new pair of tennis shoes before we rolled out of town.

The show was a big hit in the West Edmonton Mall. The mall management pleaded with us to do a few extra performances. I gave the okay as long as the promotor agreed to buy us all, including Eubanks, new tennis shoes after the run. The promotor understood the necessity completely and we had a deal. I was happy because I did not have to spend my own money on enticing Bob with a new pair of tennis shoes, everyone on the staff received a nice new pair, and even I received a pair of snappy Adidas as well. We fulfilled the promoter's wish of booking a few extra shows, and most importantly, no one had to deal with the Eau de Penguin Guano in the cramped confines of our tour bus. A producer's dream come true.

BRANSON, MISSOURI

Branson is an entertainment phenomenon that sprouted up as an entertainment and relaxation spot for coal miners and country folks in the heart of the Ozark mountains. It has now expanded into an entertainment mecca, home to at least fifty theatres and counting. Each theatre featured famous stars in their prime performing in residence at their own theatres. These stars and their showcases included such standouts as *The Osmond Family Theatre, Andy Williams Performing Arts Center, Glen Campbell, Tony Orlando, Dick Clark's American Bandstand Theatre, The Dolly Parton Stampede, The Roy Clark Celebrity Theatre, Mel Tillis, The Lennon Sisters, The Oak Ridge Boys,* and of course, *The Boxcar Willie Show.* More acts than one could possibly see in a one or two week vacation.

At the time we played Branson, most of the theatres were tin buildings with huge ornate façades out front. Management touted the success of their attractions by the number of coaches parked in their lots during any particular show. A ten coach show was great, a fifteen coach show three days in a row was definitely something to crow about. We did the *Wheel of Fortune Live!* show in the White House Theatre. The façade was an almost exact replica of the White House in Washington, DC but the theatre itself was a flimsy tin roofed building attached to the façade in front. Occasionally, during driving rainstorms, performances had to be called off due to the racket caused by rain or hail pelting the tin roof while the wind shook the walls like an eerie thunder sound effect from an amateur production of *The Tempest.* In spite of the weather, the audience loved the shows, as they were able to see all their favorite stars, Bob Eubanks included, up close in a live venue. With *Wheel* we featured a display of prizes that winners could choose from, usually from local businesses or hotels. The winners could then proudly walk back to their awaiting coaches, smiling and chattering like happy little chipmunks, prizes in hand (or in tow for the larger ones).

LAS VEGAS RESIDENCY, OR, WHAT HAPPENS IN VEGAS, MAY NOT STAY IN VEGAS

Our last stop on the tour was an indefinite residency at the MGM Grand Hotel in Las Vegas, Nevada. At the time, the Chamber of Commerce was trying to convince the public that Las Vegas was a family friendly vacation destination. To that end, the hotel constructed a state of the art amusement park as well as an elaborate pool deck with assorted slides, waterfalls, and inner tube "rivers" snaking throughout the pool deck and patio areas. *Wheel of Fortune Live!* was the perfect show for their new family friendly endeavors. We were asked to install the show in a smaller show room which, prior to our moving in, was a stand-up comedy club created when management was attempting to cash in on the comedy club craze sweeping the country at one time. As stand-up comedy no longer as popular as it once was, management decided family entertainment was now the way to go.

Las Vegas hotels employ a business model known as Four Walling. This means the hotel only supplies the four walls of the theater. Everything else within those four walls had to be supplied by the production company—sets, lighting, equipment, production orchestras, everything is brought in. This includes rebuilding the stages and interiors of the auditoriums, as in the case of more elaborate shows currently playing Las Vegas, utilizing huge swimming pools, high flying circus equipment, and so on. The hotel will supply some rudimentary advertising for the show, but only in the guise of a hotel advertisement mentioning a new show is opening on a particular date, or a listing of the show once it is up and running. In addition to all these production stipulations, shows in Vegas can only run for an hour, as management will not allow popular shows, some of which have an audience capacity of a few thousand, to keep that many potential gamblers off the floor for a longer period. A sellout crowd for our show was less than five hundred, but the time limitations remained the same. We were given fifteen minutes flex time should the show ever run over due to one puzzle taking longer to solve than another.

Las Vegas measures every square inch on the casino floor and expects a certain amount of cash generated for every inch. Even the bar surrounding our amphitheater-shaped showroom had electronic slot machines installed flush with the bar itself directly in front of every stool. For that reason, we had to set up a souvenir stand within our theatre space, as the selling of T-shirts, sweatshirts, hats, and ashtrays, as well as videotaped recordings of every show available immediately after the performance, could never compete with revenue generated from the progressive *Wheel of Fortune* slots that were magically installed all 'round the theatre's exterior.

Even though Las Vegas was making a concerted effort to reinvent itself as a family entertainment destination, there were still laws on the books that banned anyone under twenty-one years of age, particularly children, from standing within ten feet of any gambling device on a casino floor. This posed a major problem for families lining up prior to our opening the theatre before the show. The hotel solved the problem by making a slot machine-free pathway directly in front of the main doors of the show room, separating the banks of slot machines by poles and velvet ropes. Unfortunately, we were made responsible for the slot revenue lost by the removal of the machines, adding to the total revenue that the show had to generate in order to make the hotel management happy. But that's the way business is done in Las Vegas. If our show proved to be as big of a hit as was expected by all parties involved, a few extra bucks wouldn't be a problem.

The venues in Las Vegas are also extremely sensitive to being handicapped and wheelchair accessible. Management told us an organization in support of the handicapped makes it their business to visit every new installation at a casino, bar, restaurant, or showroom to insure handicapped accessibility. Because of this, most of the theatres have ramps instead of stairs in their seating areas and provide a number of tables with the space necessary for a wheelchair. As we chose contestants at random from the audience, and as our theatre was too small to build ramps to access the stage and the Wheel, we had to install a wheelchair elevator at one end of the stage. We also had to redesign our Wheel structure to have removable sections that enabled a wheelchair to slide into the proper position to give access to spin the Wheel and play the game. The wheelchair-bound contestant could choose a proxy to spin the wheel and call out the letters and solves, but only after the actual contestant made a choice and then told the proxy what he or she wanted to do. The system worked perfectly, and once the audience saw how sensitive we were to the needs of all our contestants, we always received a rousing round of applause once we utilized our wheelchair elevator, and were set up and ready to play the game.

Contestants for all our shows didn't have to endure any sort of screening process and were chosen completely at random. Occasionally, as mentioned earlier, this caused a problem with a chosen contestant who couldn't speak English, or had a hard time knowing the difference between a vowel or a consonant, but we endured. On entering the showroom, each guest was given a ticket with a number. We had a numerical computerized randomizer with huge red numbers designed by a slot machine company in Las Vegas. It was installed on the proscenium arch to the left of the stage in full view of everyone in the audience. We even hired a young local lawyer to serve as "The Judge" who sat behind a small desk on stage and operated the randomizer. The numbers would tumble rapidly for a few moments and he would then ceremoniously raise his hand. The audience would scream out "NOW!" and our lawyer would slap a large red "lock out" button in full view of the audience. A number would appear accompanied by cheers and occasional groans. The contestant with that ticket number would rush up to the stage and play the game.

On many nights, various celebrities would stop by and, with a bit of advance notice, we would set them up in the house and use their name as a puzzle on the letter board. Once identified, we would have them stand or in some cases come up on stage and take a bow.

Occasionally a private Casino Host, who attended to a High Roller's every whim or desire, would ask for a few seats. Tennis great Andre Agassiz's father was one of these Casino Hosts, as charming in an old world Italian way as he was elegant. Some of his high rollers were fans of the show and Mr. Agassiz and I met a number of times booking his charges into front row seats. I couldn't guarantee his folks would be called up to play the game, as that was made by computerized random selection protected by Federal as well as State gaming laws. Mr. Agassiz and his clients understood the rule completely, of course. If his charges were well known celebrities, we first asked their permission and then used their names or the name of their currently running show as one of the *Wheel* puzzles. Afterwards we would give them a mention and encourage a round of applause.

Louie Anderson, Tiger Woods, prop comic Carrot Top, Rikki Lake, Marc Summers, and even Vanna White herself made cameo appearances in our audience in this way. They all had numbered tickets, and if their numbers hit, they would have been invited up on stage. None was ever chosen, except once —

One night word came down from a Casino Host that Mr. Las Vegas, Mr. Wayne Newton himself, along with his wife, daughter, and some friends wanted to attend but didn't want any recognition or announcements made on their behalf. Not a problem. When Wayne and his family arrived, he was dressed in black, with a ball cap pulled down over his ears. We put them in a large round banquette against the rear wall of the showroom.

Halfway through the show, Wayne's daughter was numerically chosen at random to play the game. She nailed the puzzle after a few letters and was given the opportunity to choose a very nice prize. After the show, we ushered the audience out as usual. Once the theatre was empty, the Newtons approached, laughing and giggling and thrilled at their good fortune. We were quite happy for them as well. I introduced myself and, while shaking hands, Wayne quietly said, "Thanks for choosing my daughter."

"Mr. Newton, I assure you it's all done at random, we have absolutely nothing to do with it. It's a State and Federal gaming law."

"Sure it is." smiled Wayne, winking at me, "Sure it is."

"I swear!" I pleaded, starting to laugh, "You got to believe me!"

"No, I don't," said Wayne. Smiling, he winked again, as security shepherded them out of the theatre and through some back doors from which they originally arrived.

The very next afternoon, the Host of the show and I both received a huge bouquet of a dozen gourmet cookies in a long stem rose box. Some of the huge round cookies were covered with chocolate chips, some with white chocolate chunks, and some with a colorful array of M&Ms. The long thin peppermint stick stems were decorated with green marzipan leaves, and the whole bundle was tied with a red fondant bow. Written in thin dark chocolate script on a decorated medallion of white chocolate was, "Thanks for a great night! The Newton Family."

Always one to do the right thing, I immediately called the lawyers in the Home Office in Hollywood, and asked if I was allowed to accept such an elaborate gift.

They listened to my story and asked if I received the gift before or after their appearance. "After," I told them.

"Then no problem. Save a cookie for us!"

I enjoyed the cookies over the next few days, but I didn't save any for the lawyers.

TOM JONES, A CLOSE PERSONAL FRIEND...REALLY?

We employed various hosts for our live show in Las Vegas. We would introduce some of the lesser known fellows with a video presentation showing some of their previous credits and show business accomplishments. Once the audience was able to recognize the host from various appearances on lesser known television shows as an actor, comedian or game show host, they were ready to settle back and have a good time. After the show, most of the hosts and I would go out for something to eat, or they would return to their rooms and order something from room service, and lay low until their call the next afternoon.

One particular host we hired, we'll call him Billy, would spend the evening after the performance wandering throughout the casino as though he were a male version of Alice in Wonderland. He was on the prowl for any celebrities he might find. Better yet, he was hoping someone would recognize him from having hosting a short-lived talk show or from his regular gig as a warm-up comic for various television shows taping in Hollywood. He took great pleasure in cruising the clubs and showrooms attempting to ingratiate himself with any of the major stars performing there.

One afternoon he told me that, the night before, he had met Tom Jones and a good friend of Tom's, a legendary Vegas lounge performer named Cook E. Jarr. Mr. Jarr favored dressing all in black with his name in silver sequins running down one leg. His pants were stylishly draped over his pointed boots, decorated with silver caps on the heels and toes. He sported a jet black Moe of the Three Stooges haircut but, as his own personal flair, added a long mullet in the back. To accent his outfit he wore pounds of silver chains around his neck openly displayed on his exposed chest.

Billy told me the three of them really hit it off and they hung out until the wee hours of the morning. It seems that, as a way to relax after an evening performance, Tom would find his favorite piano lounge and, armed with his bulging "Fake Book," would play requests until four or five in the morning. A Fake Book is a large collection of popular hits and musical numbers with just the first few bars of the tune listed, enabling the musician to "fake" the remainder of the tune as he desired or as requested. After the piano bar closed at dawn, Tom would head back to his dressing room and order breakfast before finally retiring to his suite on the upper floors of the hotel. Billy told me Tom invited him along with Cook E. for breakfast and hanging out a bit longer in his dressing room. It was an experience he would never forget.

Billy considered this evening an invitation and told me he hung out with Tom in the piano bar every night after that. They became really close friends.

A few weeks later, prior to Tom's departure, Billy showed me four CDs of Tom's albums, autographed by Tom to his new close personal friend. Billy didn't tell me he purchased the CDs at Tom's swag stand and asked him to sign them. I began to grow a bit suspicious at this, as one never asks fellow performers, regardless of how friendly you may feel you are with them, for autographs. It's just not done.

After Tom left, Billy still cruised the casinos for celebrity contacts. I have to admit, it was he who invited Wayne Newton and family to the show. He met Mrs. Newton attending Sunday Mass at the Catholic Church conveniently located just down the Strip, walking distance from the MGM Grand Hotel.

Billy also claimed to know the actor and personality known for his tan, George Hamilton. George owned a cigar bar named Hamilton's across the street from the MGM Grand Hotel in the New York, New York Hotel. Between performances, he would buy coffee and muffins at Starbucks and head over the street bridge to Hamilton's to flirt with the cigar girls and enjoy his snacks. He invited me to come along one night, though I was extremely uncomfortable with the idea. I was sure that brown bagging was frowned upon by private businesses, especially in Las Vegas. Billy assured me I had nothing to worry about, as he and George were good friends, having met years ago when George was a guest on his short-lived talk show. I never accompanied Billy back to Hamilton's again. Remembering the rules of social decorum, I learned, while attending Miss Gwen's Cotillion as a teenager, brown bagging just seemed improper to me.

A few days after Tom Jones left the MGM Grand, I received a letter from management in an envelope marked "Confidential" in red. The letter stated, in no uncertain terms, that when Mr. Jones returns to the hotel, and if we were still in residence, Billy our host was not allowed to talk to him, attend his main room performances, attend his piano bar performances, or socialize with Mr. Jones or any member of his party in any way. I called the executives in the Home Office in Hollywood immediately and read the letter to them. I was told he pulled the same crap with George Hamilton a few years ago. I became a little dizzy and related the "brown bagging" incident at Hamilton's and decided the experience was so uncomfortable I didn't go back there with him again. They agreed that was a good idea, and they would talk to him about bringing personal snacks to Hamilton's. As for Tom Jones, I was told not to mention anything to our host about the letter from MGM management. When Tom returned and we were still in residence, we would talk to the host then. Billy played out his contract and returned to his job of warming up studio audiences in Hollywood. Problem solved.

THE EMERALD CITY LOUNGE

One night my agent came to see the show. He was my representative as well as the representative of the current host of the show. He came with an executive from Sony and the four of us had a drink in the Emerald City Lounge. This watering hole was located in the center of the hotel lobby, decorated in the motif of the Emerald City from the *Wizard of Oz*. In an effort to expound on its exclusivity, there were no gambling devices of any kind in the room, and the entrance was controlled by a young man manning the velvet rope in a brass buttoned uniform, sporting a top hat and white gloves. When we entered the very first time, he was able to greet us all by name. No telling how the hotel was able to figure that one out.

Intermittently throughout the room were single tables. Many were occupied by rather beautiful women, sitting alone, keeping a sophisticated eye on the goings-on within the room, sipping delicately from a brandy snifter or a champagne flute. One of these ladies was smiling aggressively and making flirty waves toward our Sony executive. All of us noticed except for him, and it was mentioned that it seems someone had some interest in him. He smiled and turned to look at her. He blushed to a shade of red rarely seen on this planet and quickly said it was nothing. For some reason we took him at his word while wondering silently how a guy as plain and straight looking as he was could raise the attention of such a beautiful woman. We all shrugged it off. No one said anything more about it, and our conversation moved on to other things.

There is an unspoken bit of Las Vegas lore that claims if you want to know something about anything that may be going on in Las Vegas, ask a bartender. They seem to have the inside scoop on everything happening in town. One afternoon while enjoying a small beverage a friendly bartender asked me if I knew the producer from Sony who shared a wild time with one of the "girls" from the Emerald City Lounge the other night. Turns out the attractive women I had noticed sitting languidly at the small private tables in the Emerald City were actually professionals known affectionately as "the girls." They were available for hire as an escort for an evening show or reception as well as for some private time, preferably the entire evening in your room—provided, of course, the price was appropriate for the time spent and the effort expended.

I told the bartender I was the only producer from Sony in attendance. Furthermore, as my wife was the self-proclaimed President of the Lorena Bobbitt Fan Club, there was no way I could sample what any of "the girls" had to offer without a close friend of mine being sliced off in revenge one night back home while I was in dreamland. He insisted it was one of our guys. Not being responsible for the crew after hours, I said maybe it could be one of them.

"Can any guy in your crew afford about five hundred dollars an hour, tip not included?" he asked. "If so, I'm getting out of bartending and become a television crew guy. Trust me, it's all over the hotel. It was one of your producers, for sure." He added a wink and went back to polishing glasses and doing whatever else bartenders do beside spreading the juiciest gossip of the day.

I thought about it for a moment and then it hit me like a thunderbolt. The flirty waves and copious smiles, the blushing network executive! Oh well, especially since I had no way to corroborate the bartender's story, I never mentioned it to anyone, though I have to admit I did think about it many times during meetings and social occasions with this same executive in the ensuing years.

Just before this Sony executive retired, he was awarded a coveted star on the Hollywood Walk of Fame. This was a huge honor for his years of service to the television entertainment industry. Invited to the event, I noticed him smiling broadly and posing with his wife and adult children as the legendary Johnny Grant, the honorary "Mayor of Hollywood," handed him a small replica of the gold star embedded forever in the sidewalk beneath your feet on Hollywood Boulevard. I looked at the adoring crowds surrounding him and didn't see any of "the girls" from the Emerald City standing around in support of this momentous occasion. Perhaps they weren't invited. Perhaps the bartender was just telling stories. Nevertheless, one thing remains as the eleventh show business commandment, "What happens in Vegas usually stays in Vegas." I'll never knnow for sure, such is the reality of life in Las Vegas.

After what we considered a rather successful year of numerous sellout crowds and packed houses, the authorities in Las Vegas decided they were bored with family entertainment. The amusement park was razed and a luxury high rise condominium was constructed in its place. We were unceremoniously canceled and, a few days later, replaced by *Crazy Horse Paris*, a flashing light and nudie revue from France. Just goes to show how quickly priorities in Vegas can switch from wholesome family entertainment to assorted naked women gyrating sensuously to electronic music while being bathed only in soft swirling lights projected from the ceiling.

HARVEY WEINSTEIN - NEED A LIGHT, SUGAR LIPS?

A few years after Las Vegas, my wife and I were having dinner in a small bistro in Paris. We were in France to attend a bi-annual international television convention in Cannes and took a few days to hang out in Paris. Harvey Weinstein and entourage sauntered in and took the table next to ours. He was not as infamous as he is today, although he was the head guy at Miramax, and my wife was first to recognize him. Okay, no big deal.

Some gent in his party was chatting incessantly throughout the entire meal about who knows what. Harvey, a bit bored, started to stare about the cluttered bistro and our eyes met. I raised my eyebrows a bit, winked, and just smiled ever so slightly in commiseration. He caught on immediately, rolled his eyes, shook his head a bit, and then turned his head and tried to be as attentive as possible to his still-chattering dinner guest.

During dessert and coffee I glanced over to his table once again and noticed him taking a cigarette out of a gold case, gingerly taping an end on the case, and then holding the cigarette up in the air between his fingers, elbow leaning on the table. A doting waiter rushed over and, with a few clicks from a silver lighter, lit it for him immediately.

A year or so later, my wife and I we were watching the news and it was a disgraced Harvey Weinstein being transferred from one jail or hospital to a rather serious prison. My wife, as is part of her charm, innocently asked, "Do you think someone will be lighting his cigarettes for him in prison?"

JOE GARAGIOLA AND THE WRANGLED AUDIENCE

Back in town, I took a job producing a small game show at the Sunset Gower Studios in Hollywood. While shooting a game show, as a money saving device, producers usually schedule five or more episodes on any particular tape day. This is done to save on studio expenses. A necessary evil for all game shows is a live studio audience serving as a source of energy that transfers to the host and contestants. Getting an ample supply of audience members, and then getting them to sit through three tapings during the day and then two additional tapings in the evening, could always pose a problem.

To alleviate the situation, a professional Audience Wrangler would be hired to bring in an energetic audience for each show. Audience Wranglers would invite groups from clubs, old folks' homes, even grabbing tourists off the street at Hollywood's Chinese theatre with the promise of a free meal at the local Spaghetti Factory after the show. Anywhere and anyone was fair game as long as the Wrangler could find a group or twenty or so with the promise of a free meal or receiving a washing machine or fridge for their clubhouse kitchen. Every now and then, our Wrangler filled the seats with assorted male and female teenagers from the Los Angeles Youth Authority. They were young, had a pulse, sported tear drops and assorted tattoos on their faces, and were always accompanied by two armed guards. When they didn't pull their shirts over their heads for some inexplicable reason they were a pretty good audience. When the Youth Authority kids were scheduled, our announcer and warm-up guy made sure to put his solid gold Rolex watch into his pocket. As long as the kids made the right amount of noise when we flashed the "APPLAUSE" sign, we were happy.

We usually shot more than one show in a day and during the break we gave away lottery tickets if an audience member volunteered to tell a joke or sing a song. A famous church choir from South Central LA came in many times as a group, informing us in advance what they needed for their rehearsal hall, after already receiving the washer, dryer, fridge, etc. The singers were all retired pros from the community, having had a fleeting moment of fame on the R&B or rock charts. During the breaks between shows they would proudly get up and sing their gold record hits of yesteryear. Particularly notable was a performance from two talented women who just happened to be ex members of the funk group Parliament Funkadelic. They gave a rousing performance of "If it Don't Fit, Don't Force it! Just Relax and Let It Go!!!" and the old roadhouse classic "If You Roll My Dough, I'll Bake Your Bread" The audience of all their church choir cohorts roared their approval, which was fine with me, getting them all warmed up for the taping of the next show. I was just relieved the Audience Wrangler had the good sense not to book half the audience with a flock of plaid skirted teens and conservatively shrouded nuns in black habits from Immaculate Heart Girls School. Along with the adult choir, the girl's school received new furniture for their bingo hall thanks to their regular attendance.

They didn't need to hear anything about something not fitting and then not forcing it.

One morning prior to taping a game show, our host, affable Joe Garagiola, was up in my office telling me funny baseball stories. While doing so, he would casually look out the window of my office overlooking the studio to check out the audience filing in below. He still held me responsible for allowing the Wrangler to fill the house with old folks from a home in Glendale. Not really a problem on paper, but it was an Armenian old folks home and most of the attendees didn't speak English. He forgave me for that one after I treated him to a few drinks afterward, but he made me swear on the life of my firstborn it would never happen again. I promised, and he continued telling even more hysterically funny baseball stories from his years in the majors.

A month or so later, Joe peeks out at the audience, and his face turns pale. He turns to me and says, "That's it. I can't go on. Show's over!"

"Joe, take it easy, what's the problem?" I stammered.

"The first row is filled with Japanese retirees." he yelled.

"So?" I asked incredulously.

"So, they don't laugh out loud. If they like what you're doing, they might smile and nod, but they don't make any noise. They don't laugh!! I'll die if I go out there!"

"Joe, are you kidding me?"

"Hell if I am! It's rude for that generation to show their teeth in public, let alone laugh. You have to move them or the whole show is going down the crapper."

In a controlled producer panic, I ran down to the studio floor and walked calmly by the quietly sitting retirees who returned my nervous smile with polite nods *en masse*. I grabbed the Audience Wrangler, pulling her off to the side, and informed her of the situation.

"No problem sweetheart, I got it covered." she said with a laugh.

Next thing I know she is chatting with the leader of the group. The leader makes a demure announcement in English and Japanese accented with a bow and a "Hi." The whole row rises and begins an orderly shuffle up the riser to an empty third row. Simultaneously, a busload of giggling teenagers was ushered in and seated in the first row.

Joe did the show. The audience, roared in laughter and enjoyment, the third row gave modest tight lipped smiles and nodded their approval. Everyone in attendance seemed to have a great time, some even going home with a spanking new washing machine.

Disaster averted.

JONATHAN WINTERS AND TWO HONEY BAKED HAMS

There is a Honeybaked Ham shop on Riverside Drive in Toluca Lake, California, a small show business enclave walking distance from the Warner Studios. The place is always busy, particularly during the run up to any holiday. One Easter season I purchased a full dinner, containers of cole slaw, potato salad, macaroni salad, an additional quart of honey glaze, and a plump honey baked ham. I then made my way toward a narrow hallway that led to the parking lot in the back. On the way I passed an open door and in that office was Jonathan Winters eating lunch at what I supposed was his desk. I was surprised seeing my comic idol. I didn't know what his relationship was with this Honey Baked Ham shop; perhaps he was the owner or simply a steady customer. Did the owners allow celebs to eat in a back office undisturbed? I'll never know, but staring at him for the moment I ran directly into the door jamb and my box of holiday goodies splashed and smashed all over the narrow hallway floor. I ended up slipping and sliding through the mess a few times as I valiantly tried to stand. The next thing I knew I felt a strong hand under my arm. It was Jonathan Winters helping me up. Having a total fan moment, I apologized for making such a mess but told him how I adored his appearances on *The Steve Allen Show* and *The Tonight Show* as well as *Mork and Mindy* and how everyone in the Improv world thought he was a god.

"Okay, okay buddy." he replied calmingly, and then called for a clerk by name. When the young fellow arrived he told him to replace my order completely and even give me an additional ham. The one I ordered wasn't damaged, wrapped as it was in their signature reddish brown paper. I mentioned as much to him and he told me not to worry about it and then told the clerk to bring a fresh T-shirt from the store's stash as well. I asked why and he pointed to me, and I noticed I was dripping with assorted holiday salads and honey glaze.

Once my order had been replaced and I donned the clean T-shirt in the rest room, I poked my head into his office. He was reading *Daily Variety* and I quickly said, "Thanks so much Mr. Winters. I really loved your Maude Frickert."

He chuckled a bit surprised, and then, as Maude Frickert replied, "So did I sonny boy, now you have a good holiday, okay?"

"Sure will." I said, "and thanks for all the laughs."

"Oh stop, you're making me blush, now beat it buster!"

He smiled and waved me off with a Maude Frickert cackle, which I took as my cue to be on my way.

LARRY KING – WIDE SUSPENDERS, THICK GLASSES AND HOT PASTRAMI

During the late sixties, Larry King had a Sunday morning radio show on WKAT, the NBC affiliate in Miami, called *Youth and the Issue*. He had already adopted his trademark thick suspenders and heavy square eyeglasses with the slightest green tint made popular by recently arrived patrician Cuban refugees. After my first appearance, I was asked back by the producer a number of times, billed as a member of the debate team from Coral Park Senior High, even though I didn't debate all that much but participated in tournaments in Oral and Dramatic Interpretation, giving speeches and performing segments of plays. My favorite was the last scene from *Of Mice and Men* when George shoots Lenny in the back of the head. It was supposed to be dramatic after all.

This one Sunday morning the subject was the CND, or Miami's black ghetto known as the Central Negro District. The area was also known as Liberty City, a racist remnant of the fifties and before. During this time the Winn-Dixie grocery had two drinking fountains, one marked "White" the other "Colored," the train station had "White" and "Colored" waiting rooms, and every African American had to ride or stand in the back of city busses, even though there were ample empty seats up front. The neighborhood consisted of ramshackle shacks and shanties, no business, and lots of crime. I suggested knocking the entire neighborhood down and rebuilding it with houses, public parks, and swimming pools like most of suburban Miami. I reasoned that if the city had money to pay for the King Orange Jamboree a parade, football game, and weeklong celebration extolling the virtue of a piece of fruit, razing and rebuilding the CND was obviously something that could be done easily and affordably.

As Mr. King hunched over his microphone with his arms folded, another of his trademarks, one of his regulars called in and said because of such a radical idea, I must have been a dirty Communist. He promptly disconnected her and, rolling his eyes silently, mouthed the words to me and the two other high schoolers participating, "FUCK HER," and jabbed his middle finger in the air. We almost fell off our chairs trying to muffle our laughter as Mr. King then held his index finger to his lips reminding us to quiet down as the microphones were still hot.

Years later I saw him eating lunch one afternoon, all by himself, in Nate & Al's, a very popular Beverly Hills deli. He still wore the heavy suspenders and eyeglasses, sans the green tint. I worked up the gumption and walked over and said hello, and reminded him of *Youth and the Issue* and his hanging up on the caller who called me a dirty Communist. He laughed and then asked if I wanted to join him for lunch. How could I refuse? The waitress, whom he knew by name, took my order, and over hot pastrami sandwiches and half sour pickles we talked almost until closing—at least the staff had begun refilling the salt and pepper shakers on the other tables, but didn't say anything to us.

When it came time to leave, I thanked him profusely for lunch, offered to pay, and he waved me off. I then handed him one of my business cards, mentioning if he ever needed a TV producer to give me a call. He said he would keep me in mind, though I never heard from him again. Certainly not a problem. He was definitely a mensch and I would never forget the time I shared with him. The hot pastrami wasn't bad either.

MERV GRIFFIN

A Production Bible is a production manual for television shows that have been sold in the international market. When you buy a format, a bible is sent by the producer informing you how to produce their show. Over the years, I have had the pleasure of being hired to create over fifty production bibles for American, European, and Asian companies. It seems the people at Merv Griffin Enterprises were interested in taking out a few of their newer developing properties internationally and wanted to talk with me about creating proper bibles. They contacted my agent, my agent called me, and a few days later my agent and I were waiting for Merv Griffin in his Beverly Hills office.

    His office, if you could call it that, was actually a museum to Hollywood and the years Merv was part of it. The walls were lined with photos of Merv posing and smiling with every celebrity imaginable, as well as with every President since Eisenhower. They weren't simply government issued 8x10s with a hurriedly scrawled signature. These were photos showing Merv smiling and posing with all the presidents and their families, at dinners, casual barbecues, weddings, and even funerals. One of the standout curios sitting on a lower shelf of a wall-to-wall mahogany book case, filled with a number of Emmy® awards and assorted memorabilia, was a two-and-a-half-foot tall brass shell casing. I picked it up, curious about its heft. It was quite heavy. I sniffed at the opening and it still had the faintest hint of gunpowder. It was certainly authentic. At that very moment Merv sauntered in and noticed I was checking out what seemed to be spent ammunition from a canon. I quickly stepped away, somewhat embarrassed at being so nosey, but it just couldn't be helped.

    "I see you noticed my Howitzer shell. It's actually one of my proudest possessions." he said modestly, "Nancy gave it to me. It was one of shells used during the twenty-one gun salute at Ronnie's funeral."

It took a nano-second for me to realize he was talking about Nancy Reagan and President Ronald Reagan's formal state funeral. Talk about a way to totally intimidate a writer coming in to pitch his services.

Intimidation proved to be the furthest thing from his mind. He was just ingenuously stating the facts. He then listened attentively as my agent sang my praises, much to my surprise, as he never said anything as glowing to me in private. I explained what I had to offer, as well as showing him some hardbound copies of international bibles I had created and brought in for him to take a look. He thumbed through both volumes and then set them aside. He had decided it was time for lunch.

Conveniently, Merv's office building was situated directly alongside the venerable Beverly Wilshire Hotel. His office overlooked the driveway approach to the hotel, so I suppose in earlier days he could keep an eye out for the comings and goings of the international as well as Hollywood elite. Rumor had it that he was even a part owner of the hotel along with many other snazzy properties around the world. On our way to lunch, the three of us—Merv, my agent, and me—crossed the little side street to the hotel driveway. Helicopters were uncharacteristically buzzing the neighborhood; it seems on that particular day King Abdullah II of Jordan and his family were in residence at the hotel. The usually elegant and understated lobby area was filled with intermittently placed American as well as Jordanian secret service agents all wearing dark sunglasses with a wire coming from their suit collars attached to an ever present earbud protruding just slightly from their left ears. The American agents all wore tiny American flags pins in their lapels, the Jordanians, a tiny stripped Jordanian flag. Every pillar, every potted palm, every entrance or archway had one of these dour lads standing there, hands at their sides or folded in front of them. A few, holding an arm up to their faces, were mumbling to the inside of their wrists. As Merv and our group passed each guard, Jordanian or American, they broke their steely non-descript gazes, and in their coolest, secret service way, acknowledged Mr. Griffin with a slight nod and just a wee sliver of a smile. Those not wearing dark glasses even winked. Merv smiled back and with a friendly wave and his signature chuckle and returned a friendly gesture to each and every one. Seemed to me the usually stoic agents realized some sort of acknowledgment, however subtle, was quite apropos. Even though their orders of the day were to protect a Hashemite King, they couldn't very well ignore a beloved King of Hollywood.

Lunch went off without a hitch. Merv was gracious and friendly to everyone in the restaurant. By the time we left, the lobby was completely empty. Every agent in dark glasses, hiding behind the potted palms had disappeared. Merv looked around and quipped, "Guess the King and his family are off to Disneyland. Too bad we didn't bump into him, I would have comped him for a few of my shows. Oh well." We headed back to his office to continue our meeting. Before leaving his museum-office, he ordered bibles for three shows.

ROGER AILES, RUSH LIMBAUGH, AND MISS EARTHA KITT

Years before his days at Fox News, Roger Ailes was hired to spearhead a very early venture into cable television by NBC. Roger claims he came up with the idea that the new network should be all talk, all day, and cover the talk show gamut from light entertainment to serious news, politics and current events.

Before Roger hired me to produce a one hour show called *Pork*, a supposed exposé of graft and excess government spending, he called me into his office to "see if my head was on straight." Sitting between an American flag and a yellow Don't Tread On Me banner, he asked me to sit down and immediately asked me about my political affiliation.

A bit taken aback by this odd question, I mentioned the illegality of asking such a thing. He smiled nicely and said, "You want the job? Answer the question."

I told him I was a registered non-partisan voter as there were planks of each party I agreed with, and planks I disagreed with.

"Being a non-partisan voter is usually rather arrogant. What do you agree or disagree with?" he asked, rather arrogantly I might add.

I told him I completely support abortion as it is the law of the land. Should my daughter ever need the procedure, it should be made available to her, quietly, cleanly and without anyone holding signs and screaming outside any clinic of her choice. On the other hand, I wasn't all that supportive of all-inclusive gun control, as I really didn't see the need for automatic weapons, but I was an avid trap shooter, and enjoyed an occasional pheasant or duck hunt.

He listened sagely and, while I was talking, rose from his desk, crossed to a wall with all sorts of photos and such. He ceremoniously straightened a framed certificate attesting to the fact he had been a passenger on Air Force One. He returned to his seat, and said, "You're a Kempian Republican," making a reference to Jack Kemp, considered a liberal Republican who ran for Vice President under Bob Dole.

I quickly replied, "Roger, you can call me anything you want but 'shithead.' I'm not changing my political affiliation or lack of it just to get a job."

I was officially hired within the hour.

A week or so later my staff and I were called to his Manhattan office and told to explain our plans for the show we were assigned. Because *Pork* was supposed to be an exposé of sorts, I came up with the byline, adjusted from Kennedy's inaugural speech, "Ask not what your country can do for you, ask what your country is doing *to* you!" He loved it! Told us we were all doing a great job, and sent us back to the studio and our offices which were just over the George Washington Bridge, in Fort Lee, New Jersey.

A few weeks later I was channel surfing in my office and came upon *The Rush Limbaugh Show*. Not a fan in the least, I was curious to see the show. Roger Ailes was responsible for creating Rush Limbaugh as well as currently producing the television show.

The first words of his spiel before the opening credits, "Ask not what your country can do for you, ask what your country is doing *to* you!"

I almost did a spit-take, sending a half-eaten bagel and sip of coffee spraying across my office. I immediately marched into Roger's office. He too was enjoying a bagel, sipping coffee, and watching *The Rush Limbaugh Show* on his office monitor.

"Roger," I announced proudly, "I wrote that as a byline for my show, not for a pompous nit like Limbaugh!"

Munching on his bagel, and not looking away from the screen, he scowled, "Thanks for your opinion about one of my best friends. You wrote that line for me. I own it. I can do whatever I want with it. Now get out of my office."

The next day I was promoted to Network Executive Producer in charge of five hours of entertainment programming. I never mentioned Limbaugh again. I screened his show occasionally and never heard any of my material, or that created by my other producers, used again, either.

Although I didn't agree with Roger's politics in the least, I had to admit he was brilliant, in addition to having a great sense of humor. I booked my wife Geraldine as an emergency replacement on a comedy talk and entertainment show we had on our daily schedule when a comic we originally booked was arrested for lewd and lascivious behavior, on the Jersey side, under the George Washington Bridge.

We flew her out from Los Angeles on a Sunday afternoon, and she was ready to roll on Monday morning. Her improv alter ego and character was "Candy Lee Hargrove, Arch Anti-Feminist and Fascinating Female." She claimed her husband, Maurice, owned an auto body repair and gourmet coffee shop in the area. The specialty of the house being Café Fort Lee was a double espresso with a cigarette butt floating in it. Supposedly it was the favorite drink of their best customer, a hefty television producer "that hunka, hunka burning love, Rupert Ailes" The host of the show choked and cut to commercial, and Geraldine was replaced with a musician during the break. Afterwards, people came running to my office, claiming I might as well start packing because there was no way could I get away with a guest on one of my shows saying something like that about Roger.

Not only did Roger love her performance, he insisted we book Geraldine back as a regular, as well as flying out our six year old daughter to be with us.

Fox News—and all that horrible behavior which proved to be his demise—came much later.

My favorite show in the schedule was a late night talk entry featuring live bands looking for a big break or at least some late night exposure, and an assortment of celebrities eager to plug a new book, Broadway run, or movie premiere. Geraldo Rivera was a frequent guest, always having something to announce. Gossip columnist Cindy Adams would appear, but not before we promised to pick up the tab for getting her hair done as well as a limo from the Upper East Side to our studio in Fort Lee. Adam

West, the original Batman from the TV series during the sixties, was the nicest guy on the planet. Soft spoken, entertaining, and interesting, a perfect talk show guest. Staff favorite was any of the owners from Katz's Deli on the Lower East Side. They would arrive with a giant platter of deli sandwiches and assorted sides for everyone to enjoy, and we certainly did.

My all-time favorite had to be Eartha Kitt, appearing on our network to tout her new (1991) autobiography called *Confessions of A Sex Kitten*. Prior to taping, I poked my head into her dressing room, introduced myself as the Executive Producer for the network, and welcomed her to the studio. She smiled coyly, as only Eartha Kitt could, and purred, "And just what does an Executive Producer do, Mr. Bruce?"

Her question threw me for a moment, and just as I was going to muster a reply, a production assistant, burst into the room with a small white paper cone of water.

"Miss Kitt asked for some Perrier, but we didn't have any, so I got her this from the bubbler." he said trying to make his way into the room.

"Whoa! Hold on!" I said, pointing to the softening cone of water, "This will not do. Now listen carefully. Run across the street to the liquor store, get a few bottles of chilled Perrier." I asked her, "sparkling or still, Miss Kitt?"

"Sparkling, Mr. Bruce, by all means sparkling," she said with an appreciative grin.

I turned to the PA, handed him a twenty and said, "Get two still and two sparkling. Make sure they're chilled. Now go!" He was off in a flash, leaving motes of dust spinning in a dervish where he once stood. I then closed the door, turned to Miss Kitt, and said, "That's what an Executive Producer does, Miss Kitt."

She smiled and winked, "*Touché*, Mr. Bruce, *touché!*" her fluttering eyelashes sending chills up and down my spine, "*Merci beaucoup.*"

"*Je vous en prie.*" I replied with a wink in my best French, "You are most welcome."

Eartha Kitt lived up to her famous reputation and was as charming and alluring as she ever was while doing her segment on the show. When her limo arrived, I handed the driver the leftover bottles of Perrier with a hand written note on my personal network stationary, *Thanks so much for visiting us this evening. You were fabulous! This is just one more thing an Executive Producer does. Bonsoir! (Good evening!)*

GERALD FORD AND TALES OF A FLY-AWAY PRODUCER

A "Fly-Away Producer" is a producer hired by any number of production companies and sent to the studio of a production entity who purchased one of the formats belonging to the production company. For example, *American Idol* is actually a Dutch format purchased from a company in Holland. *Dancing With The Stars* is an English format, and *The Masked Singer* originated in Korea. American formats are also very popular worldwide with *Wheel of Fortune* as a format having been sold in over twenty-six markets worldwide. *The Price is Right, Cash Cab, Pyramid* and many others are American formats playing all over the world, as well.

On assignment to install *The Gong Show* in Jakarta, Indonesia, I had a hard time convincing the producers that a man sticking long pins through his lips, cheeks, and face, was not a great act. They couldn't understand why, so I mentioned what if a child tried to do the same stunt at home with his mother's knitting needles, would you claim responsibility? They thought about it for a minute and then decided a singing pig might be better family entertainment. I immediately agreed.

Prior to taping the first show, I was invited to participate in what the producers called an "atavistic ritual" for good luck. Right around lunchtime, they brought in a large round table covered with banana leaves with a huge mountain of rice in the center. All around the rice were bowls of various Indonesian delicacies made with beef, chicken, fish, duck, and who knows what else. It looked fantastic and smelled even better. The entire cast and crew entered and each shook hands with me and, in the charming Muslim tradition, touched their hearts and modestly bowed after each handshake. They then stood around the table holding hands. The producer said something in what I was told was the ancient language. Everyone nodded while saying what I imagined was a sort of "amen." The producer then took a precut square of banana leaf and, with the thumb, index finger, and forefinger of his right hand, scooped a bit of rice in the center of the banana leaf, as well as a few finger scoops of the various meats and assorted goodies surrounding the mound. With two hands, and a bow, he presented the loaded banana leaf to me. I look around and see all the young faces, still holding hands staring at me in anticipation, so I accepted the banana leaf with a bow as well. They were all still staring at me. I figured you are only young once, so with three fingers of my right hand, I sampled a bit of the rice. Savored it for a moment and then said, "Delicious! Terima kasih! Thank-you!" and bowed again.

They all applauded while laughing and cheering, and then dug into the rice and assorted dishes as a catered lunch. It was enjoyed on banana leaves, with their fingers, as well. I joined in with my portion, as one of the more helpful producers helped me identify each finger scoop as I was eating. It was without a doubt the best Asian food I had ever tasted. I figured the worst that could happen would be a Kaopectate milkshake in my hotel room later that evening, so I hoped for the best. Nothing negative happened. I actually looked forward to dinner the following night when I was promised a communal meal at a famous fish restaurant on a giant Chinese junk floating in a local river.

At that dinner, everyone sat on floor cushions around another circular table. A small bowl of warm water with a slice of lemon floating in it was supplied to each diner before dinner in order to wash up. We were served a huge fried fish to share, placed on a spinning Lazy Susan in the center of the table with the commensurate sides in bowls, with a spoon, this time, sticking out of each bowl. An individual bowl of warm sticky rice for each diner replaced the banana leaves. Dinner service, included tearing off chunks of the fried fish with ones fingers and ladling assorted sides and relishes into ones bowl with the spoon. The actual eating was still accomplished with ones thumb, index, and forefinger. As the honored guest, I was presented with the fish's head.

Everyone had a wonderful time. No one died. The fish head was delicious.

Some months later, Sony International in Los Angeles received word their counterparts in Mumbai, India had contacted Mark Burnett about doing their version of *Survivor*. He flatly refused. Undaunted, the Indians decided to move ahead with their version of the show anyway. Sony management sent me to Mumbai to insure whatever they came up with could not in any way be close enough to the original or Burnett would sue Sony for infringement. They could produce a show that resembled the original, but it couldn't have any of the elements used in the original show.

After twenty hours of flight time, ten to London and then ten to Mumbai, I arrived around three in the morning a bit bleary eyed but in good shape. The guide books I read prior to arrival mentioned the air in the city was "smoky," so I thought this referred to the smog and such I was used to dealing with in Los Angeles. As I was being driven to the hotel in a comfortable limo with moist towels and cold bottled water in the back seat, I noticed out the window that the bulk of the population, even at this early hour in the morning, were cooking meals or tea on small wood or charcoal fires right on the sidewalks. There were thousands of them. It seems hefty numbers of residents in Mumbai, if they are lucky, live on the streets in ramshackle tents and abodes resembling the many homeless encampments that have sprung up under freeway overpasses and bridges here in the United States. Every sidewalk, every patch of green, every concrete island between every busy intersection and every culvert had people living there. As soon as the car passed through the gates of my hotel, the Mumbai Oberoi, it was as though I was magically transformed to the grounds of any five star hotel anywhere in the world. Fountains, gardens, manicured lawns, magnificently dressed Sikhs, with silver swords in their belts and feathered turbans, opened my door. Young men in crisp white waistcoats took my bags and escorted me to the front desk, and then up to my room. In the elevator ,there was a young lad in a brass buttoned uniform, who was in charge of pressing the buttons of the requested floor. In addition, he was tasked with initialing "small talk". "Did you have a good flight, Sir?" "Will you be staying with us long, Sir?" "First time in India, Sir?" "Have a good evening, Sir". The next morning, I was met with, "Did you sleep well, Sir?" "Enjoy your breakfast, Sir." "Have a good day, Sir."

My driver and a spotlessly clean car were waiting for me early the next morning. Cold bottles of water and sodas in a small ice chest resting on the back seat.

It seems rental cars in India all come with drivers, which is a good thing; traffic in Mumbai competes with huge red double-decked English Leyland busses, thousands of cars, three-wheeled scooters, wallas on bicycles balancing hundreds of tin cylinders carrying lunch to office workers and, of course, a healthy sprinkling of elephants, camels, long-horned buffalos, and other assorted wildlife pulling a variety of carts, wagons and two-wheeled chariots. My driver, named Hari, was able to navigate it all like a champ. Interesting thing about Hari. As I mentioned before, he came with the car. After dropping me off at the Sony offices, he stayed in the parking lot with the other drivers who all hung out under a thatched roofed overhang waiting for their charges to emerge at any time during the day or evening. Hari was a pleasant young fellow with a rudimentary knowledge of English, though he spoke his "mother tongue," the language of the state where he was born, and Hindi perfectly. I suppose he was also a fan of chewing on betel nut leaves, because every time he smiled at me, which was often, he revealed a mouth full of purple stained teeth.

Once inside, the Sony offices resembled any production office anywhere in the world. Uniform built-in desk units, neon lighting, production posters decorating the walls, and an occasional rubber chicken hanging from a lighting fixture. Young teen boys in uniforms of light brown shirts and dark brown pants, known as "walla" boys, popped up in every office and conference room moments after you sat down asking the helpful question, "Nes-Coffee, Tea. Sweets?"

I came to learn "Nes-Coffee" was instant coffee with canned milk and sugar, the tea was strong and black, and sweets could be anything from hard candy to Cadbury chocolate bars. Nary a meeting took place without a platter of something being brought in and placed on the table for snacks by the walla boys. My cohorts were quick to warn me if it was something I could eat, meaning it had been ordered from a Domino's Pizza or Colonel Sanders across the street, or if it was something I shouldn't touch, meaning they bought it from a street vendor lining the neighboring streets.

Meetings were all in English as everyone in the television business were highly educated, as I was to learn, indicative of their caste. At times during a heated argument they would revert to Hindi, and then apologize to me and assure me they would translate everything later. During casual times the staff loved questioning me about my life in America. How many servants did my family have? Did I have a "love marriage" or was it arranged? As for the servants, I told them we didn't have any. They all started laughing and questioning, "Do you take your garbage to the dump?"

"No the city picks it up every week." (One servant.)

"Does your wife iron your shirts?"

"No, we take our stuff to a laundry." (Two servants)

By the time they were finished with the rigorous cross examination, it was determined I utilized ten servants in order to survive in America.

Answers to the arranged marriage question were quite surprising. Most of the folks agreed that a "love" marriage was the way to go, but the station manager, a well-educated sophisticated man in his mid-thirties, the same age as most of us in the room, admitted to having an arranged marriage. In a rather blasé, matter-of-fact way, he told us his parents knew the girl's parents, he met his bride on their wedding day, and they have been married for fifteen years and have two children. I noticed he didn't say "happily married." The more vociferous in the room claimed they would emigrate to America, even England, before letting that happen to them.

Walking around the studio lot, located on the northern edge of town, I couldn't help but notice barefoot security guards sauntering around armed with a machete hanging from their belts and a long barreled rifle slung over their shoulders. When I asked why they were so heavily armed, the reply came back,

"Tigers."

"Really? Here in Mumbai?" I replied incredulously.

"Don't you have lions and bears walking around your backyards and swimming in your pools in Los Angeles? We hear about that on CNN all the time."

They had me on that one. How could one argue with a report from CNN.

We decided on creating a competition show, called "Moksh" based on the levels of enlightenment popular in Hindi culture. A person would not be required to eat rats, something no self-respecting Indian would ever do, but would demonstrate through various contests how well they could achieve a level of enlightenment through singing, dancing, self-defense, the ability to show love, and so on. Basically all the attributes heroes in Bollywood films possess in bushels.

Later on, during a day of sightseeing at the Gateway to India arch built by Queen Victoria during her reign, I snapped a photo of a turbaned man posing nearby with a basket of cobras. I suppose he didn't like the tip I gave him, so he decided to follow me around the square screaming and waving the basket of cobras in my face. My driver tried to run interference but the guy finally relented after a policeman in a red jacket and white helmet smacked him with stick.

The question remained, "How much do you tip a guy with a basket full of cobras?"

Every time the car stopped at an intersection, we were mobbed by beggars of all shapes and sizes. They would press their faces against the windows to see who was inside and then the wailing and pleading would begin. One guy kept rubbing his fingerless hand on the window and looked like what I thought to be a leper. When I told the people at the office about the fingerless hand, they laughed and said he was a professional. Meaning as a child his parents snipped the fingers off one of his hands so he would look like a leper, making his life a lot more profitable as a beggar. I should just ignore them. I did, but unfortunately, I will never forget him.

On the ride back to the airport, we drove through the teeming neighborhoods to get to the highway to the airport. I noticed a man sitting on a bucket practically nude giving himself a soapy bath right on the street and a little farther up the same street I noticed a man laying spread out on the sidewalk with greasy stained newspapers covering his face. When I asked my driver what was up with the guy laying there, he glanced out his window and then turned to me with a smiling purple grin and said, "He dead." and we continued driving. No one on the busy street, men with lunch cans hanging from a pole, women wrapped in saris lugging groceries or children in matching uniforms and book bags skipping off to school, seemed to notice the corpse. More importantly, no one seemed to care. They had their own lives to be concerned about.

Waiting in the First Class lounge at the airport, I noticed a young boy terrorizing what looked like a little black Schipperke dog built with the characteristic short front legs and taller back legs. The racket was incessant as he chased the critter under the seats, against a wall, crashing into chairs and knocking some down. Looking a bit closer I realized he wasn't chasing a dog at all, but a very large black rat. In a strange way I suppose I was happy to be leaving India. But I realized I would never forget it.

On another occasion, I was sent to Belgrade, Serbia to assist in the production of a two-hour Italian extravaganza known worldwide as *Ciao Darwin*. Hoping to attract international production business, the Serbian production company had just built a state of the art studio facility on the outskirts of town. So new were the buildings that the streets between the buildings were not even paved as yet, so when it rained the streets turned into a quagmire. Not only did it slow down production, but it made it very difficult to get an audience in and out for each show. They also found it quite expensive to pay for bus transportation from downtown Belgrade to the outlaying studio, six times a day. I suggested it wasn't necessary to bring in a fresh audience for each show. Simply bring in one audience by bus for the first show. Have a large supply of assorted sandwiches, lots of sugary soda pop, no sugar-free beverages, and boxes and boxes of hard candy and chocolate bars delivered to the studio. Between the first and second shows, hand out the sandwiches and a can of soda, between the second and third, handfuls of candy and more sweet soda. After the third show, send everyone home on the same bus that brought them out earlier in the day. Tape day accomplished. I didn't mention anything about possibly raffling off a washing machine, in addition to the free lunch and snacks, as this concept would have been simply way too mind blowing for their production sensibilities. A few sandwiches, some cans of soda and assorted bags of candy were fine, but a washing machine? If I mentioned that, I'm sure they would have politely suggested making an appointment with a local psychiatrist. Nevertheless, they were impressed beyond belief with my simple suggestions on how to keep one audience happy and excited for three shows.

During another season, the same Italian company that sent me to Serbia as the Fly-Away producer for *Ciao Darwin* sold the same show to Vietnam and sent me to Ho Chi Minh City, nee Saigon, to assist with their production. A word about *Ciao Darwin*. It's not your ordinary game show. Rather it is a two-hour Saturday night extravaganza predicated on the idea of natural selection articulated by evolutionary scientist Charles Darwin and testing, if glibly, summarized as, "the survival of the fittest." The show features one hundred contestants on stage, perhaps fifty fat men against fifty skinny men, or fifty married women against fifty single women. The show opens with a Vegas-style dance number featuring twenty or more dancers (bare breasted women clothed only in feathers) and assorted lions, camels, and an occasional elephant. The show goes on for two hours with various stunts and games testing which team of fifty is more adept at the assortment of goofy stunts they have to endure. The final stunt of every show placed one contestant from each team in a large cylindrical tube on stage, equipped with a diving mask and snorkel. He or she must answer true or false questions about what has happened during the show that just transpired. Each time he or she is incorrect, the tank fills with a few gallons of water. The first contestant to be covered with water loses for his or her entire team and the other team are declared the winners.

The show is extremely popular all over the European Union and Asia. I was hired to install the show in a number of cities including Belgrade, Jakarta, Vilnius, Reykjavik and, finally, Ho Chi Minh City, still called Saigon by the locals, as they feel it is a prettier name.

A Vietnamese television company bought the show from the Italians and decided to produce the format. The first time I was sent to Saigon was to serve as the Fly-Away Producer for their production of *Ciao Darwin*. Even though it seems every citizen in Vietnam owns a motor scooter, and it was not uncommon to see up to five family members sharing a ride on one tiny motor bike, it is still an extremely Communist country, meaning that people were quite capitalistic, but the government was arch conservative. Every few blocks there were huge billboards done in the social realism style extolling the wonders of farm life, the wonders of family, service to the people and, most importantly, the avuncular love of Ho Chi Minh.

For most young people working in television, the war with America, referred to as the "American War," was as distant and ancient as the Korean War or World War II is for most Baby Boomers and subsequent generations. They ignored the propaganda of the socialist realism billboards and delighted in wearing Levis and Polo shirts, and loved fancy rock and roll tattoos. Hookers would still cruise likely prospects on the street, but now they rode on the backs of motor scooters. If you looked promising or a bit lonely they would hop off the back of the idling scooter, quickly and directly proposition you and, if you refused, would hop back on the bike and give you the finger as they rode off. There were Colonel Sanders Kentucky Fried Chicken shops throughout the city, as well as Starbucks, Old Navy, Adidas, Pizza Huts, and The Gap on almost every other street and corner. The only visible reminder of the American War was the old American Embassy with a large red Vietnamese flag with the bright gold star flying from the flagstaff. The entire building, now reconditioned in gleaming white, with its new name in large gold letters over the entrance reading *War Remnants Museum*. The adjoining yard was filled with rusting hulks of helicopters, a few large guns, and a disabled tank or two. Adorning the grounds as well were a few social realism signs praising the victory of the noble Vietnamese peasant over the big Evil. Regardless of the time of day I was driven by, the museum and grounds were always empty.

When viewing the first dress rehearsal of the show, I started sweating profusely. Instead of casting fifty skinny men against fifty fat men, provided they could even find fifty fat men in Saigon, in order to get the government's okay, the show had to extoll the wonders of their new society. They claimed, and I suppose rightfully so, they were the original Asian culture and everyone else stole from them. They were forced to endure five hundred years of Chinese hegemony and then one hundred years of colonial occupation by the French and finally fifty years of unwanted protection from the Americans. It was now most important for young people to be fully versed in their history, both ancient and modern. To that end, the contestants consisted of fifty students from the Saigon College of Optometry verses fifty students from the National Agricultural College of Hanoi, or some such combination of schools or colleges. There was a dance number at the beginning but, instead of "tits and ass" and elephants, the dancers were covered from head to toe with only their hands and feet exposed, and did a charming classical Vietnamese dance resembling the "Run Eliza" number from *The King and I* with Yul Brynner. Two opposing contestants didn't have to sit in a tank that filled with water for the finale, but the entire team had to present a choral rendition of a classic Vietnamese song. The winning team received a tractor or some sort of practical item for their school.

Panicked, I immediately called Italy on my cell phone, as I was hired to do, and told them what was happening, They listened intently and then said, "Their check arrived a few days ago and cleared this afternoon. Let them do whatever they want." I did, and I hoped everyone was satisfied. They must have been, because about two years later I was called back to run a seminar for the Saigon International Film School. I was blown away by how much the society had changed in the few years that I was gone. The old Tan Son Nhat airport originally looked like any one of the small one-story American airports from the fifties, not unlike the Bob Hope Airport in Burbank. No doubt the original was built by the Americans during their disastrous visit. It was now a huge super modern multi-storied edifice with a level for picking up arriving passengers and a level for dropping off departing passengers. Elsewhere around town, the old propaganda signs and billboards had been replaced with flashing neon billboards extolling the virtues of giant flat screen televisions and vacuum cleaners, and had every coffee shop and retail international clothing shop imaginable, including Gucci, Chanel, Dior, and Prada. In fact, I bought my wife a Prada bag. When I gave it to her, she was very impressed. When I told her I was sure it was authentic because I actually saw the guy sew it together inside the huge Ben Thanh market in downtown Saigon, she threw it at me, never to be seen again. Oh well.

In Ho Chi Minh City, *nee* Saigon, the motor scooter was still king during my second visit, but an occasional Harley-Davidson would roar by, and many people, like the owner of the film school, tooled around town on a BMW scooter and kept his Mercedes sedan parked in a garage on the outskirts of town.

The seminar went perfectly. Although all the participants spoke English, I worked with two required interpreters who took turns translating what I was saying live, during my lectures. I later learned this was at the insistence of the government, and for all I know I was being recorded as well. I was sure not to cast any aspersions on the character of honored Uncle Ho Chi Minh. Not that I would, as I never met the man.

At the end of the seminar the school threw a lavish ten-course banquet that started with salmon sashimi flown in from Norway and just got better after that. At the end of the hall was a classical

Vietnamese string orchestra playing classical Vietnamese tunes, or so I thought. After listening closely I heard Asian string renditions of "Raindrops Keep Falling on My Head" as well as popular ditties of the Beatles, Rolling Stones, and Aretha Franklin, plus show tunes from Les Misérables and Cats. A Communist government, no question about it, the music was not supplied by a rock band, but a cosmopolitan society for sure! True to their capitalistic nature, CD recordings of the orchestra's music were available for sale. I bought one, of course, as Asian string renditions of pop music and show tunes was truly a unique souvenir. Playing the CD a few days later, all the tunes were classical Vietnamese ditties, sounding just shy of stepping on a cat's tail. Nothing by Aretha, the Beatles, or Andrew Lloyd Weber. Obviously, the government in Vietnam is more involved with everyday life than with the ever-present Starbucks lattes, buckets of Kentucky Fried Chicken, or pop music played at a formal dinner receptions.

Tipping the musicians revealed a charming custom. Rather than rudely hand each player cash, the host of the banquet, company CEO Dien Quan, who was also the owner of the restaurant and The Saigon International Film School, was given five long stem roses. Around each stem he wrapped a 500,000 VD, Vietnamese Dong note (about twenty dollars, US), and then handed the flower to one of the attending guests, who brought it over to the orchestra, and placed it in a classically decorated silver vase on the small stage. This was done throughout the evening, until there was a rose for each musician.

A few months after returning from Viet Nam, Sony Pictures International hired me to install *Wheel of Fortune* in Vilnius, Lithuania. I was booked on a First Class flight on Lufthansa to Stuttgart on a Boeing 747. My flight continued from Stuttgart to Vilnius on a Russian built Tupolev TU-134. Suffice it to say, the First Class meal on the Lufthansa 747 began with a chilled one-ounce jar of Beluga caviar and all the accompaniments, served to all the passengers in the Upper Deck First Class cabin. The five-course meal after the caviar was exquisite, even at ten thousand feet. We were served a fresh salad of wild greens, a shrimp cocktail, crisp asparagus, and a grilled filet mignon. The meal was topped off with a hand scooped ice cream sundae with hot fudge for dessert. Granted, the flight from Stuttgart to Vilnius was only a few hours, and the Lithuanians, having recently thrown out the Russians, were struggling to join the capitalist world. They designated their First Class from Coach in their Tupolev TU 134 with what looked to be a shower curtain attached to the ceiling of the plane with thumb tacks. The seat configuration remained the same, three on each side of the aisle, but in First Class there was a pillow and blanket in the middle seat, for whomever grabbed it first I suppose. During meal time, the First Class bourgeoisie received a small packet of some sort of smoked meat and a choice of unwrapped crackers. No telling what was served in Coach. Before we landed, everyone in First Class received a small ceramic cream pitcher as a souvenir.

The hotel booked for my stay was a recently converted monastery furnished with stylish Scandinavian furniture no doubt purchased from companies located conveniently just across the Baltic. A small typewritten sign hung in the bathroom:

We would like to inform you the water which flows from the tab (sic) might be of dark color. Please do not panic. That is because of the old pipe system which cannot be changed in a short time. For getting clear water please keep the water run (sic) for a few minutes. Sorry.

One morning at breakfast two well-dressed businessmen were chatting in their musical Scandinavian tongue when the waitress arrived and asked in halting English what would they like. They answered in a schooled English, she thanked them, and then they returned to chatting in Swedish or Norwegian. This proved to me once again that English was now an international language.

Arriving at the studio, Televizija Radijas, an imposing brick building obviously built during the Soviet era, I noticed a shrine on the grounds consisting of large crosses, statues, wreaths, and incense burners swinging in the breeze. I asked what it was. The folks replied, rather offhandedly, "Oh that. When we threw the Russians out, ten of our friends died defending the television station."

It took a moment for that to sink in. I then thought, would I, or any of my compatriots here in town be willing to die defending CBS in the Fairfax District? Would we demand catering from Canters Deli up the block? Would we be willing to set up gun batteries below the huge sculptures of the dwarves at the entrance of Disney Studios in Burbank? How about machine gun nests at the gates of Paramount or Universal? These guys did—without catering, without wavering—and ten were slaughtered in the process. The reality of their sacrifice, enabling friends of theirs to purchase *Wheel of Fortune* as a daily format some months later, made me shiver.

The host of the show was a tall, austere man sounding more like Bela Lugosi than Pat Sajak. The letter turner was a beautiful young woman named, surprisingly enough "Vanya." A comparison with the original American Vanna White was made many times during the taping of the show.

The show had a problem with vowels as classic Lithuanian, one of the oldest languages on Continental Europe, possessed fifteen. After a brief discussion, we resolved they actually had five vowels, as in English, but each vowel could be pronounced three different ways. We compromised with a rule created on the spot (known as a "vest pocket" rule a producer pulls out of his vest pocket, as needed) which gave a contestant credit for a vowel regardless of the form it took within a word or phrase.

Prizing was also a bit of an issue, as the prizing ranged from a set of ornate drinking glasses for third place, curtains for your flat for second place, and a slightly used Moskovitch 408 four seater family sedan as the Grand Prize. So pleased by the selection of prizes available, I noticed the winner of the set of glasses posing with his family after the taping, proudly holding the glasses. They asked if I would take a few photos with their camera and I gladly agreed, thinking if this were the prize for an American game show, the "winners" would be chasing me about the studio, throwing the glasses at me like hand grenades.

Before the fifteen hour flight from Los Angeles to Vilnius I was ushered into the First Class Skyway Lounge to get my tickets.

Leaning on the desk, I looked to my left and a man was quietly standing there. He was shorter than I was but looked like an older version of Gerald Ford. I stared at him for a moment and our eyes met. He seemed to be getting a little annoyed with my staring at him.

"You know," I said, in a way to diffuse what could have been a weird situation, "You should call Ron Smiths Look-Alikes. He's an agent in town who books celebrity look-alikes because you are the spitting image of Gerald Ford. Has anyone ever told you that?"

His eyes narrowed, attempting to figure me out, and then sneered, somewhat defensively, "I am Gerald Ford."

A brief moment transpired as I registered what he just said, and then I lost it completely. Any pretense I might have had on entering the exclusive lounge, as a sophisticated international television producer, flew right out the window. I immediately became a babbling school boy. "Oh my god, Mr. President! I've never met a President before! You really do look like Gerald Ford! I mean, I don't know what to say."

"Try good evening Mr. President, that's always good for starters." He smiled slyly.

So like an idiot, I repeated exactly what he said, word for word, "Good evening Mr. President, that's always good for starters." I then realized how ridiculous I must have sounded, and we both started laughing. Recovering quickly I then asked, "Would you mind signing something for me?" I asked politely.

"Sure, of course" said the former President.

I then leaned over to my left to open the canvas and leather shoulder bag I always traveled with. I was immediately surrounded by five gorillas wearing dark suits, a few sporting dark sunglasses who, to this day I will swear were not standing there before, or anywhere in the vicinity. They just appeared in a flash like menacing genies from a lamp someone had just rubbed. I looked up and nervously realizing who they were, and, and why they appeared, as well, I said, "Oh. Hi guys, I guess you travel with the President, I'm just looking in my bag for a piece of paper for an autograph."

They weren't impressed. Their serious expressions didn't change one bit, until one looked over to the President. He winked and nodded ever so slightly, and they backed off, disappearing once again into the ether. I pulled out my travel wallet with its note pad and handed it to the President. He signed it, "Have fun in Lithuania! Best Regards, Gerald Ford"

Just as he handed my wallet back to me, the goons reappeared, and he was shuffled off to a very private area to wait for his flight.

I stood there in awe, startled out of my stunned silence by the ticket agent calling my name and handing me my checked-in ticket to the charming Vilnius, Lithuania. I have to admit, the destination lost some of its anticipated exotic appeal. After all, I just had a little chat with a one-time President of the United States of America!

I called my wife to tell her what had just happened. She listened patiently and said, "That's wonderful darling. It's almost midnight. I'm in bed. Have a safe flight. Kissy-Huggy, Bye-bye."

She hung up with a loud click.

JAY LENO, AND A PA SYSTEM HITLER USED AT NUREMBERG.

Attending college in the Back Bay area of Boston from 1969 to 1973, a number of drama students became well acquainted with another downtown neighborhood known affectionately as the "Combat Zone." How tough was this neighborhood? In addition to having back-to-back strip joints and bars that reeked of rancid beer and pickled eggs, it was also well known for hookers who could occasionally be seen pummeling sailors on the sidewalk because the swabby might have said something "fresh."

Although a Mass Communications major at the same school, Jay Leno was also enamored with stand-up comedy. He was able to get emcee jobs at numerous strip-clubs and honed his stand-up routines while introducing Fatima of the Seven Veils and her Twirling Twins. Having gigs at numerous clubs allowed Jay to buy a car, a luxury none of us could afford, let alone pay for all the parking tickets cars collected on a regular basis in the Boston Back Bay. To support the parking tickets Jay would offer rides to Manhattan on Friday nights, with a return on Sunday night. He may have charged ten dollars for the round trip, cheaper than a Greyhound, so it was a great deal. During one of these rides Jay mentioned that his roommate was a drama major named Fred. I knew Fred, as I was a drama major as well, and we shared a number of classes. I mentioned that to Jay while he was driving and in his characteristic high pitched voice, he quipped, "Fred has two pairs of patched jeans hanging in our closet and a PA system Hitler used at Nuremburg!" It was so true, so funny, and it kept us laughing all the way to Grand Central Station.

Years later I was having lunch at Jerry's Deli with Jan Smith, the owner of Igby's Comedy Cabaret, a small club in Santa Monica favored by working comics as a great place to try out new material.

Jay, wearing his usual Levis and jeans jacket, was working the dining room in the deli as everyone did for various professional reasons. Walking by, he noticed Jan. He gave Jan a big hello as he sidled into our booth, extended his hand toward me, and said, "Hi, I'm Jay Leno."

While shaking his hand, I said, "I actually know you Jay, we went to Emerson College together, Class of '73."

"Hey me too!" he said rather surprised, "But I don't remember you. I'm really sorry."

"Don't worry about it, but you gave me a number of rides on Friday nights to Grand Central Station for ten bucks a trip."

"Oh yeah," he said remembering vaguely, "I had '66 Ford Galaxy 500 convertible back then. I loved that bucket of bolts!"

"In fact, you also had a drama major named Fred for a roommate, and you had the best line about him. You said Fred had two worn out pairs of Levis hanging in his closet and a PA system Hitler could have used at Nuremburg!"

"That's my line!" Jay yelled.

"Yes, I know it is. It was funny then and it's still pretty funny now."

"Hey, so you really do know me." said Jay, his surprise starting to sink in a bit, "How's Freddy doing?"

"We really don't keep in touch, but the last time we spoke he was selling insurance in Saint Petersburg and plays Merlin on weekends at Universal Orlando."

"Still a tall guy, he must have been six-six if he was an inch."

"Yeah," I agreed, "I don't think he's gotten any shorter."

"Funny." said Jay pointing his finger at me, but not cracking a smile. He then turned to Jan and said, "Hey Jan, I can't make it on Friday or Saturday, but I'd like to try out some new stuff on Sunday night. Do you have a spot for me?"

"Anytime Jay, just let me know when you arrive."

"Great, I'll see you Sunday night." He got up to leave, not before saying to me, "Say hello to Fred for me next time you guys talk." He touched me on the shoulder and then moved off to schmooze another table.

SIR JOHN GIELGUD, SIR RALPH RICHARDSON, MOHAMMAD ALI AND ELAINE STRITCH.

The reason I relied on Jay Leno's bargain rate ride to Manhattan was that, as a theatre student, it enabled me to see as many full length Broadway shows as I could possibly afford, and then "Second Act" the rest. "Second Acting" was the mischievous custom of loitering outside a Broadway theater until intermission. When the audience came out for a smoke or a chat, you would mingle with the milling crowd and, when the lights flashed, you joined them as they re-entered the theater to take seats from people who had left during Intermission. You would head for the upper balconies and enjoy the second act of the show, maybe the third as well, if there was one. After the show, at least what we were able to see of it, my cronies and I would head for Tads $1.49 Steak House in Times Square. We would treat ourselves to an oily baked potato, a slab of garlic bread, and a strip of steak that was always served, regardless of how you requested it, extremely well done. A soda pop to wash it all down was an additional ten cents and we were living the high life. One night after our sumptuous meal I decided an Orange Julius was in order for desert. I stepped into the Orange Julius shop and, standing in front of me, was Muhammad Ali and a nice looking young woman. He was appearing in a Broadway play at the time, and I suppose this was after hours. He noticed me staring at him, and said, "You want one?"

I was a bit at a loss for words as I didn't know how to address him. He had just changed his name from Cassius Clay to Muhammad, so I said, "No thanks Champ. But you can sign this for me."

I presented a white paper bag with a pound box of Schraft's chocolates inside that I was planning to give to an Aunt later on.

He signed it "Muhammad Ali," and then said, "You sure you don't want a Julius?"

"No thanks Champ we are off to see a show."

"Really, you mean you haven't seen mine?"

"No yet, but we are planning on it."

"Okay, I'll be looking for you." He feigned an angry expression, miming a shot to my nose, then smiled his classic friendly grin. Years later I met him again with his "people" for a meeting about being a guest on a talk show I was producing. He was already in advanced stages of whatever his particular brain affliction was and took great delight in walking up behind people and rubbing his thumb and forefinger together making a squeaking cricket like chirping sound. Totally out of the blue and so surprising, it made you jump every time. He really enjoyed that and would smile that wonderful Mohammad Ali smile, not unlike the same smile he shot to me that night in the Orange Julius stand on Broadway.

During another evening, David Storey's drama *Home* was playing at the Morosco Theatre starring John Gielgud and Ralph Richardson. We splurged and bought orchestra seats for $6.50 each, the usual price for an orchestra seat at the time. *Hair* was playing on Broadway during the same period and orchestra seats were an outlandish $25.00 each. All prices on Broadway doubled on New Year's Eve, so to take a date to see *Hair* would run over $50.00! Who had that kind of money? Certainly not college students from Boston, or any where else for that matter. It's interesting to note orchestra seats to Broadway shows these days can run anywhere from $300 to $500 or more for each seat! Times have certainly changed.

The show was about two elderly gents sitting on a park bench chatting with each other about lives and past loves. It's not until the second act you realize they are in an insane asylum, hence the title *Home*.

After a rousing back-to-front standing ovation, we left the theatre. We decided not to wait on the sidewalk as most people did for the actors to leave, but found our way into a dank alley where the stage door was located. First to exit was Elaine Stritch with two stalwart fellows in tow. Recognizing her I stammered, "You're, you're. . ." and before I could say another word, she cackled, "That's right honey, I am!" and she stormed through the double doors separating the alley from the sidewalk, her two escorts following obediently behind.

What a bitch, I thought, but before I could dwell on it, the stage door opened once again and Sir Ralph Richardson walked out in a deerstalker cap, plaid overcoat, and smoking a curved Meerschaum pipe.

"Mr. Richardson." I said.

"Yes that's right, page seventeen," he grumbled, referring to the page on which his bio and photo appeared in the program. I hastily turned to the page in my yellow Playbill, he snatched it from me and quickly scrawled his name over his photo. Thrusting it back to me with a muffled few words and harrumphs, he left the alley via the doors to the sidewalk.

Well, I thought, at least he wasn't as creepy as Elaine Stritch. The stage door opened once again and out walked Sir John Gielgud. He was wearing a glistening black fur coat with a small round fur cap to match, He walked directly over to us and said,

"Good evening."

Somewhat gob smacked, as they say across the pond, I was able to muster, "Good evening, Sir John. I have never said hello to a knight before."

He smiled and said, "Well you can start with, good evening Sir John, I enjoyed your sterling performance."

"Absolutely Sir John you were fantastic. It was a back-to-front standing ovation, by the way," I added.

"Back to front? Are you a theatre scholar?" he smiled. I was referring to the three types of standing ovations, "front to back," "back to front," and "simultaneous." The "back to front" being the most appreciated, means that the people who bought the less expensive seats in the rear of the theater appreciated the show more than the fat cats sitting down front.

"Actually I'm a theatre student from Boston, we come down on the weekends to catch as many shows as we can."

"Boston? A wonderful town actually. I've done shows there at the Colonial and the Shubert." He smiled and gently loosened the program from my hand, turned to the appropriate page, and signed it with his own pen and handed it back to me. "Well, it's getting late and I have a television interview in the morning. We are headed uptown; can I offer you a lift?"

"Thank-you, Sir John, thanks for asking, but I'm headed for the Port Authority, just a few blocks away."

"Well then, tell all your fellow theatre students about the show. Have a nice evening." He winked and headed for the doors. His assistant opened them wide and he walked out through an adoring crowd who were applauding politely. He doffed his black fur cap, bowed slightly, smiling to everyone as he walked, and then entered the waiting limo. His assistant got in and shut the door, and the car drove away from the Morosco Theatre curb into the bustling Broadway evening.

STEVE LANDESBURG – COMEDIAN, ACTOR, DADDY

I first met *Barney Miller* star Steve Landesburg in the early 1990s during our daughters' kindergarten orientation held at a small private school on Laurel Canyon Boulevard in Studio City, California. Other fathers and mothers attending included Bobcat Goldthwait and his daughter, Billy Idol and his son, George Wendt and his son and daughter, as well as Eric Idle, and Macy Grey with their kids, and many others. My daughter and Steve's daughter hit it off and eventually became best friends, as did our wives. This translated into a myriad of sleepovers for the girls, weekend meetings for breakfast and dinners (particularly at restaurants that had Steve's photo hanging in the vestibule), whale watching trips to San Diego, family trips to Las Vegas, and sojourns to every amusement and theme park in the Los Angeles area. Steve would be recognized occasionally either from his stint on *Barney Miller* or sitting in for Johnny Carson on *The Tonight Show* or his numerous appearances on various late night and daytime talk and game shows. Even though he was obviously not "on stage" at the moment he was recognized, usually getting on or off a roller coaster at an amusement park or waiting to be seated at a local sushi bar, he was always gracious, signed an autograph or two, chatted just a bit, and then excused himself, saying he was with his family. The autograph seeker would usually understand, take the hint, and back off. Sometimes they didn't. Steve was never nasty, but he would just brush them off in an elegant manner, and we were off to our table or the next nauseating ride.

One summer we sent the girls to a sleep-away camp in the foothills of the High Sierra. The girls assured us they were having a great time and eventually it was time to come home. The busses were scheduled to drop them off in a high school parking lot, so we all arrived early to wait for them. Steve and I decided coffee might be a good idea, so we crossed the street to a coffee shop and ordered an assortment of lattes. While waiting for the coffees, the busses pulled in, and Steve rushed out of the shop in a flash, leaving me behind to deal with the coffees. When I got to the parking lot, Steve's daughter was first off the bus and leaped into Steve's arms, kissing and hugging him and laughing. The other kids leaving the bus did the same with their parents. My daughter was a few kids later and the first words out her mouth, before stepping foot on the pavement were, "Why did you send me tuna fish in my care package?"

She failed to mention the Peanut M&Ms, Hershey bars, Oreos, and Snickers bars. She got off the bus, retrieved her stuff, and didn't say anything to us for the entire trip home. By the way, her diet at home consisted primarily of tuna, so we figured it might be funny to send her a few cans just in case the camp chef had run out. She didn't get the joke.

Steve would regale us with hysterically funny stories about his days hanging out either at the Improv in New York, The Comedy Store in Los Angeles, or breakfasts on Saturday mornings at a local deli, where a table was reserved for some of the funniest minds in the country, enjoying lox and eggs, and never-ending carafes of decaf. They would talk (or *kibbitz*, as some of the older ones put it) about gigs past, present, and future. It was even rumored that, while at the Comedy Store, Steve had a special relationship with Mitzi Shore, the Queen and owner of the establishment, but that could never be verified. If truth be told, Steve was not the only one, so it really didn't matter.

Steve met his wonderful wife, Nancy, during a Ryder Truck commercial she was producing with Steve as the spokesman. Sparks flew, and they were happily married for many years, quite an accomplishment for Hollywood relationships. Nancy and my wife adored each other—partners in crime. you might say. Case in point, during the "Beanie Baby" craze the two of them decided to get their daughters every Beanie Baby in existence. It turns out McDonalds was giving away a Beanie Baby with every Happy Meal purchased, so the two of them descended on every McDonalds in town, bought every Happy Meal with a Beanie Baby they didn't already have, and then gave the meals away to homeless folk gathered in the neighborhoods and under the freeways. It was a win-win as far as they were concerned. They were accomplishing a civic good deed and getting dozens of collectable Beanie Babies in the bargain. For at least the last twenty five years the Beanie Babies have been stuffed in a cardboard box somewhere in our garage, ignored and useless. Oh well, at least dozens of homeless folk got Happy Meals.

Steve never went out without some index cards and a pen in his top pocket. He was always on the prowl for an interesting line, funny concept, or turn of phrase he could use in a stand-up routine. He was as good a listener as he was a storyteller. Later on in his career, Steve teamed up with a group of well known comedians and they formed a troupe of traveling entertainers playing condos and auditoriums across the country. I was told way in advance that Steve was going to play my mother's condo in Sunrise, Florida. I mentioned this to Steve and he agreed to give her a mention during his act. Sadly, my mother passed away two days before Steve was scheduled to appear at her condo. I rushed over to his house to pick up my daughter, who was playing with his daughter; she was going with us that night to Florida for her grandmother's funeral. I told Nancy to warn Steve not to mention anything about my mother, and she said he would take care of it.

The funeral was a day after we arrived, and when I reached the podium to say a few words, I scanned the attending gathering of elderly faces and coiffed gray-haired neighbors, anticipating the deli buffet after the ceremony. I noticed that, sitting there, though standing out in the third row, wearing a black yarmulke compliments of the Abramowitz Funeral Home, was Steve Landesburg.

How he found out where the cemetery was and the time of the service, let alone how he got there, I will never know. I brought him back to the condo afterwards for the buffet and cake, and he endured all the questions from the assortment of Uncle Sols and Aunt Esthers about his being "the funny cop on the *Barney Miller* show" or "the time he sat in for Johnny Carson." After a few autographs and a few hours he excused himself politely, as he did have two shows to do that night one for the "Early Birds" at 6 p.m. and one for the "Fancy-Shmancy" crowd at 9 p.m.

I drove him back to his hotel and, before he got out of the car, he leaned over and he gave me a quick kiss on the forehead. He smiled knowingly, and was gone.

Many years later, I was able to reciprocate that sweet unspoken gesture by gently kissing his wife Nancy on her forehead after Steve's funeral and memorial.

CHARLTON HESTON – LILLA HESTON'S BIG BROTHER ... CHUCKY

Even though my daughter's elementary school was less than a mile from our home, there was no way we would ever let her walk home alone. Every afternoon after a morning of writing, I would drive over to the school and wait in the schoolyard along with dozens of other parents for the kids to be released. One afternoon I looked to my left and there was a wizened older guy standing there, a bit stooped over, but still taller than my 6'2" frame. Our eyes met, and he gave me that characteristic sardonic grin that I recognized as the same grin I had seen on Major Dundee, Ben Hur, and, yes, even Moses himself! I was standing next to Charlton Heston!

I suppose he noticed I was staring at him, so he winked at me. This startled me out of my reverie, and I extended my hand and said, "Mr. Heston, excuse me for staring, but it's not often one meets a biblical hero in a Studio City schoolyard."

He smiled and said, "My grandson goes here. This is our day."

"Of course I understand" I said, "By the way, I took a master class from your sister Lilla once upon a time."

He recoiled just a bit, and said, "You went to Northwestern?"

"No, I went to Emerson College in Boston actually and Lilla was brought in as a Guest Lecturer in Oral Interpretation. I was a drama major with a speech minor so we were all invited to attend a few of her lectures."

"You still acting?" he asked, surprising me.

"No, I gave it up years ago for producing and writing."

"You're better off." he chuckled, with a wave of his hand.

"Were you a student of hers at Northwestern?" I asked.

"How did you know I want to Northwestern?"

"During her talks she would occasionally mention her brother Chuck, or Chucky, so we just put two and two together and figured that had to be you."

"I never took any of her classes because I figured there wasn't much I could learn from my baby sister. But I have to admit, she did have lots of good things to say about oral interp, and acting, and things like that. I never learned that from her in a classroom."

"Did she ever give you any pointers on parting the Red Sea?"

"Absolutely," he laughed, "keep your feet dry!"

We both laughed and at that very moment the school bell rang and his grandson came bounding out of the classroom building and leaped into his grandfather's outstretched arms. They snuggled for a moment, and he put him down, looking at me and saying, "They get heavier every day," and he rolled his eyes.

"Tell me about it." I said, just as my daughter walked over and handed me her computer bag with a groan.

We watched as, hand-in-hand, the two of them walked toward the parking lot. The little boy, jumping and gamboling like a puppy, while Mr. Heston's gait was much slower and labored. I later learned he had hurt his knees in one of the action movies he did, something to do with horses colliding with each other or some such movie set accident. He was paying the price for it now. For the moment he was Grandpa, walking slowly with his grandson, to a bright red, late model Corvette convertible. They got in, lowered the top, and zoomed off into the afternoon. It was his day after all.

"Who was the old guy?" asked my daughter.

"Just a very famous actor. Remember when we saw *The Ten Commandments*? He played Moses. Do you remember *Ben Hur*, the movie with the chariot races and Jesus getting crucified and all that? He was Ben Hur!"

She listened attentively as long as one can when you are ten, and then said, "What do you know about spread sheets? I have to create a spread sheet for tomorrow's computer class."

"No problem," I said, a bit disappointed she wasn't at all as excited as I was about who I was just chatting with. "I'll show you when we get home. Let's go."

"Can we stop at Ben & Jerrys too? Please, please, please?"

"Sure. You had me at the first please, by the way."

"I know.' she smiled, cocking her head like a cutie pie, and off we went for ice cream.

LION TAMER CLYDE BEATTY, OTTO THE DWARF, AND GRANDMA ON A SKATEBOARD

My father, nicknamed "Lefty," worked as a midway "Talker" with the Ringling Brothers and Barnum & Bailey Circus during the thirties. Known as a "Barker" in literature and lore, the "Talker" was actually an early form of a rapper. He possessed a spiel for every attraction on the midway leading up to the main entrance of the three ring performance tent: The "Blood Sweating Hippopotamus" (all hippos sweat red), the "Abominable Snowman" (actually a nice fellow from Mexico with a clotting condition that caused his legs and feet to swell to an enormous size), and my favorite, the "Hootchie-Kootchie" show, featuring dancers who, according to my father, "The girls are on the inside, the boys are in the outside... so don't push, don't shove... there's room for all... These girls can wiggle and waggle like jelly on a plate on a frosty morning!"

World War II interrupted my father's circus career and getting married was the final straw. In addition to that, the Ringling show went indoors during the fifties, so the midway was eliminated. Most of the carnies moved over to the Clyde Beatty and Cole Brothers Circus which was still a "mud show" with tents and a midway. By the time the show pulled into Miami it was the end of the season, the tent was patched in various places and the costumes had become a bit faded, but the performers were still as energetic and exciting as though they were performing for royalty. I always thought it strange that an overweight woman in a two piece red, white, and blue sequined costume could simply hand a juggler a small hoop to add to his act and then strike a glorious pose and take a bow. There's no business like show business.

Every Sunday morning when the show was in town my father would bring his pals a load of bagels, lox and cream cheese, and they would all share them in the mess tent. He was known as "Lefty" while on the circus grounds, and I remember him introducing me to Clyde Beatty, the lion tamer, always wearing tan riding jodhpurs, high black boots and a pith helmet. I noticed he always had a big pistol in a holster on his belt. When I pointed out the gun to my father, he said, "Relax, it only fires blanks. Besides, those damn lions are over a hundred years old, if he ever shot at one, the lion would collapse with a heart attack, and old Clyde would be out looking for a job!"

My father introduced me to Otto the Dwarf who was smoking a cigar while we shook hands. I noticed I was about a foot taller than he was. He smiled and said to my dad, "Hey Lefty, be careful, he's going to be bigger than you in no time! Hey kid, you want a stogie?"

"No!" said my dad, "He doesn't need a cigar, thank you very much!" and everyone started laughing. I couldn't figure out what was so funny.

When we returned home later that morning, I tried to roll part of the Sunday funnies into a stogie and tried to light it. When my mother asked what I was trying to do, I told her Otto the Dwarf was smoking a cigar and I was taller than he was. Mom flipped out, grabbed my "cigar" out of my hand, and shaking it in my father's face, accused him of leading me down the road to ruin by introducing me to all "those circus people." He ignored her, of course, and we all left the house to arrive in time for the matinee performance.

We always had front row center ring seats, as Lefty was part of the family. The show always began with Clyde Beatty and the lions and, while the cages were being taken down, the attention was directed up to a trapeze act. During the show the Wallendas performed on a tightrope with seven of the family balancing on bicycles forming a pyramid. The last act was always a guy and his wife being shot out of a huge cannon in the first ring, flying over the second ring, and landing in a huge net set up above the third ring.

I always looked forward to the final "spec," or spectacular, when all the performers walked around the circumference of the three rings for their final bows, and then the big finale: twenty-five elephants holding each other's tails with their trunks, charging around the rings, causing the seats in the first few rows to vibrate. Sitting in a flimsy folding chair vibrating because of elephants charging by was something an eight year old could never forget. Occasionally they would stop and raise their front legs up onto the backs of the elephant in front, so close to our seats that I once tried to reach out and touch them, but a swat from my father's left hand put an end to that idea rather quickly.

Years later, the Ringling show was playing the Forum in Los Angeles. I had not seen the show in years, so I invited a date and for old time's sake, bought front row center ring seats. I didn't expect the concrete floor of a modern arena to vibrate from elephants charging by, but surprisingly enough, it did. Almost a 4.0 on the Richter Scale, I would guess.

During one of the parades, I noticed a clown dressed as an old woman, riding a skate board. He looked vaguely familiar, even with all the makeup. Looking closer I realized he was a classmate of mine from college. When he looked my way I yelled, "Hey, I know you, don't I?"

He smiled and nodded yes.

"We went to school together didn't we?"

He smiled and nodded yes again.

"Lubin, is that you?"

He finally whispered, "Bruce, you're killing my act. Meet me behind the curtains after the show."

He skated off acknowledging the crowd and doing his clown thing.

Turns out the clown was the famous Barry Lubin with his Grandma on a Skateboard character. He had gone to school with me majoring in directing, but after graduating was accepted in the Ringling Brothers Clown School in Sarasota. We went out to dinner after the show and then I took him back to his train car parked in a train yard in Palos Verdes. His cabin was the length of his bed with a small closet and desk. Showers and bathrooms were at the end of the car and a dining car was a few cars down. I asked why he didn't have a trailer or van of his own like most of my father's carny friends did and he said the show traveled thousands of miles in a season and who could afford the gas. I suppose being a featured clown for the Ringling show wasn't as high paying as being a carny and charging "whatever the traffic will bear."

Barry had won all sorts of international clowning competitions and eventually left Ringling and became a headliner and partial owner of the European style one-ring "Big Apple Circus" appearing in New York's Central Park. The one ring, no animal, idea predating the Cirque Du Soliel by many years.

While working as the Executive Producer of *America's Talking*, I invited Barry to be a guest on our late night talk show. He leaped at the opportunity and then showed up with five of his fellow clowns from the Big Apple show. How does one deal with six professional clowns on a talk show? You don't. We decided all bets were off; I rescheduled the other guests for another night and dedicated the entire show to the Big Apple Circus clowns. It was a night to remember.

Barry retired a few years ago and currently lives with his wife in Sweden.

HOTEL RITZ PARIS

Twice each year an international television convention takes place in Cannes, in the Provence region in the south of France. During one particular visit, my wife and I decided to spend a week in Paris afterward to celebrate our twenty-fifth wedding anniversary. At the time, our daughter, Peregrine, was on a field trip with her Spanish class to Spain. We chose Hotel Ritz as our home base, and let's just say, even though we secured a package deal, a week's stay still cost more than the first brand new car I purchased off the showroom floor in 1977. Breakfast was included, as well as transportation to and from Charles de Gaulle Airport, so I suppose it was a bargain.

Arriving at the hectic airport, we retrieved our luggage and moved to the drivers' waiting area. A herd of drivers waving hand scrawled signs with various names and companies scribbled on them eagerly shook their signs at us as we passed by. Off in a corner, I saw a tall older man dressed in a black suit with a white handle bar moustache. In an extremely blasé manner, he was holding a machine-printed sign reading *Les Starins. S'il vous plait.* or The Starins, if you please.

We were quite pleased and made our way over to him. *"Bon jour, je suis Monsieur Starin, et c'est ma femme."* I said, (Good day, I am Mr. Starin and this is my wife).

"Bon. Merci" he replied. *"Suivez-moi, s'il vous plait."* (Good, thanks, follow me please.)

He took our carry-on luggage and led us to an exquisite white Mercedes Maybach with The Ritz logo in gold on its sides. The car was parked immediately outside the arrival gate, by the curb. He opened the door, and with a very gracious wave of his hand said, *"Madame, Monsieur, s'il vous plait."* (Madame and sir, if you please.)

"Merci beaucoup, Monsieur," and we climbed into the unbelievably spacious white leather seats in the back. There was a fully stocked bar and a pyramid of rolled moist towels sprinkled with fresh mint leaves in a silver tray nearby.

Once he was satisfied we were comfortable; he gently shut the door and went around back and deposited our luggage in the trunk. He climbed into the front seat separated from us with a lightly tinted window and we were on our way to the Place Vendome in the First Arrondissement, Paris. In the center of the Place Vendome, a tall spire had been erected by Napoleon in 1805 after melting down one hundred-eighty cannon captured during the Battle of Austerlitz. Ninety-three years later, in 1898, Cesar Ritz opened the doors to his Le Hotel Ritz and it has been charming guests ever since. Celebrating our wedding anniversary, we became two more of those fortunate guests.

The room was very comfortable in a fluffy Louis XIV sort of way, with curved French doors opening out onto a small terrace. We had a view of the rooftops of Paris in front of us, the domes of the Paris Opera dominating the view to the left, and the angular Louvre to the right. The bathroom came equipped with double sinks with gold faucets shaped like swans. There was a silver vase between both sinks, in which a fresh long stem red rose was placed every morning. The bathtub was the huge claw foot type with two porcelain-handled chains hanging down from the ceiling. One said *Maid* the other *Valet*. We never tugged on either of them. fearing who might show up.

Even a meal as simple as breakfast was memorable at the Ritz. *Le petit-dejeuner* was served in the Michelin two-star dining room, L'Espadon, decorated in a pastel Louis XIV style, with open floor to ceiling French doors overlooking a formal garden. This one spring morning, after dining on small bright yellow omelets and side salads of wild greens sprinkled with white and black truffles, we were enjoying our cups of thick French coffee. The waiter, wearing white gloves and a tuxedo with tails and gold brocade, rolled over a trolley with a slab of dripping honeycomb on it, about two inches thick, two feet wide and some three feet long. He gave us each an ample square, and brought another basket of warm croissants and fresh French breads, along with a tub of softened butter to our table. Croissants with drizzled honey and crusty French bread with a shmear and a drizzle. Could anything be better?

After a breakfast like this, one could easily grow to adore Paris in the springtime, in fact, one could also learn to love Paris in the fall and, as Maurice Chevalier concluded, "I don't know when I love Paris most of all!"

One afternoon while my wife and I were waiting in the lobby for a car to take us to the Eiffel Tower again, an obvious American tourist wearing meticulously clean and creased Bermuda shorts, as were the two teenage girls alongside her, showed up and headed for the Concierge podium right by the entrance. The woman and the two kids were wearing what Parisians likes to call "marshmallow feet," or those huge sparkling white sneakers every American tourist seems to wear when visiting Paris. Very politely, in a voice reserved for a church, she asked the Concierge, "Do you mind if we look around just a little?"

The Concierge looked down his nose at their eager little faces, and then said, with a disdainful sneer, "Non, this is not the Disneyland," adding a shooing motion with his hand toward the three of them. Disappointed and dejected, they turned and left.

That was a bit severe, I thought, but moments later our driver arrived and we were off for to the Eiffel Tower.

PIERCE BROSNAN & MOHAMED AL-FAYED

A few years before my wife and I visited Paris for the first time she insisted we go to the Eiffel Tower. The base area was filled with what I have come to call "Flag People," ant-like single file lines, or gaggles of tourists following obediently behind a tour guide holding a cane or umbrella with a small pennant flying from the crook. These lines of tourists by the tower legs were all waiting for an elevator ride up to the first level observation floor and there were hundreds of lines. I refused to join any of them and my wife has never forgiven me for that bit of stubbornness.

In order to preserve marital bliss, and as were in town to celebrate, I relented and agreed to re-visit the Eiffel Tower. The legs of the base were still crowded with thousands of Flag People but I noticed there was one leg without a line. In fact, there was just a young man wearing a long white apron and a dark blue shirt with thin white stripes, standing behind a wooden podium. We made our way directly over to him and asked why there wasn't a line like at all the other legs. He told us this was the entrance to the private elevator to the Michelin starred *Le Jules Verne* restaurant on the highest level of the tower, four hundred and ten feet in the air. He told us there was one table for two available for *Dejeuner* and asked if we wanted it. We leaped at the opportunity and in seconds found ourselves in a small private elevator lined in an opulent red and gold brocade speeding up to this aerial temple of *haute cuisine Françoise*.

We were shown to a table alongside a floor-to-ceiling window overlooking the Seine with the Trocadero and all of the Left Bank stretching out below us. We must have been giggling like children at our phenomenal good fortune as the couple siting at the table next to us were staring at us and smiling. Our eyes met and I asked them when made their reservations. The fellow replied a few months ago, and I immediately blurted out we made our reservations ten minutes prior and told them the whole story. While telling our tale, I realized I was chatting with Pierce Brosnan and his wife. I was making small talk with Bond, James Bond!

"Honey," I said to my wife, "we have Paris to our left, and Bond, James Bond to our right." He rolled his eyes. "Sorry, Mr. Brosnan," I laughed, "but I recognized you immediately, so I was just trying to be subtle. Wasn't very successful was I?"

"No, not really." he chuckled, "Where are you from?"

"Los Angeles," I replied, "we are on our way back from a TV market in Cannes, so we thought we would spend a week in Paris to celebrate. It's our anniversary."

"You were at MIPCOM? So were we." he said.

"No kidding! What a small world! Provence is unbelievable, don't you think? We would love to get a place there someday. I take it you are on your way back to Hawaii?" I asked innocently.

He grew a little suspicious and asked, "How do you I know I have a place in Hawaii?"

"Oh sorry," I said, a bit embarrassed, "I was sitting in on a table read for a Jaguar commercial some years ago. Your name came up and the producer said you lived in Hawaii and we could shoot it there as well. The client didn't want palm trees or a tropical look, they wanted something a bit more rugged. So they decided on the cliffs of Northern California along the Big Sur coast instead."

"I wondered why my ears were burning," he joked. As he and his wife began to leave, he added, "Be sure to order Floating Islands for dessert. It's fantastic."

I noticed, just before getting on the private elevator, he whispered something in the Maître D's ear, nodded toward out table, and left. Moments later, I saw the Maître D' walking toward us with the Sommelier, wine tasting spoon dangling from his neck, walking obediently behind with a bottle of wine and a silver ice bucket on a stand.

"A gift for your anniversary from Monsieur Brosnan. Rosé from Provence. Bon Appetit!" cooed the Maître d' and he motioned for the Sommelier to set things up.

After our meal of fresh oysters, lobster ravioli, and an exquisite rabbit ragout, we took Pierce's advice and ordered Floating Islands for dessert. A large flat bowl was brought to our table with mounds of freshly toasted meringues floating in a "sea" of a bright red sauce of assorted *fruits rouges* (red fruits).

I do not know what level of heaven we were in, but I can assure you, it far exceeded the seventh!

We decided to take the public elevator down as we thought a stop on the main observation deck might be fun. Stuffed into in a huge elevator car holding upwards of at least seventy-five people shoulder to shoulder, I could not help notice a glaring sign above the sliding doors ominously announcing in five languages:

Fate attenzione ai borseggiatori!
Cuidado con los carteristas!
Vorsicht Taschendiebe!
Mefiez-vous des pickpockets!
Beware of pickpockets!

Quite a bit different from the brocade-lined private elevator for two on the way up. Ah, *c'est la vie*.

We arrived back at the hotel in the early evening. The lobby was humming with activity, with the owner, Mohamed Al-Fayed, sitting in front of the Hemingway Bar enjoying an aperitif with friends. This was supposedly the same bar Hemingway liberated at the end of World War II. Legend has it Hemingway immediately mixed a pitcher of Martinis to celebrate, while the remnants of the German occupation were hightailing it back across the Rhine. Two taciturn gents in navy blue suits, wearing dark aviator style sunglasses, indoors, were standing with their arms folded, directly behind Mr. Al-Fayed's small table.

Without a care in the world, my wife bounces right up to Mr. Al-Fayed and bubbled, "Oh, Mr. Fayed, we just love your hotel. We're having the time of our lives here!"

Al-Fayed looks at her suspiciously for a moment and then rose, smiling broadly, and said, "You like my hotel?" He then puts his arms around our shoulders and walks us to the center of the lobby.

"Yes, it's beautiful." we chirp in unison.

"Where are you from?" he asks. We tell him California and he then asks, "Do you have any children?"

"Yes" we reply, at what seemed to be a strange question, but I went on, "Just one and she is currently attending university in Northern California majoring in art."

"Beautiful!" he says with a charming smile, "Here, these are for you."

He takes my hand and places two baby blue pills in my palm, and closes my hand with his. "Now, go up to your room in my beautiful hotel, and make more children!"

Somewhat surprised, my wife and I start laughing. Mr. Al-Fayed starts laughing. I notice the Front Desk Staff are laughing; even the crabby Concierge who, earlier in the day threw out the three American tourists with marshmallow feet, is laughing as well. The security guards were even smiling, slightly.

A few months later after we returned home I was watching the news and it was covering a story about Whitney Houston and Bobby Brown visiting Harrods in London. Mr. Al-Fayed shows up, as he was the owner of Harrods as well. He greets them, puts his arms around their shoulders, and hands Bobby two baby blue pills just as he did to me. Bobby swallows them immediately and starts acting goofy, and that was the end of the news story. I had my pills framed by the way, and they are still hanging in my office. I have no idea if they are authentic or not, but admittedly, just the memory makes me stiffen with laughter.

ITHACA

When you start on your journey to Ithaca, then pray that the road is long, full of adventure, full of knowledge. Do not fear the Lestrygonians and the Cyclops and the angry Poseidon. You will never meet such as these on your path if your thoughts remain lofty. . . Pray that the road is long. . .that you will enter ports seen for the first time

With such pleasure and with such joy!

But do not hurry the voyage at all; it is better to let it last for long years.

—Excerpts from "Ithaca" C.P. Cavafy

Whether it's eating sticky rice from a palm frond with your fingers, running amok in a brothel, chatting casually with Hollywood legends, or eating lunch in four-star gourmet restaurant on the top floor of the Eiffel Tower, I took poet Cavafy's advice to heart, though I never met a Lestrygonian, a Cyclops, or Poseidon. I must admit, many of the folks I dealt with over the years acted like all three. By the way, Odysseus met the Lestrygonians on his journey back to Ithaca. They were a charming race of cannibal giants. When Odysseus sent emissaries to meet with the giants, they ate them.

Granted, not everyone is lucky enough to get a shot at sailing off as an officer on a cruise ship, soaking in volcanic thermal pools in Iceland, exploring the ruins of Crusader castles, riding camels, and performing as a cowboy in westerns shot in the Middle East. Yet even to a casual observer, there are certainly more places and experiences available to those who seek them that far outpace, as Thoreau put it, "lives of quiet desperation."

Certainly not everyone would even have the slightest desire to grab at any opportunity that promised travel to exotic places, as well as, for example, the need to learn to say "please" and "thank-you" in Vietnamese, Russian, or Tagalog. Yet to those of us who possess the wanderlust gene, I'm reminded of a quote I read at a very young age by Norwegian playwright Henrik Ibsen:

"When we dead awaken, we know we have not lived."

Upon reading that passage I vowed to spend as much of my life as possible blazingly wide awake. There is so much more to life than simply dreaming about how you might want to experience it all and, sadly, so little time to get it even partially accomplished.

Leap at every opportunity to travel and come face to face with the hungry Lestrygonians, Mr. Cyclops, or King Poseidon, the adventures will follow along naturally.

Bruce J Starin, Spring, 2021

www.ingramcontent.com/pod-product-compliance
Lightning Source LLC
Chambersburg PA
CBHW071906230426
43671CB00010B/1491